D1305642

CREATED BY **JOSS WHEDON**

JEREMY **LAMBERT** VALENTINA **PINTI** MARIANA **IGNAZZI**
CLAUDIA **BALBONI** RAÚL **ANGULO**

Buffy the Vampire Slayer™

VOLUME TEN

WE ARE THE SLAYER

Published by
BOOM! STUDIOS

Designer
Madison Goyette

Assistant Editor
Gavin Gronenthal

Editor
Elizabeth Brei

Special Thanks to **Sierra Hahn**, **Jonathan Manning**,
Becca J. Sadowsky, & **Nicole Spiegel**.

Ross Richie Chairman & Founder
Jen Harned CFO
Matt Gagnon Editor-in-Chief
Filip Sablik President, Publishing & Marketing
Stephen Christy President, Development
Lance Kreiter Vice President, Licensing & Merchandising
Bryce Carlson Vice President, Editorial & Creative Strategy
Hunter Gorinson Vice President, Business Development
Josh Hayes Vice President, Sales
Sierra Hahn Executive Editor
Eric Harburn Executive Editor
Kate Henning Director, Operations
Ryan Matsunaga Director, Marketing
Stephanie Lazarski Director, Operations
Elyse Strandberg Manager, Finance
Michelle Ankley Manager, Production Design
Cheryl Parker Manager, Human Resources
Dafna Pleban Senior Editor
Elizabeth Brei Editor
Kathleen Wisneski Editor
Sophie Philips-Roberts Editor
Jonathan Manning Associate Editor
Allyson Gronowitz Associate Editor
Gavin Gronenthal Assistant Editor
Gwen Waller Assistant Editor

Ramiro Portnoy Assistant Editor
Kenzie Rzonca Assistant Editor
Rey Netschke Editorial Assistant
Marie Krupina Design Lead
Crystal White Design Lead
Grace Park Design Coordinator
Madison Goyette Production Designer
Veronica Gutierrez Production Designer
Jessy Gould Production Designer
Nancy Mojica Production Designer
Samantha Knapp Production Design Assistant
Esther Kim Marketing Lead
Breanna Sarpy Marketing Lead, Digital
Amanda Lawson Marketing Coordinator
Alex Lorenzen Marketing Coordinator, Copywriter
Grecia Martinez Marketing Assistant, Digital
José Meza Consumer Sales Lead
Ashley Troub Consumer Sales Coordinator
Harley Salbacka Sales Coordinator
Megan Christopher Operations Coordinator
Rodrigo Hernandez Operations Coordinator
Jason Lee Senior Accountant
Faizah Bashir Business Analyst
Amber Peters Staff Accountant
Sabrina Lesin Accounting Assistant

BUFFY THE VAMPIRE SLAYER Volume Ten, August 2022.
Published by BOOM! Studios, a division of Boom Entertainment, Inc.
© 2022 20th Television. Originally published in single magazine form
as BUFFY THE VAMPIRE SLAYER No. 33-34, 25th Anniversary
Special. © 2022 20th Television. BOOM! Studios™ and the
BOOM! Studios logo are trademarks of Boom Entertainment, Inc.,
registered in various countries and categories. All characters, events,
and institutions depicted herein are fictional. Any similarity between
any of the names, characters, persons, events, and/or institutions in
this publication to actual names, characters, and persons, whether
living or dead, events, and/or institutions is unintended and purely
coincidental. BOOM! Studios does not read or accept unsolicited
submissions of ideas, stories, or artwork.

BOOM! Studios, 5670 Wilshire Boulevard, Suite 400, Los Angeles,
CA 90036-5679. Printed in China. First Printing.

ISBN: 978-1-68415-842-3, eISBN: 978-1-64668-740-4

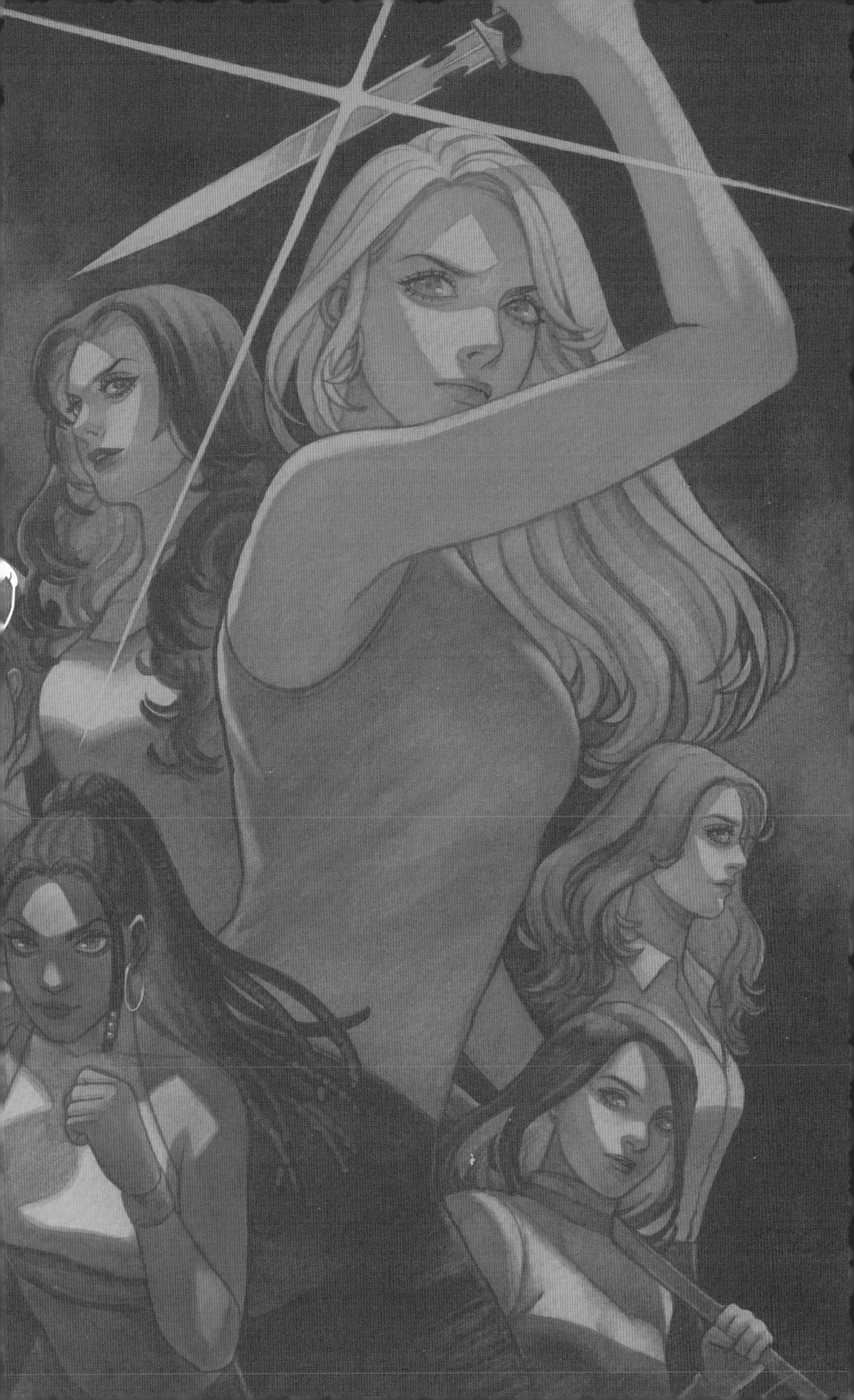

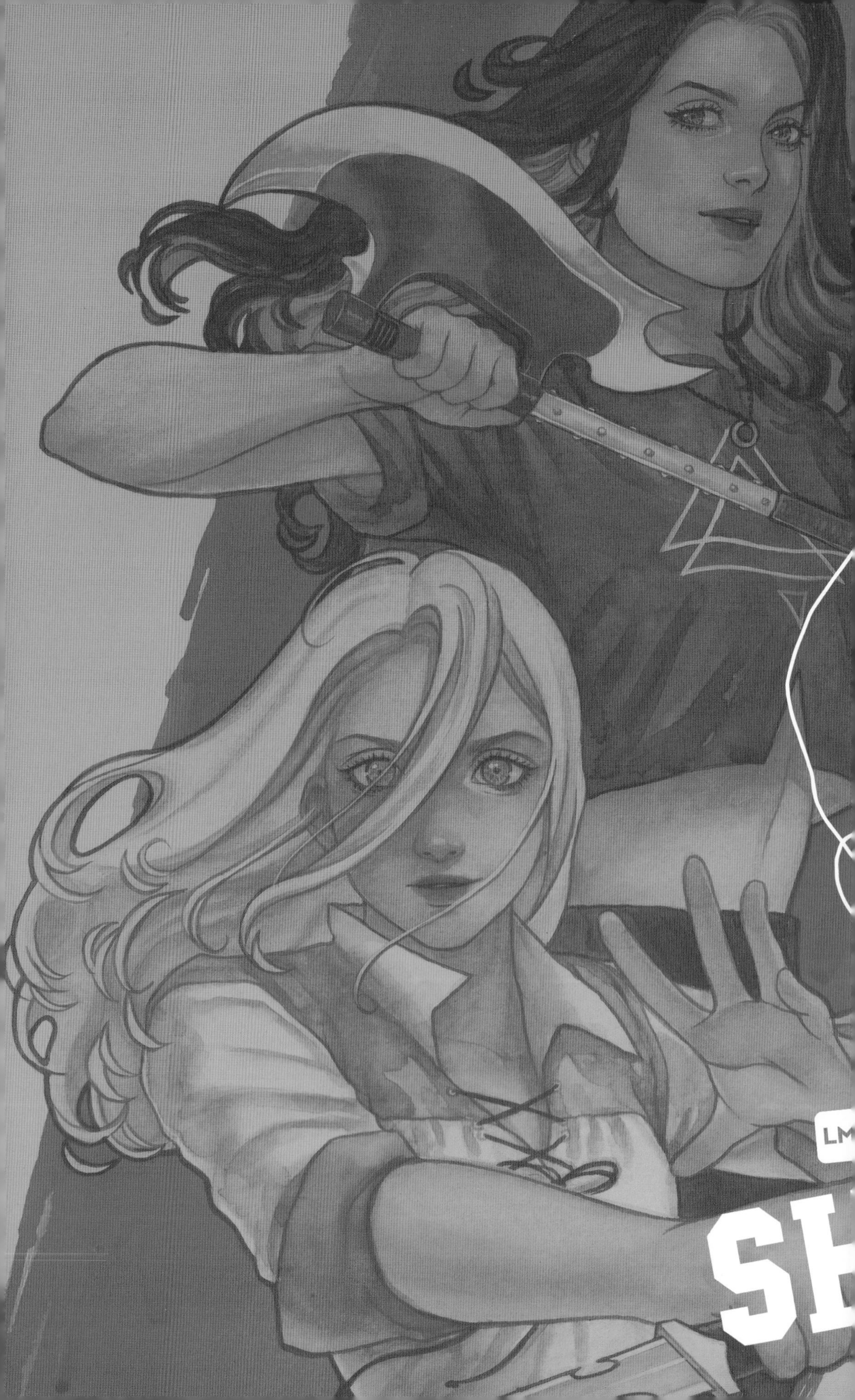

Created by
Joss Whedon

Written by
Jeremy Lambert

Illustrated by
Valentina Pinti Chapter 33
Marianna Ignazzi Chapter 34
Claudia Balboni Epilogue

Colored by
Raúl Angulo

Lettered by
Ed Dukeshire

Cover by
Frany

CHAPTER
THIRTY-THREE

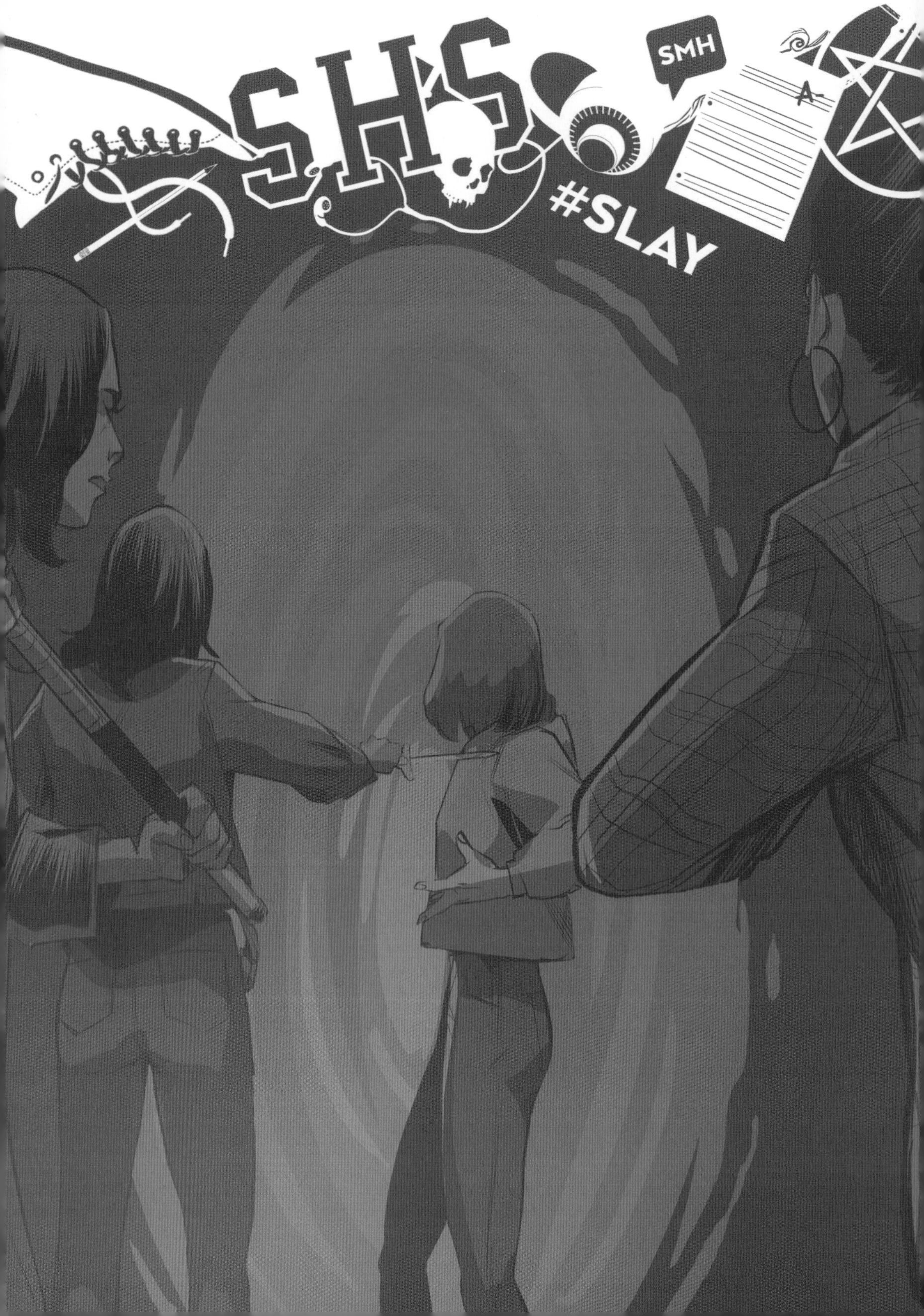
S.H.S.
SMH
#SLAY

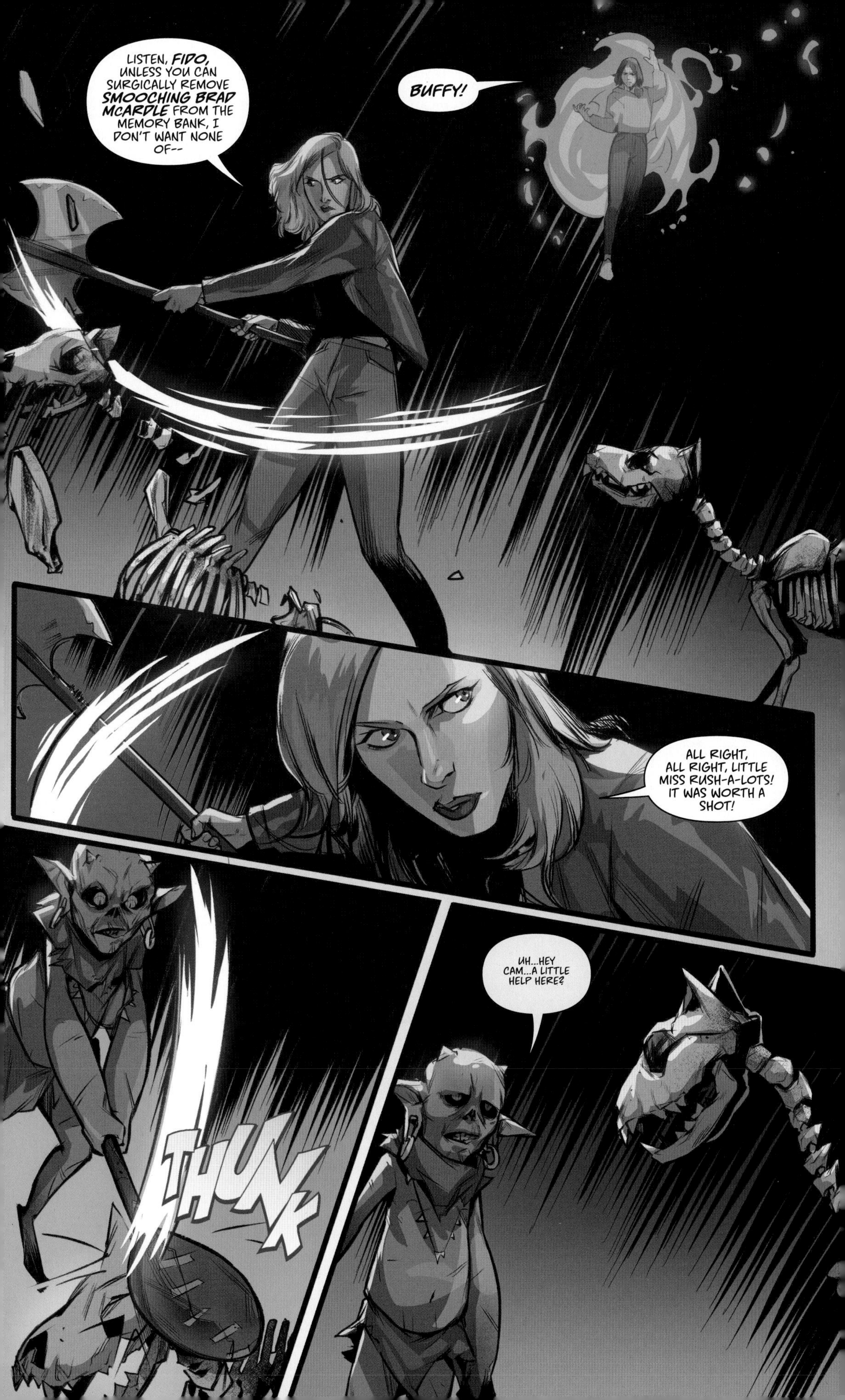
LISTEN, FIDO, UNLESS YOU CAN SURGICALLY REMOVE SMOOCHING BRAD MCARDLE FROM THE MEMORY BANK, I DON'T WANT NONE OF--
BUFFY!
ALL RIGHT, ALL RIGHT, LITTLE MISS RUSH-A-LOTS! IT WAS WORTH A SHOT!
THUNK
UH...HEY CAM...A LITTLE HELP HERE?

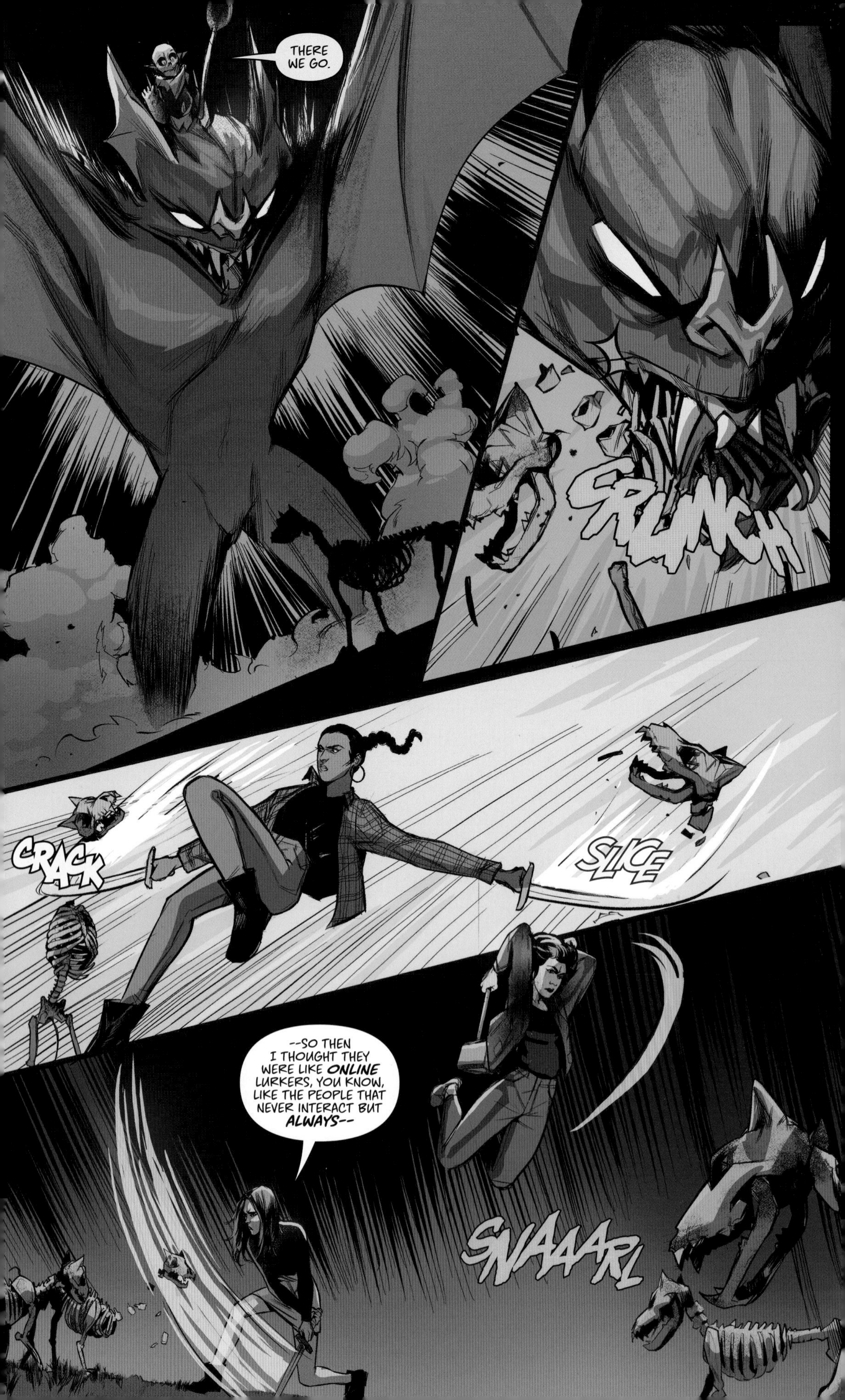
THERE WE GO.
CRUNCH
CRACK
SLICE
--SO THEN I THOUGHT THEY WERE LIKE ONLINE LURKERS, YOU KNOW, LIKE THE PEOPLE THAT NEVER INTERACT BUT ALWAYS--
SNAAARL

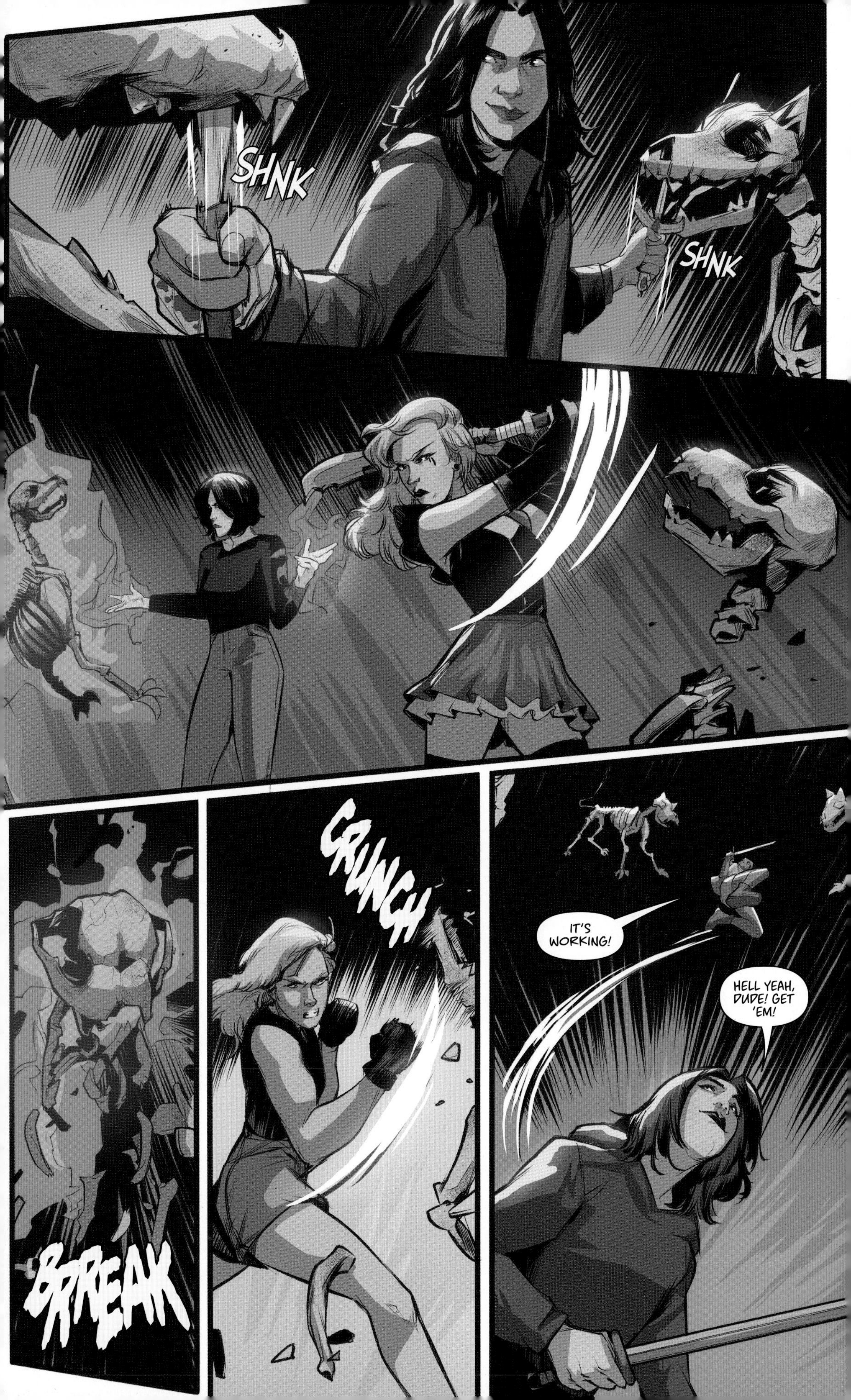
SHNK
SHNK
BRREAK
CRUNCH
IT'S WORKING!
HELL YEAH, DUDE! GET 'EM!

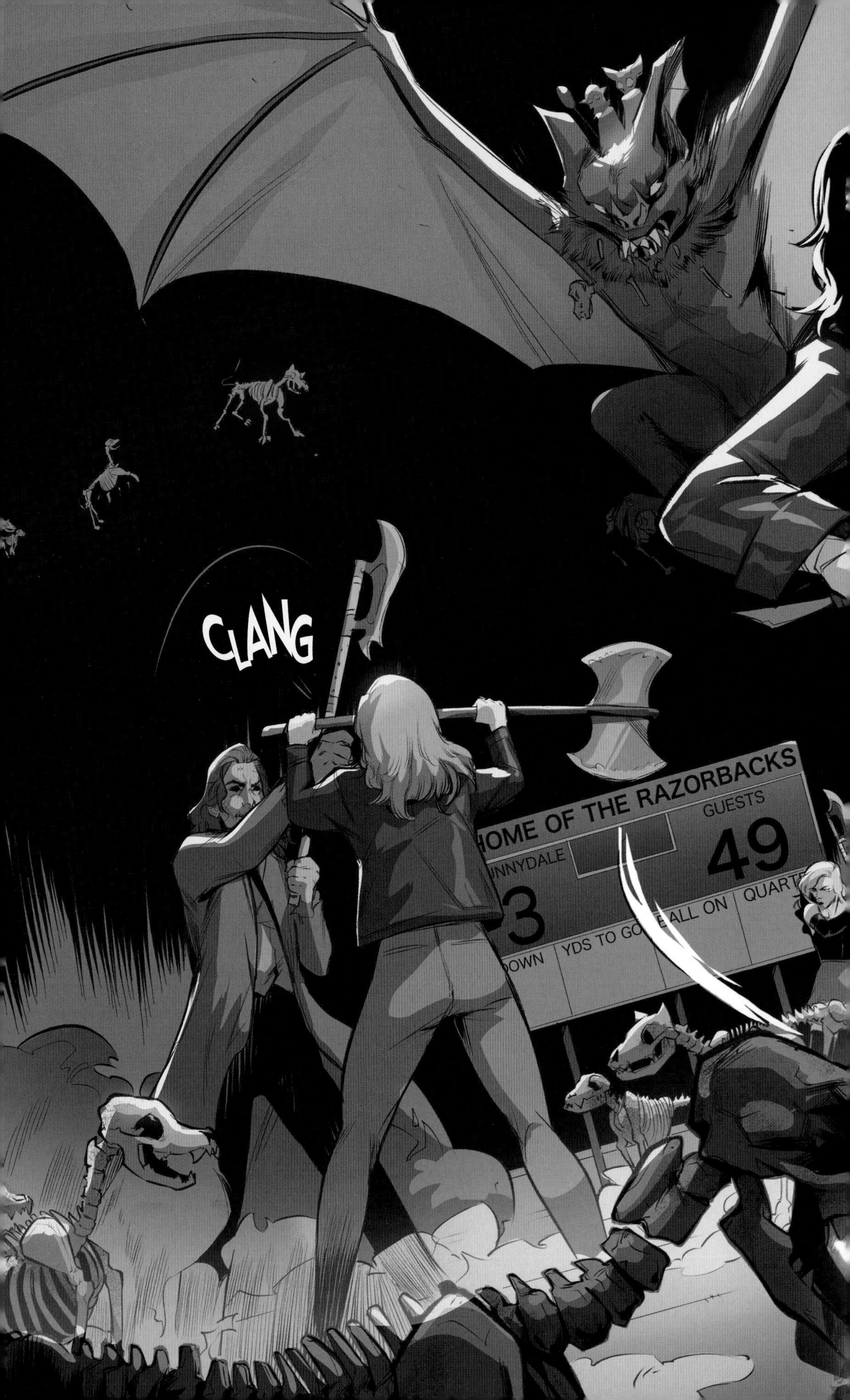
CLANG
HOME OF THE RAZORBACKS
GUESTS
49
YDS TO GO
BALL ON

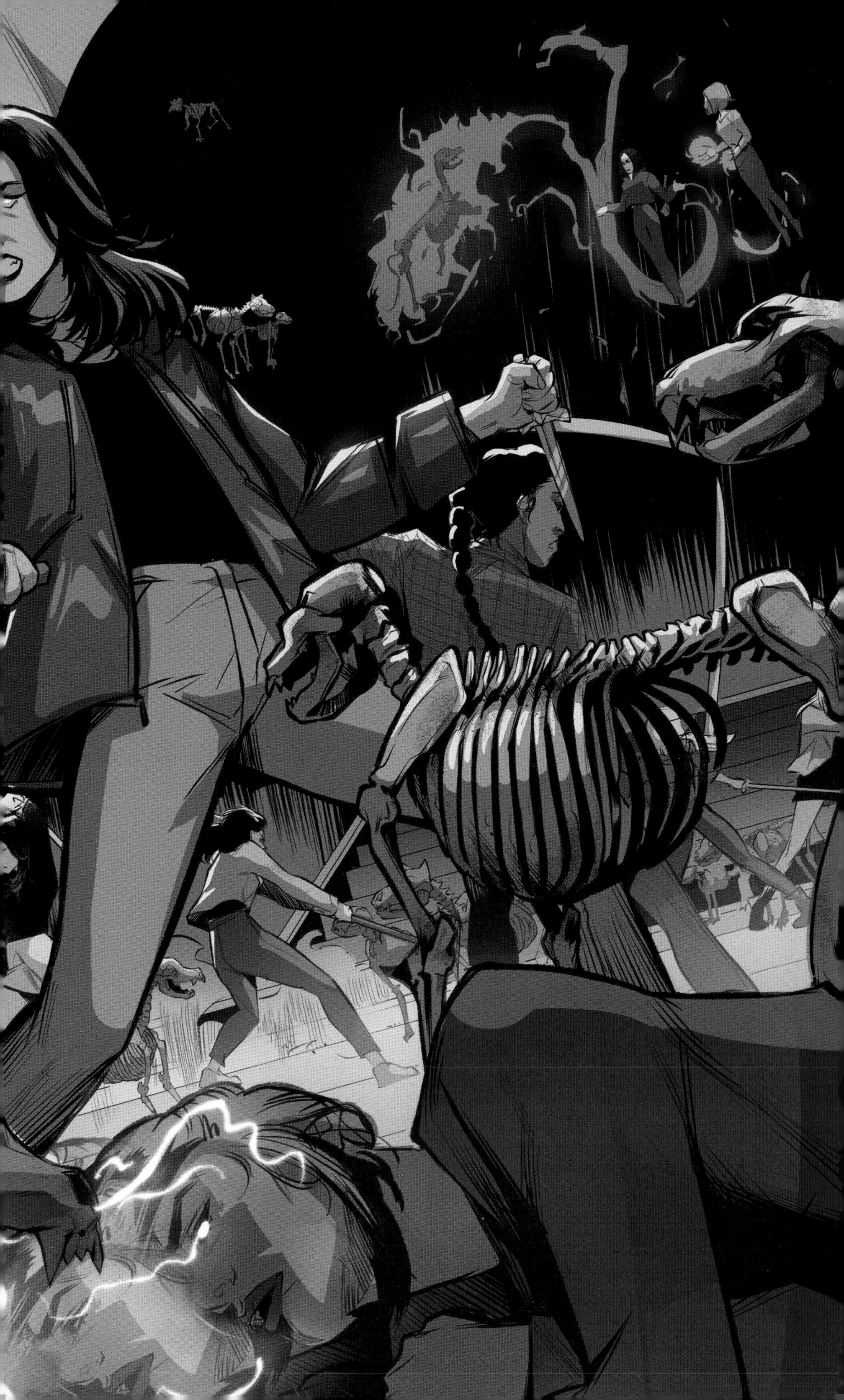

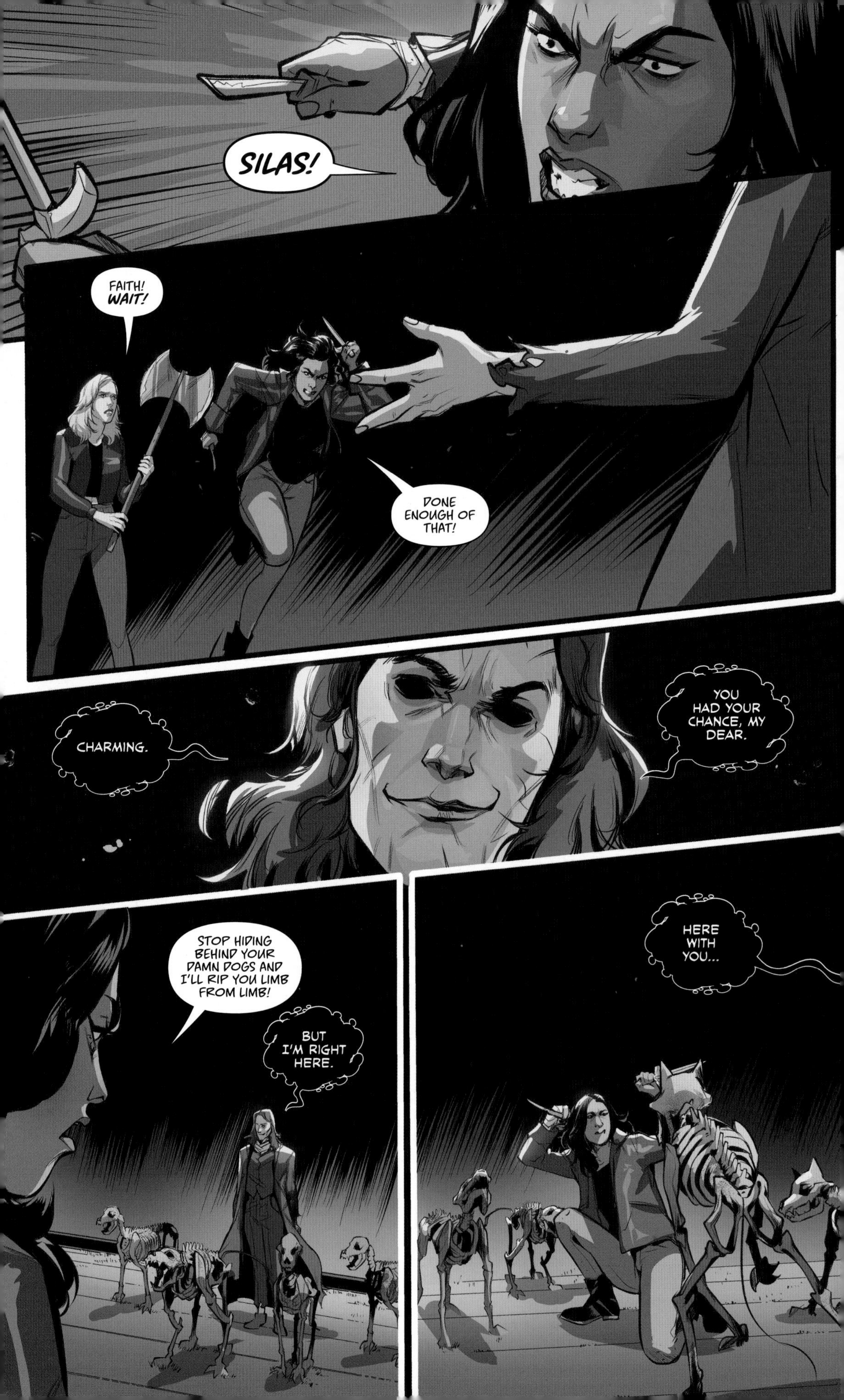
SILAS!
FAITH! WAIT!
DONE ENOUGH OF THAT!
CHARMING.
YOU HAD YOUR CHANCE, MY DEAR.
STOP HIDING BEHIND YOUR DAMN DOGS AND I'LL RIP YOU LIMB FROM LIMB!
BUT I'M RIGHT HERE.
HERE WITH YOU...

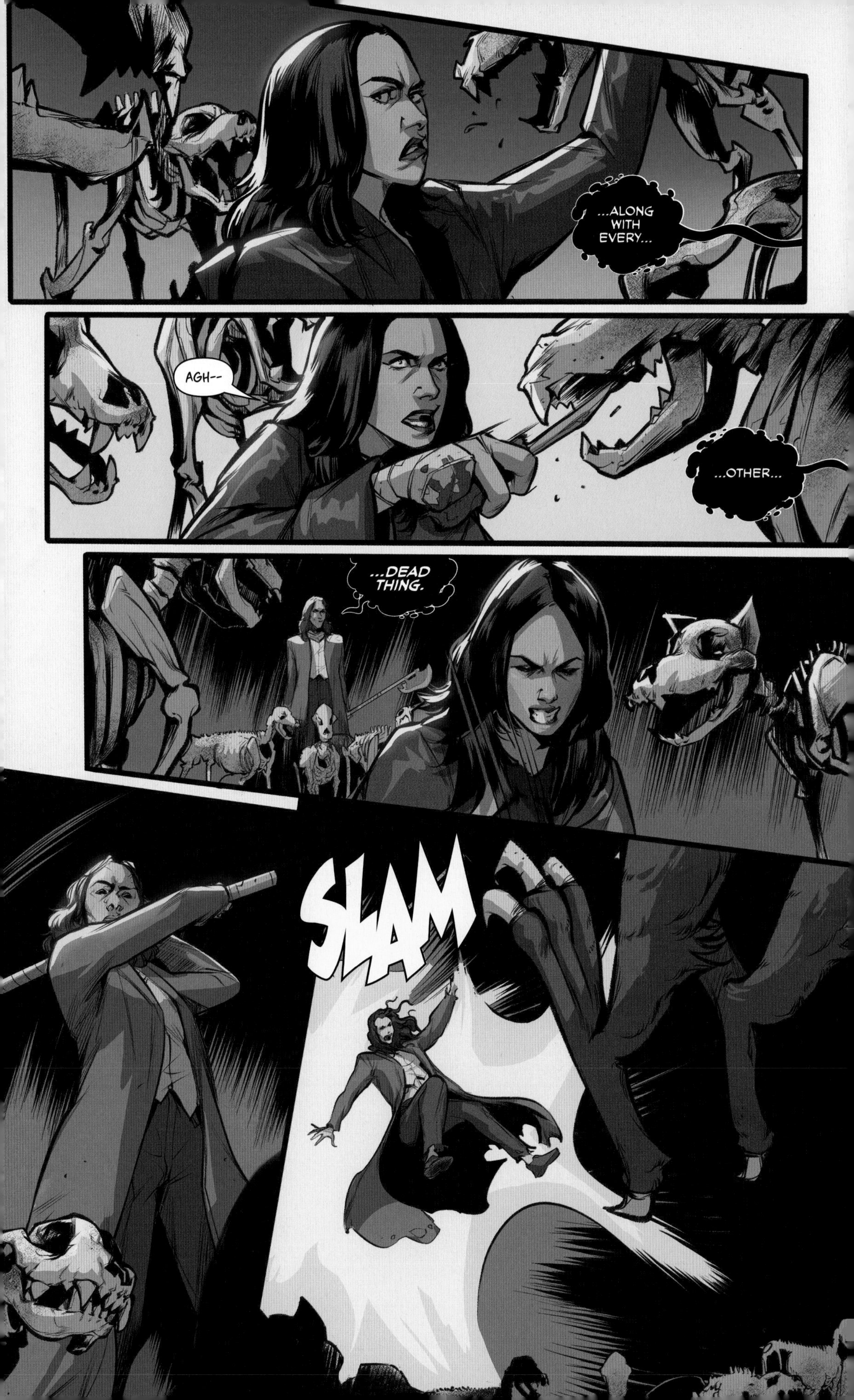
...ALONG WITH EVERY...
AGH--
...OTHER...
...DEAD THING.
SLAM

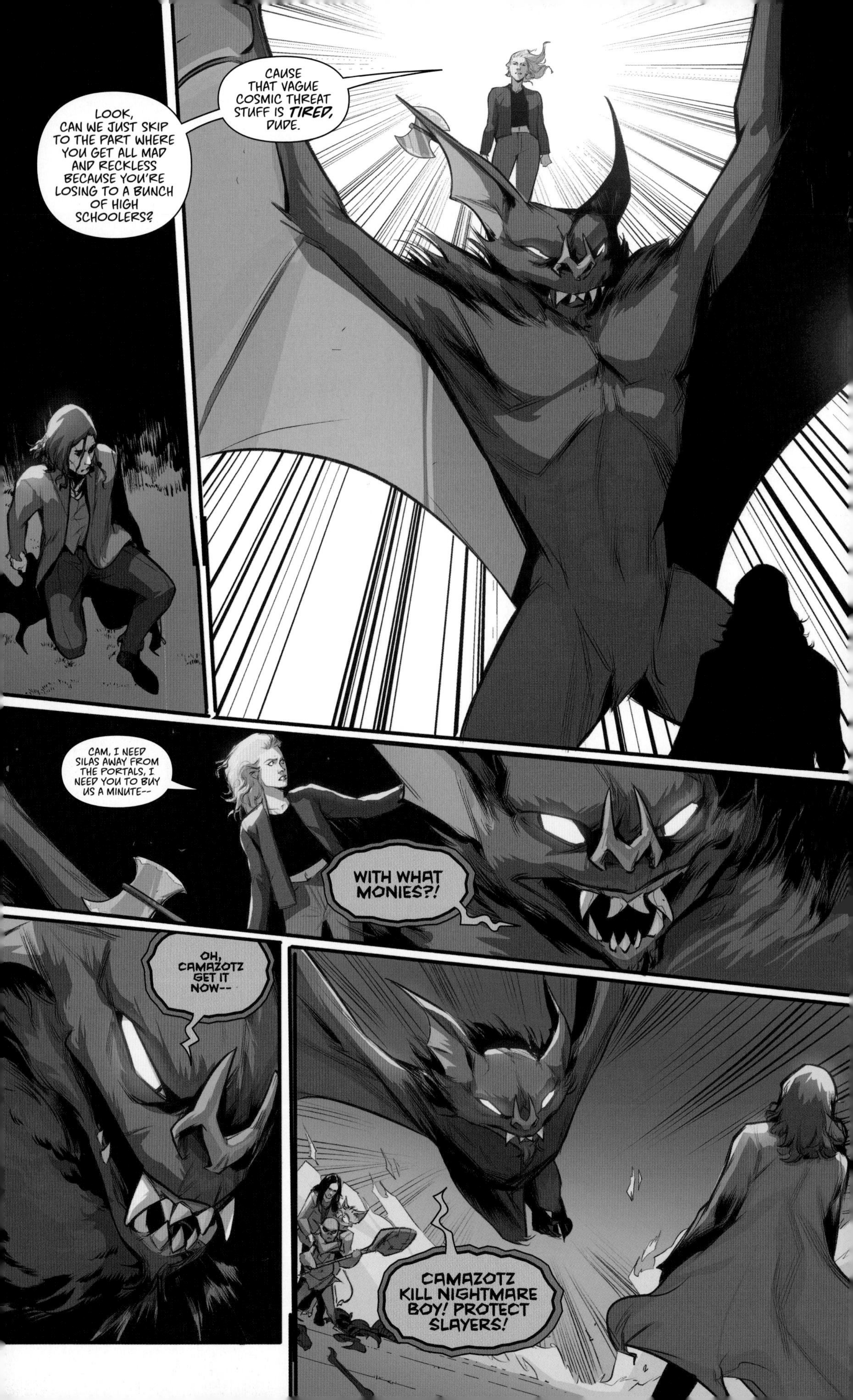

LOOK, CAN WE JUST SKIP TO THE PART WHERE YOU GET ALL MAD AND RECKLESS BECAUSE YOU'RE LOSING TO A BUNCH OF HIGH SCHOOLERS?
CAUSE THAT VAGUE COSMIC THREAT STUFF IS *TIRED,* DUDE.
CAM, I NEED SILAS AWAY FROM THE PORTALS, I NEED YOU TO BUY US A MINUTE--
WITH WHAT MONIES?!
OH, CAMAZOTZ GET IT NOW--
CAMAZOTZ KILL NIGHTMARE BOY! PROTECT SLAYERS!

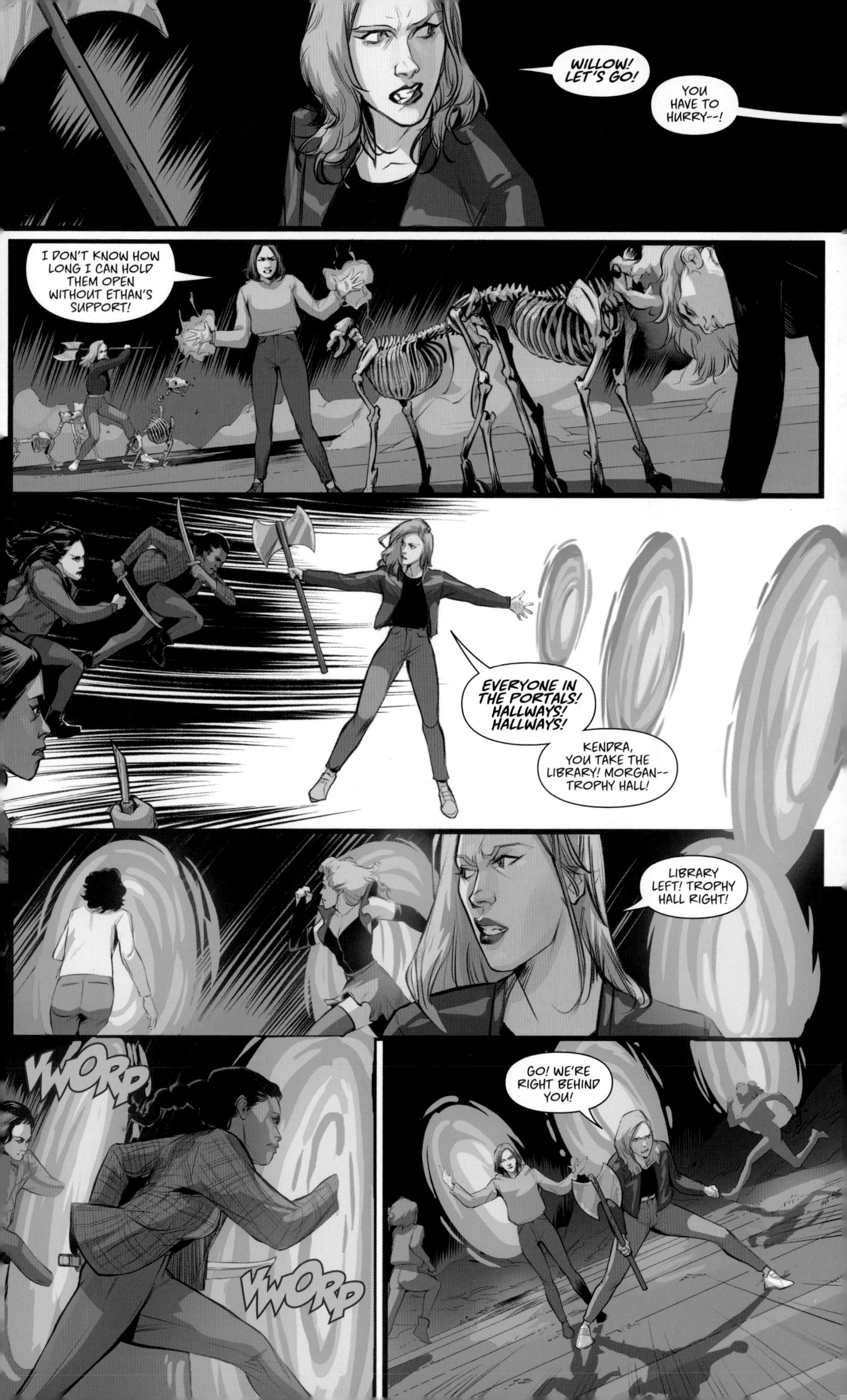
WILLOW! LET'S GO!
YOU HAVE TO HURRY--!
I DON'T KNOW HOW LONG I CAN HOLD THEM OPEN WITHOUT ETHAN'S SUPPORT!
EVERYONE IN THE PORTALS! HALLWAYS! HALLWAYS!
KENDRA, YOU TAKE THE LIBRARY! MORGAN-- TROPHY HALL!
LIBRARY LEFT! TROPHY HALL RIGHT!
WWORP
WWORP
GO! WE'RE RIGHT BEHIND YOU!

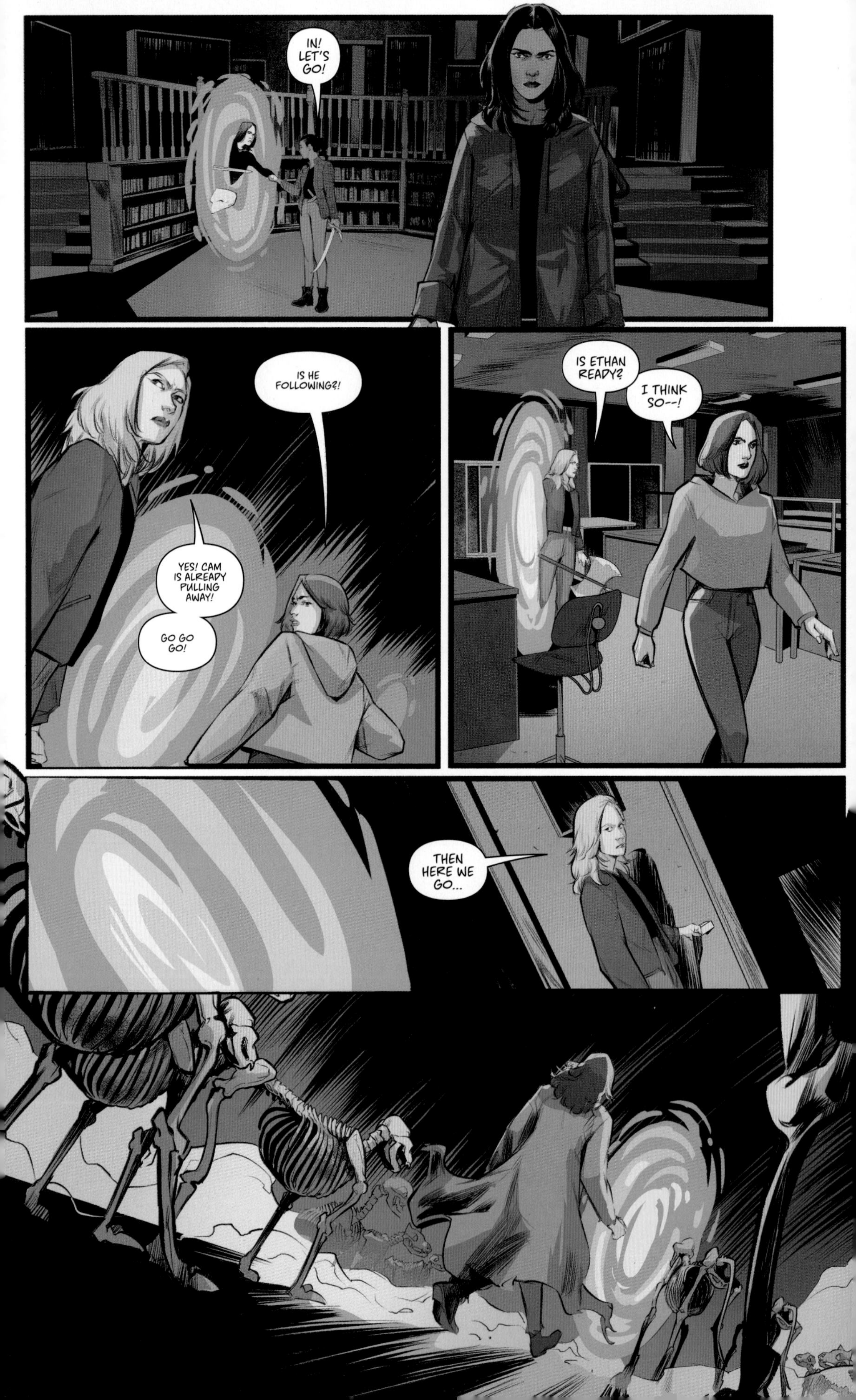
IN! LET'S GO!
IS HE FOLLOWING?!
YES! CAM IS ALREADY PULLING AWAY!
GO GO GO!
IS ETHAN READY?
I THINK SO--!
THEN HERE WE GO...

CREEEAK

JUVENILE...

LIKE WALLS COULD STOP ME.

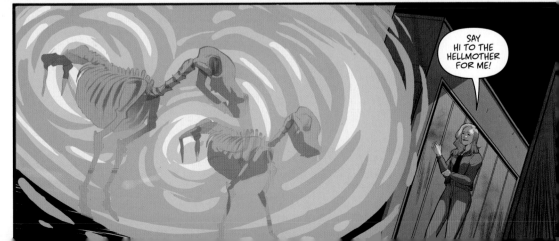

SAY HI TO THE HELLMOTHER FOR ME!

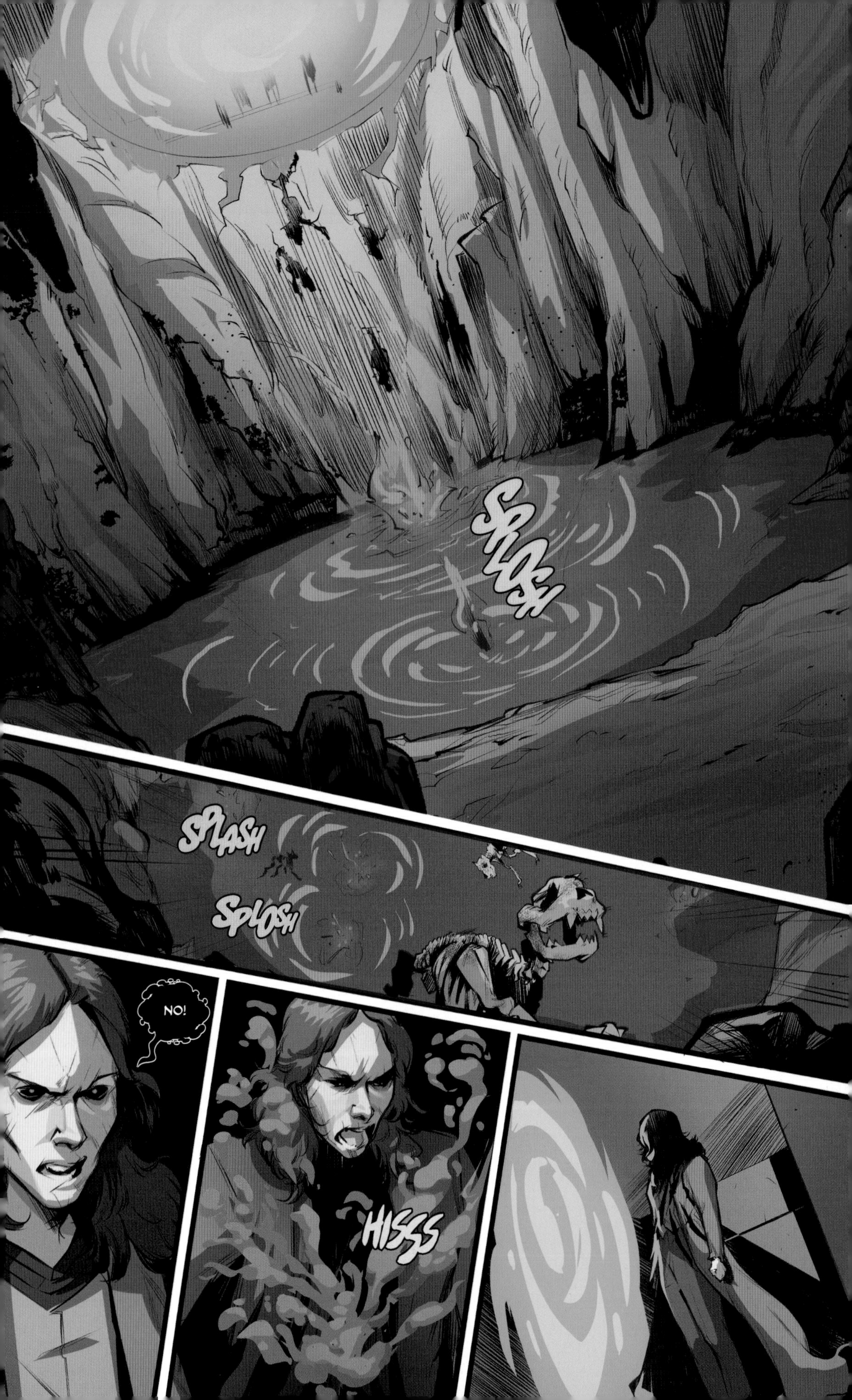
SPLOSH
SPLASH
SPLOSH
NO!
HISSS

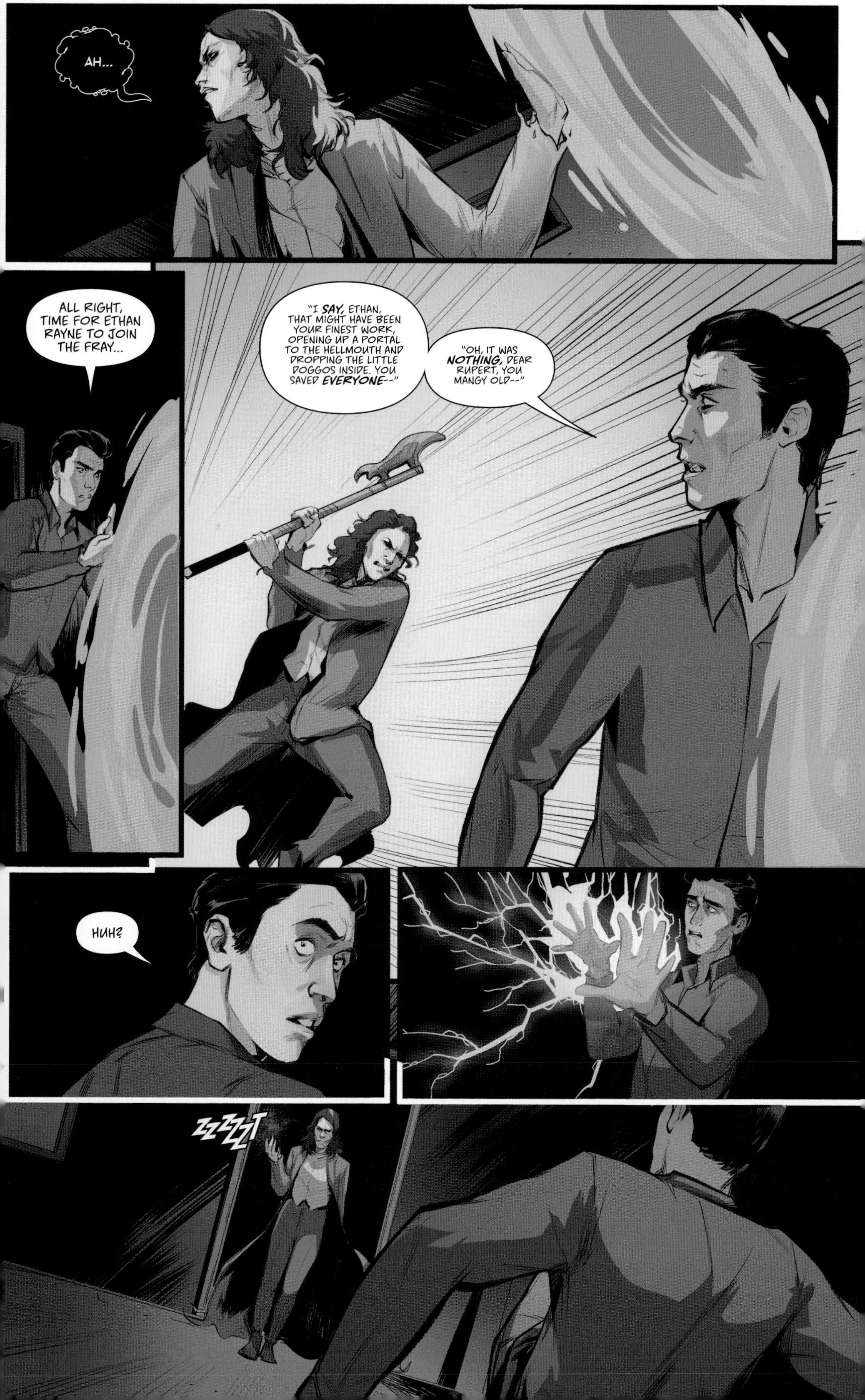
AH...
ALL RIGHT, TIME FOR ETHAN RAYNE TO JOIN THE FRAY...
"I SAY, ETHAN, THAT MIGHT HAVE BEEN YOUR FINEST WORK, OPENING UP A PORTAL TO THE HELLMOUTH AND DROPPING THE LITTLE DOGGOS INSIDE. YOU SAVED EVERYONE--"
"OH, IT WAS NOTHING, DEAR RUPERT, YOU MANGY OLD--"
HUH?
ZZZZZT

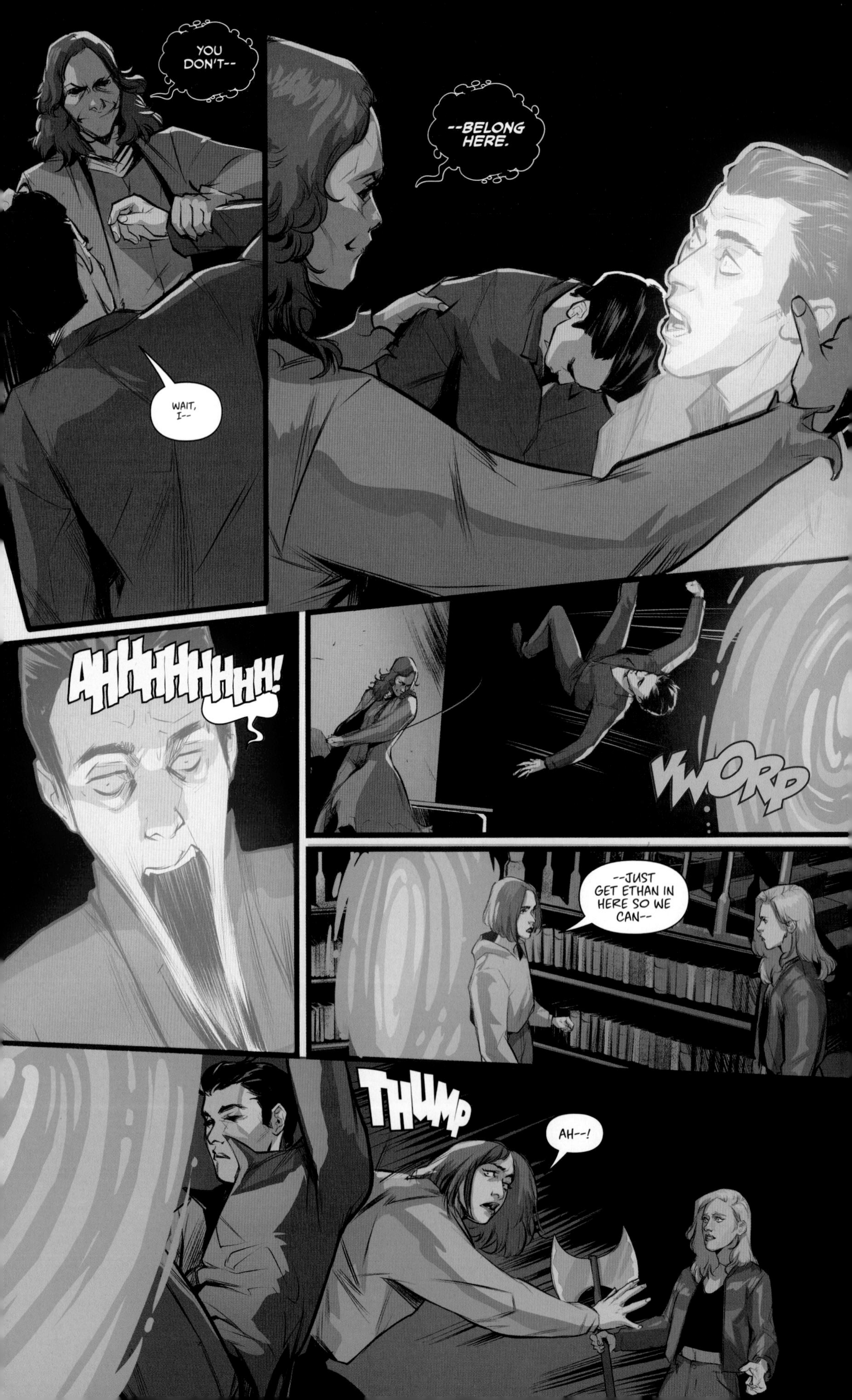
YOU DON'T--
--BELONG HERE.
WAIT, I--
AHHHHHHHH!
VWORP
--JUST GET ETHAN IN HERE SO WE CAN--
THUMP
AH--!

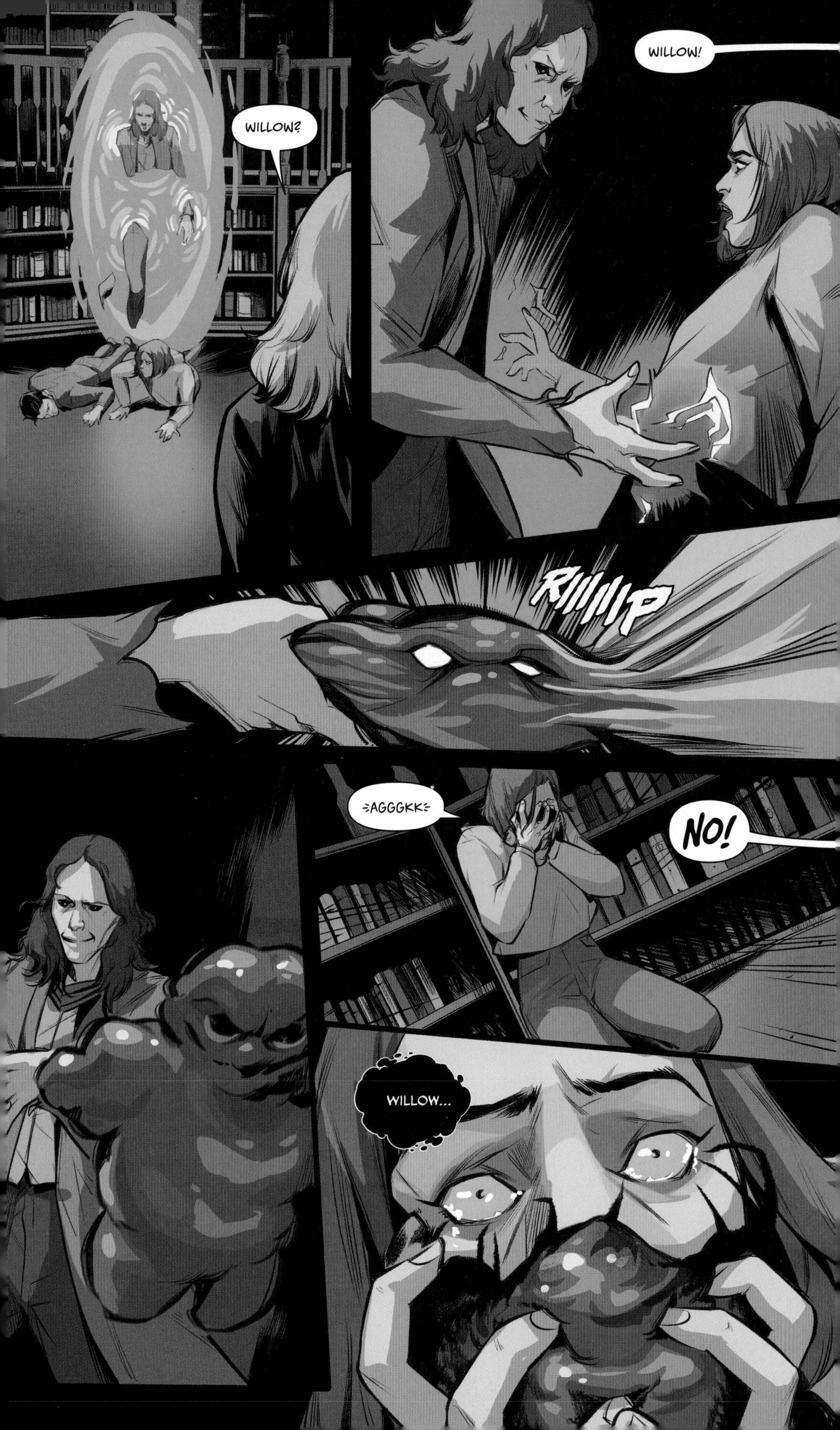
WILLOW?
WILLOW!
RIIIIIP
=AGGGKK=
NO!
WILLOW...

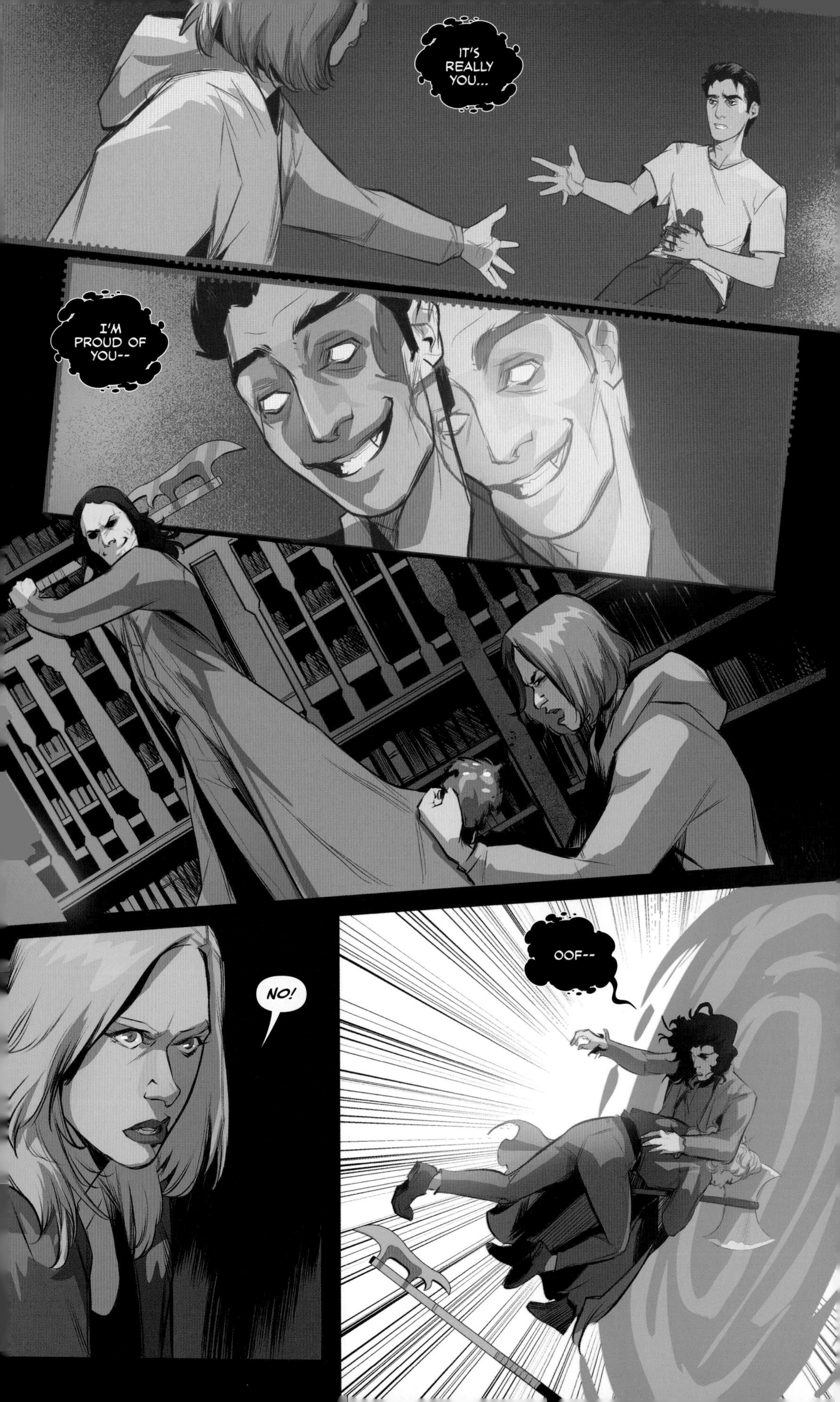
IT'S REALLY YOU...
I'M PROUD OF YOU--
NO!
OOF--

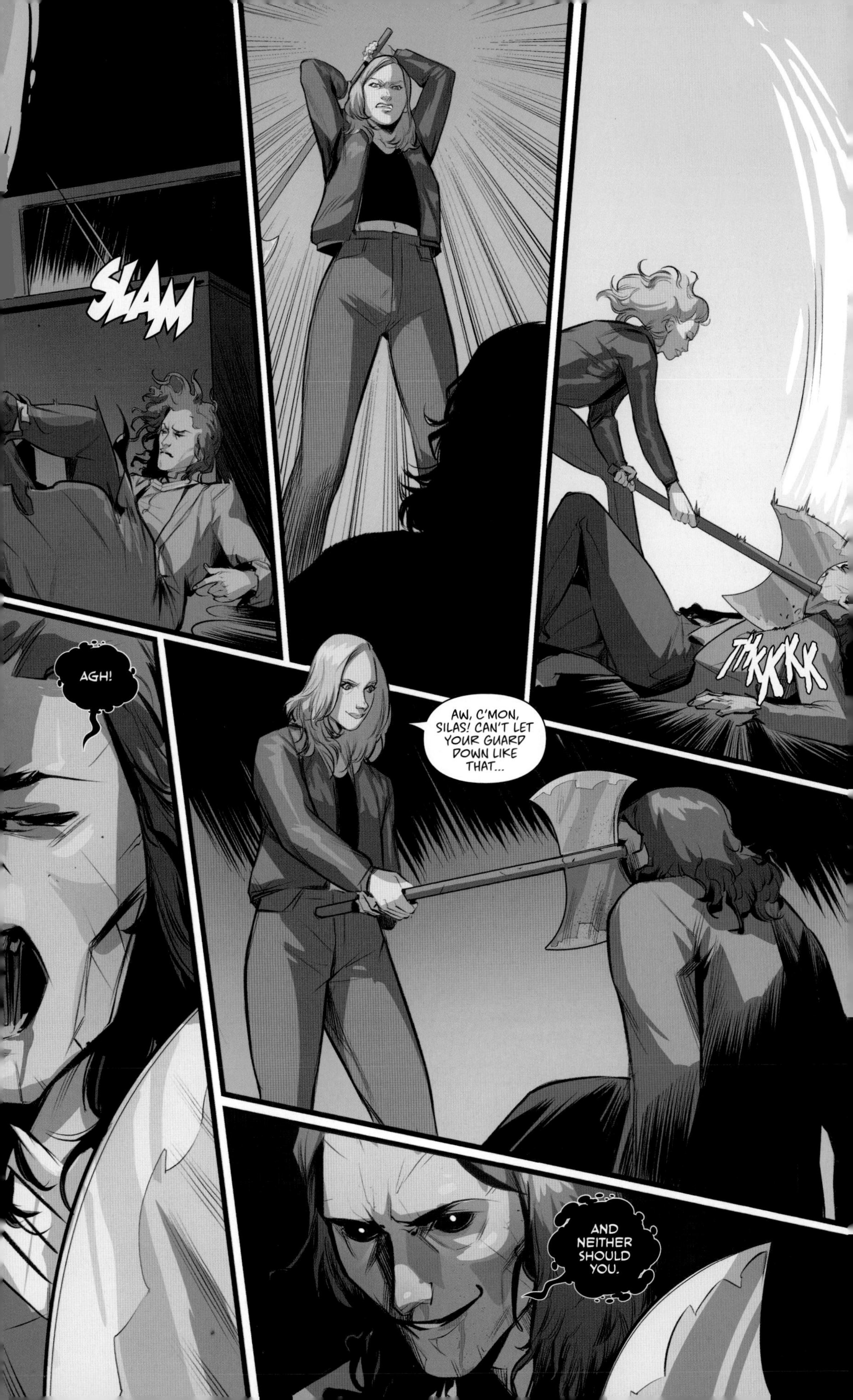
SLAM
THKKKK
AGH!
AW, C'MON, SILAS! CAN'T LET YOUR GUARD DOWN LIKE THAT...
AND NEITHER SHOULD YOU.

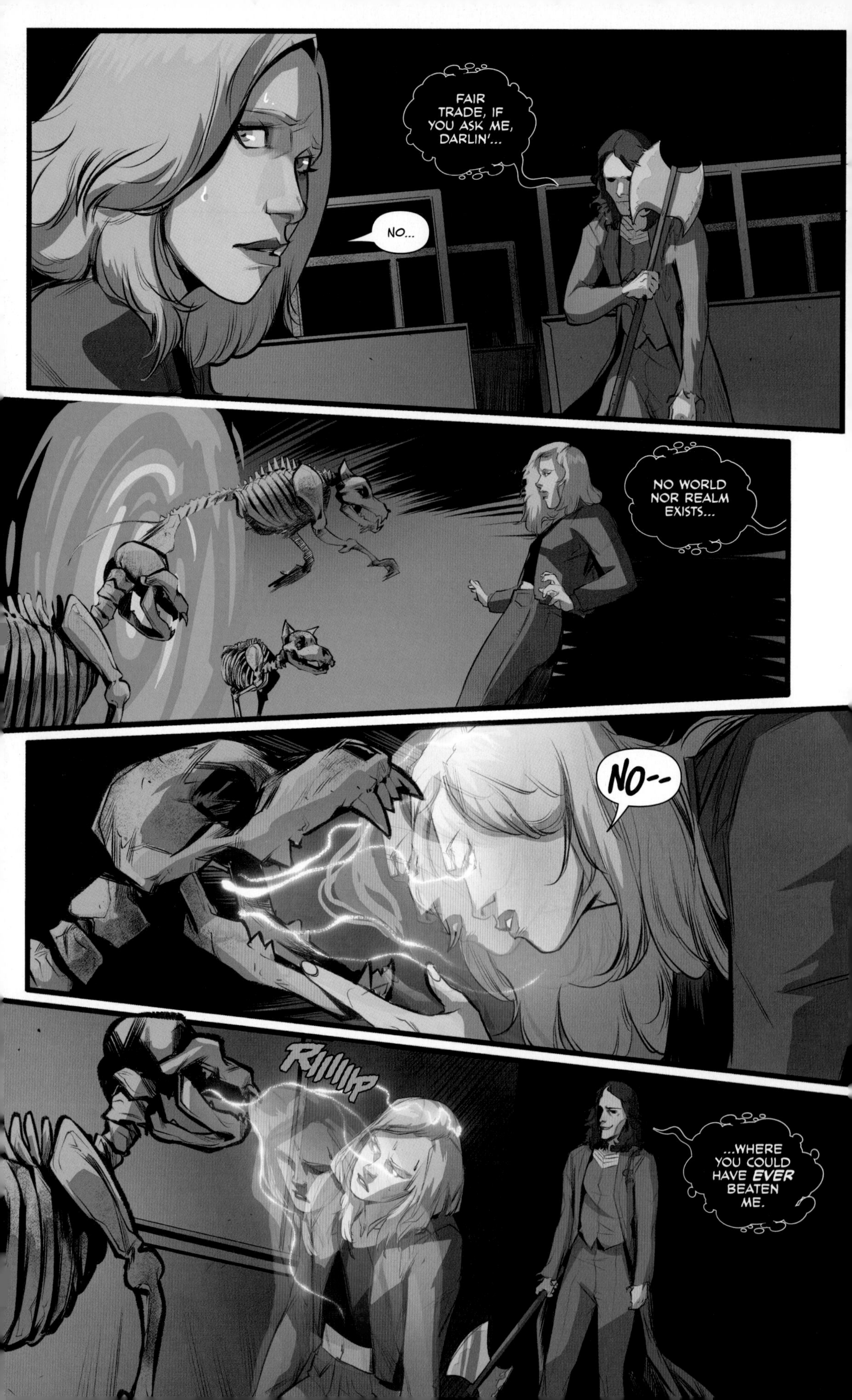
FAIR TRADE, IF YOU ASK ME, DARLIN'...
NO...
NO WORLD NOR REALM EXISTS...
NO--
RIIIIIP
...WHERE YOU COULD HAVE *EVER* BEATEN ME.

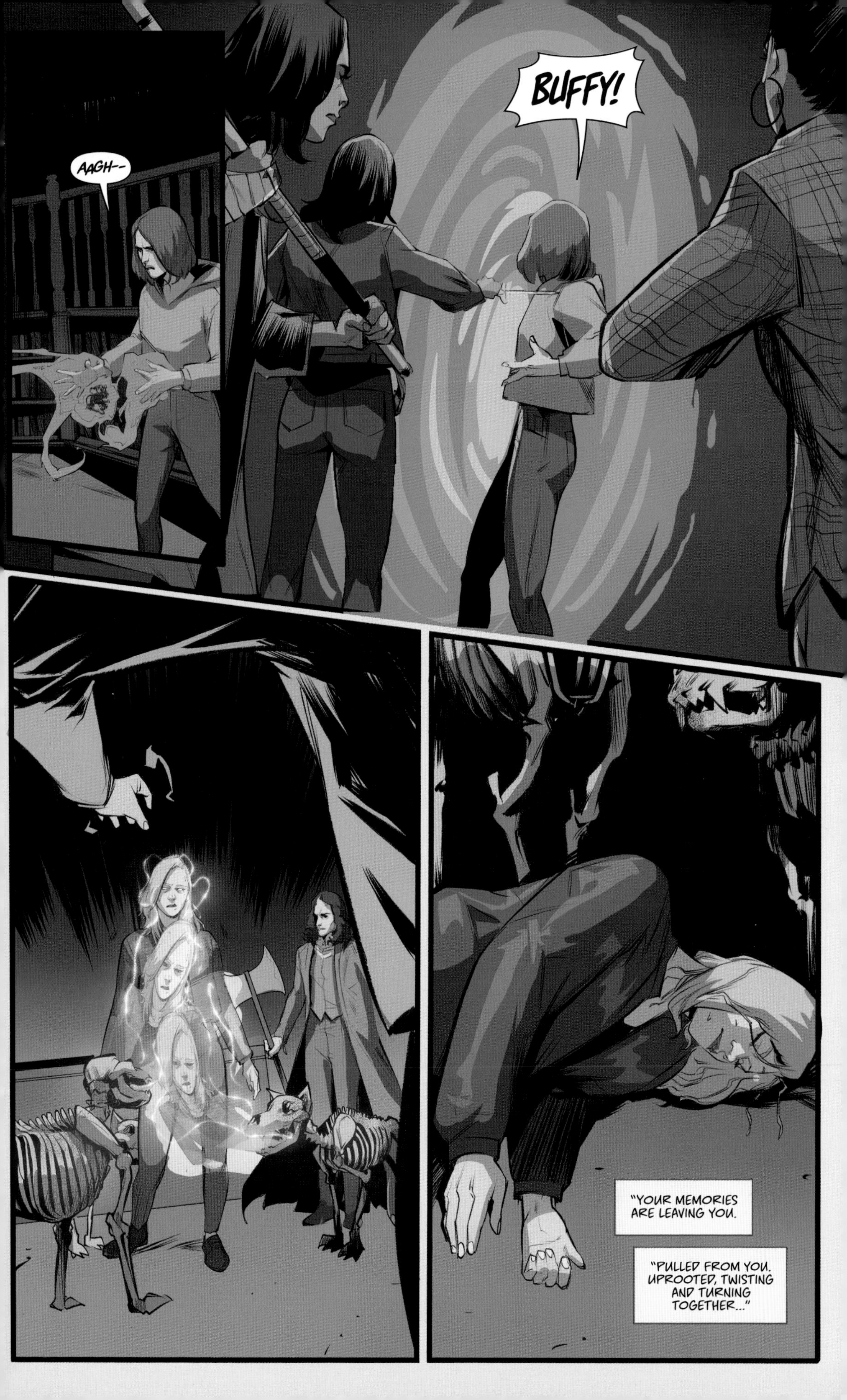
AAGH--
BUFFY!
"YOUR MEMORIES ARE LEAVING YOU.
"PULLED FROM YOU. UPROOTED, TWISTING AND TURNING TOGETHER..."

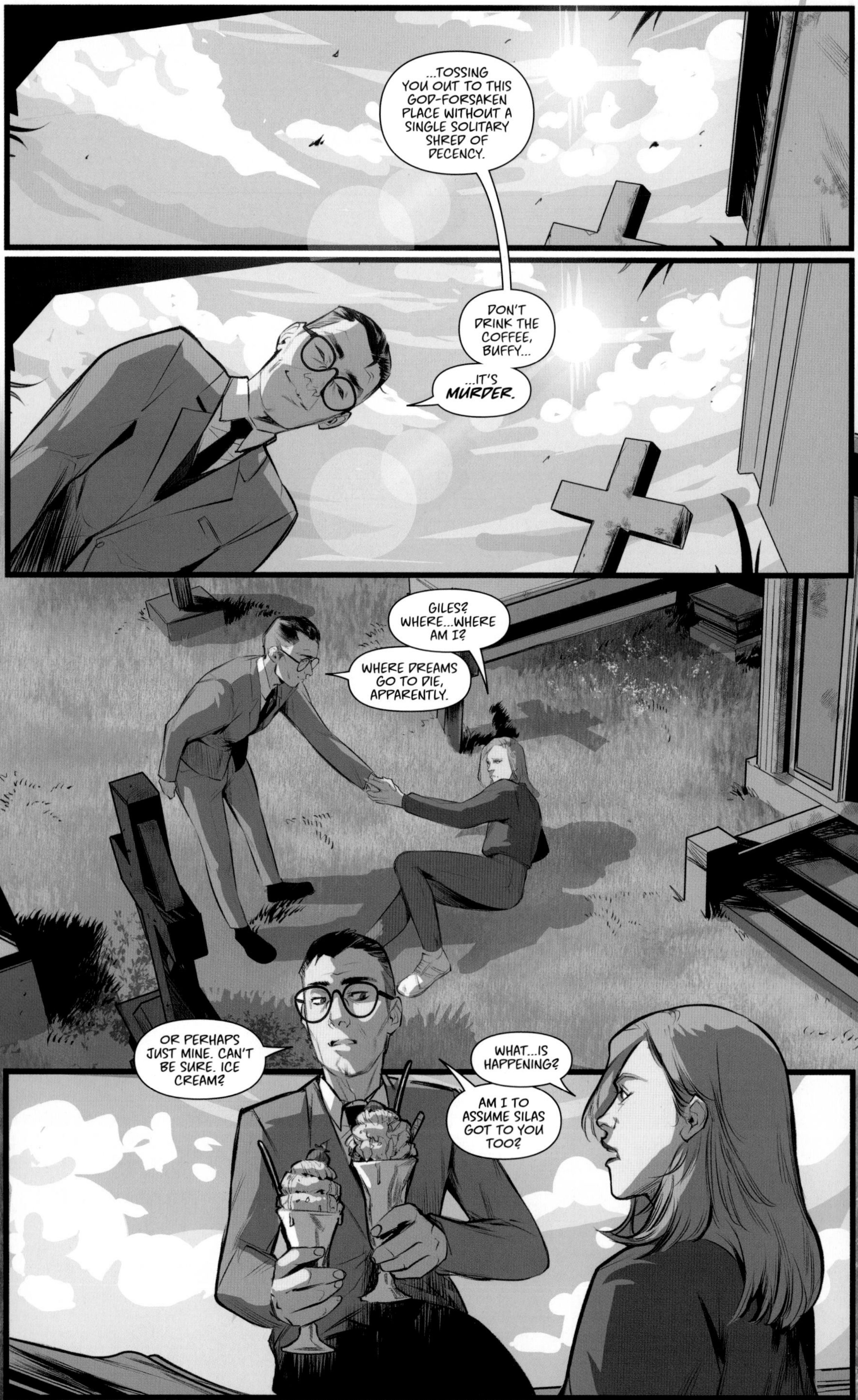
...TOSSING YOU OUT TO THIS GOD-FORSAKEN PLACE WITHOUT A SINGLE SOLITARY SHRED OF DECENCY.
DON'T DRINK THE COFFEE, BUFFY...
...IT'S *MURDER.*
GILES? WHERE...WHERE AM I?
WHERE DREAMS GO TO DIE, APPARENTLY.
OR PERHAPS JUST MINE. CAN'T BE SURE. ICE CREAM?
WHAT...IS HAPPENING?
AM I TO ASSUME SILAS GOT TO YOU TOO?

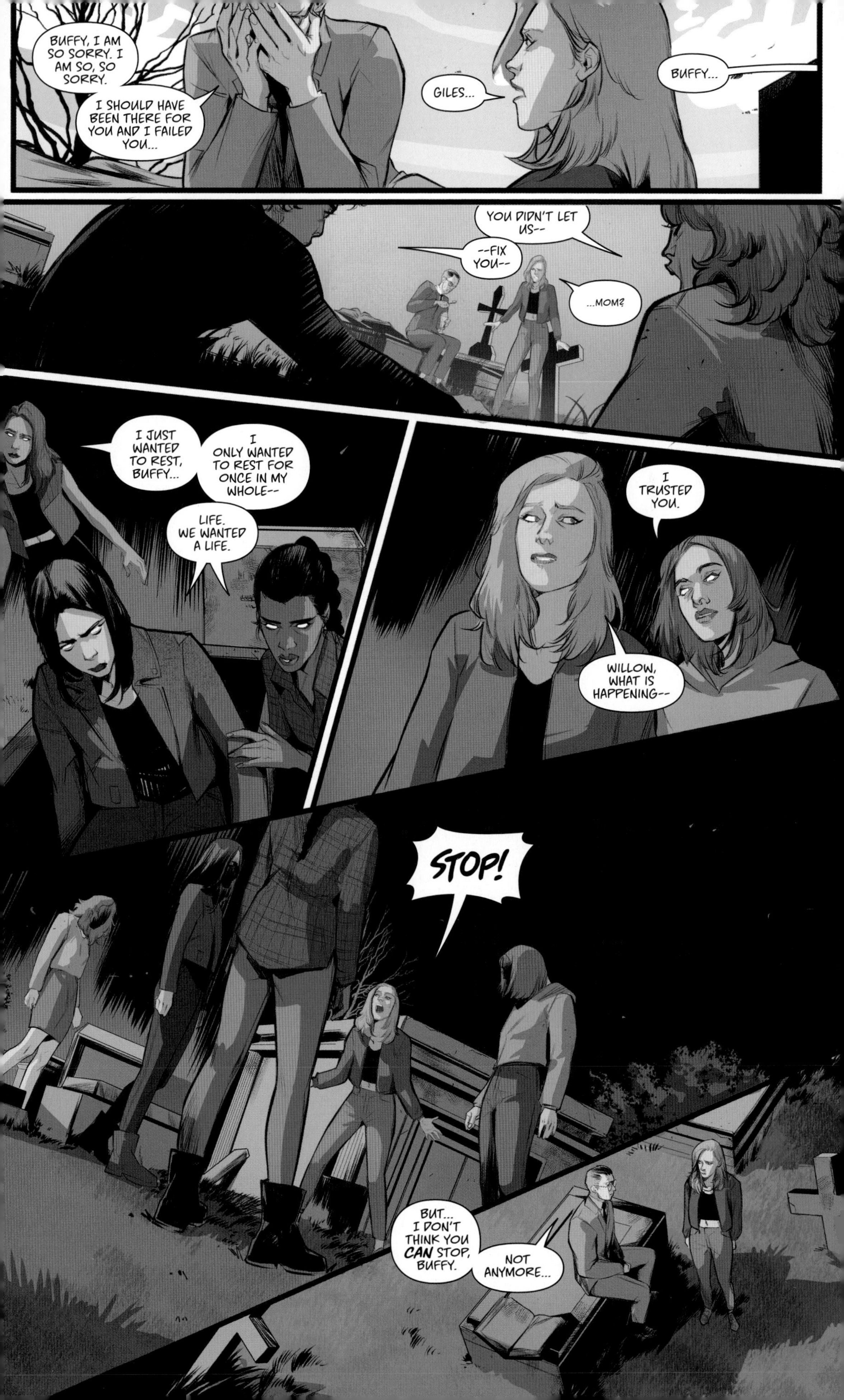
BUFFY, I AM SO SORRY. I AM SO, SO SORRY.
I SHOULD HAVE BEEN THERE FOR YOU AND I FAILED YOU...
GILES...
BUFFY...
YOU DIDN'T LET US--
--FIX YOU--
...MOM?
I JUST WANTED TO REST, BUFFY...
I ONLY WANTED TO REST FOR ONCE IN MY WHOLE--
LIFE. WE WANTED A LIFE.
I TRUSTED YOU.
WILLOW, WHAT IS HAPPENING--
STOP!
BUT... I DON'T THINK YOU CAN STOP, BUFFY.
NOT ANYMORE...

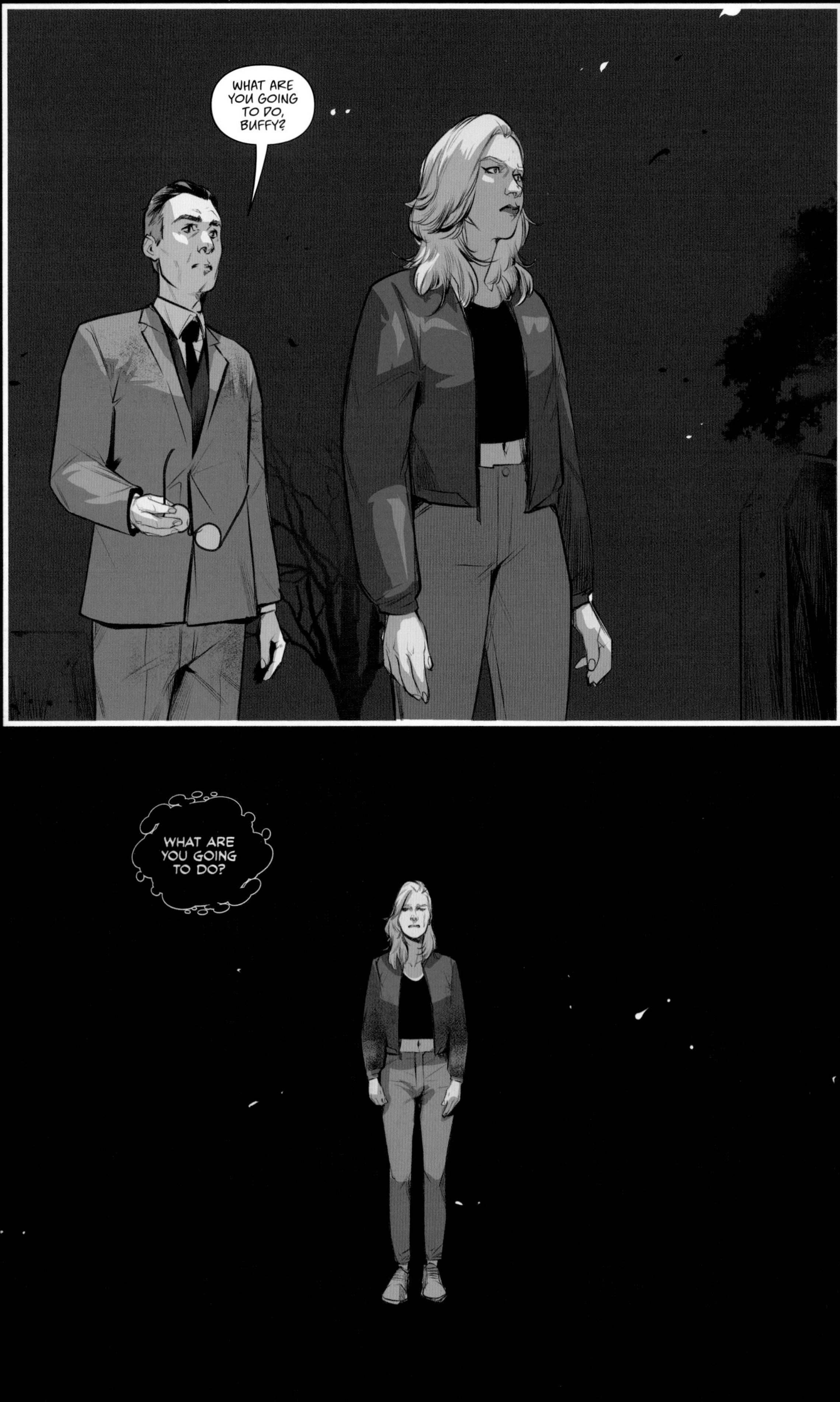
WHAT ARE YOU GOING TO DO, BUFFY?
WHAT ARE YOU GOING TO DO?

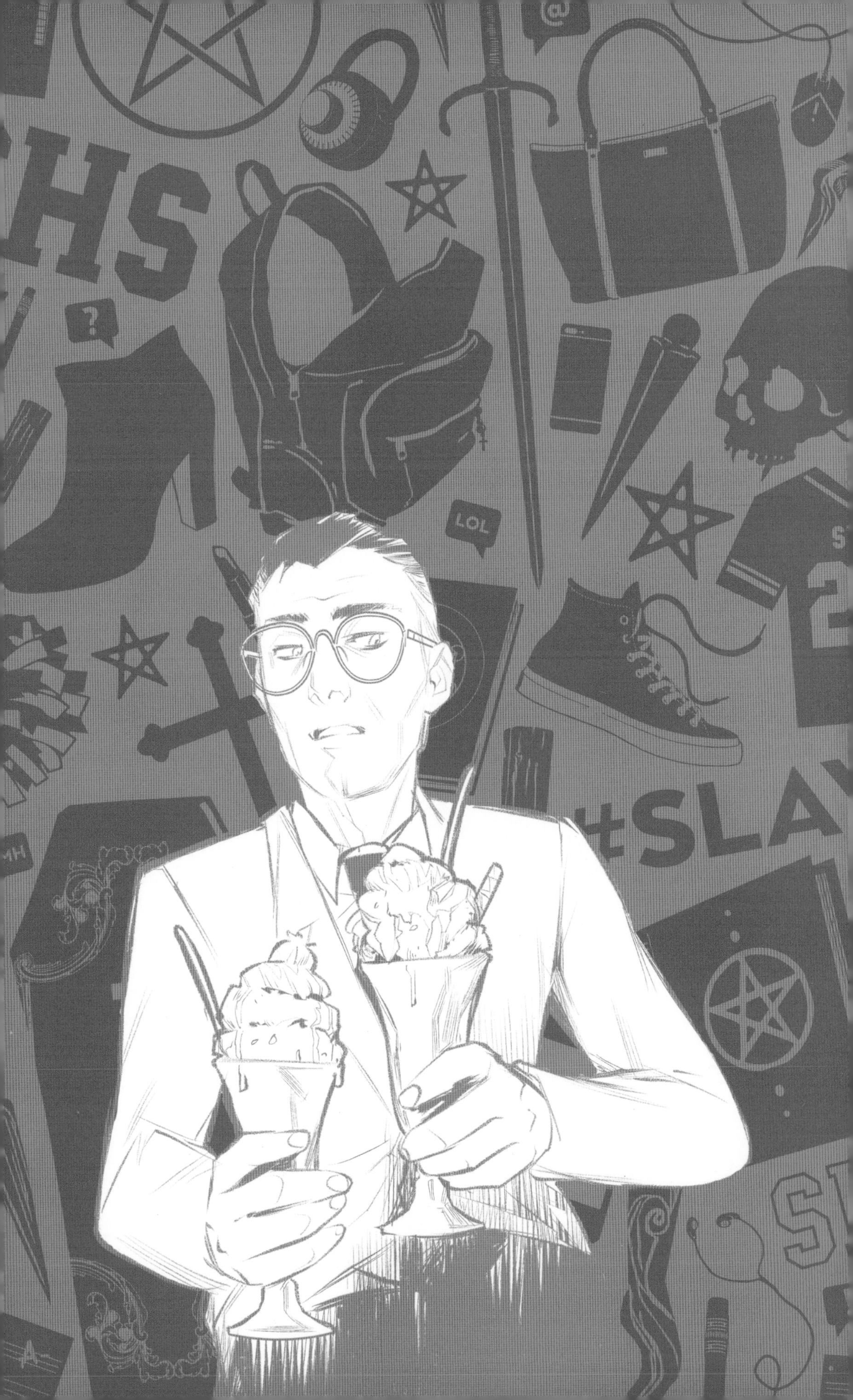
HS
LOL

CHAPTER THIRTY-FOUR

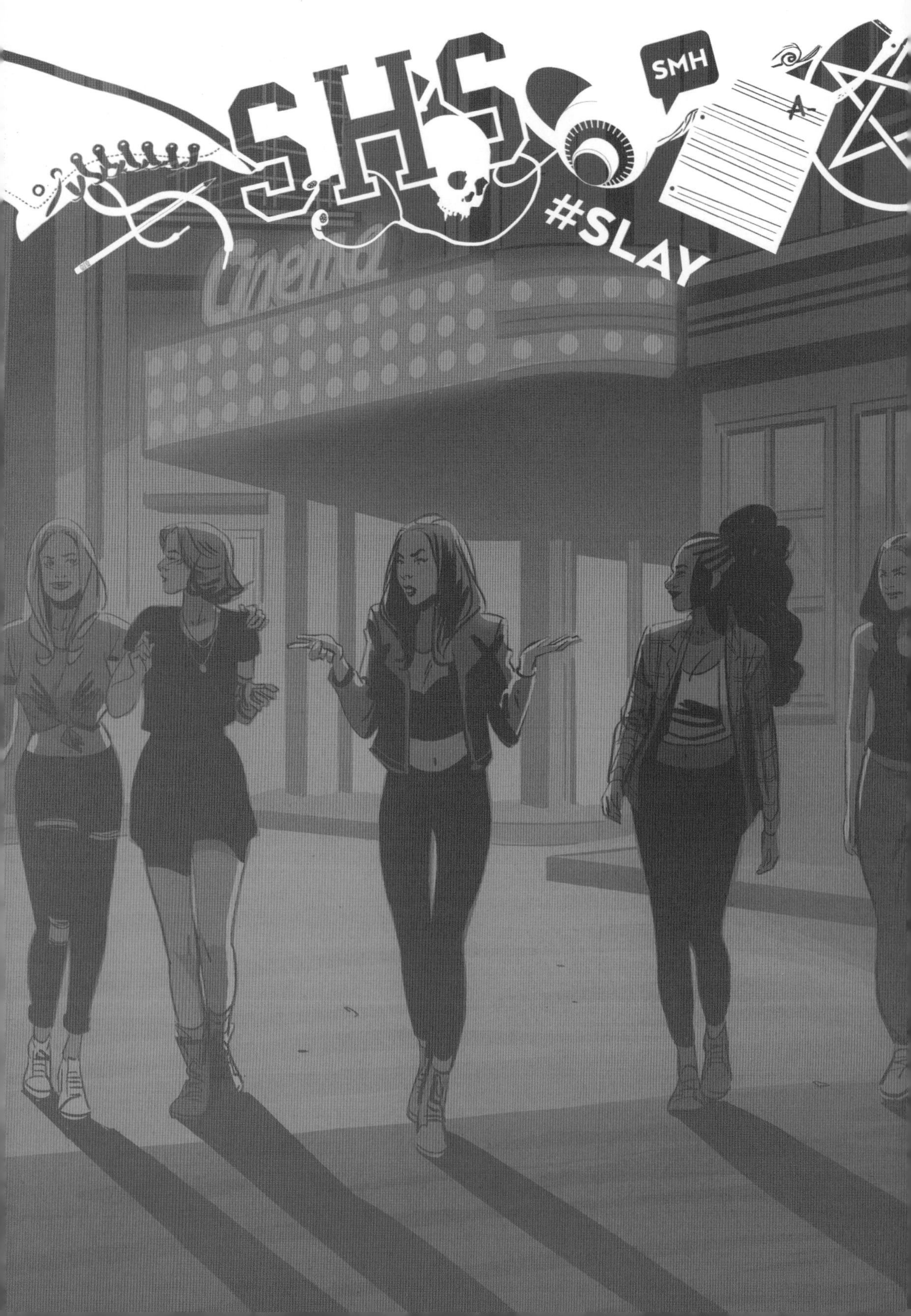
S.H.S.
SMH
#SLAY
Cinema

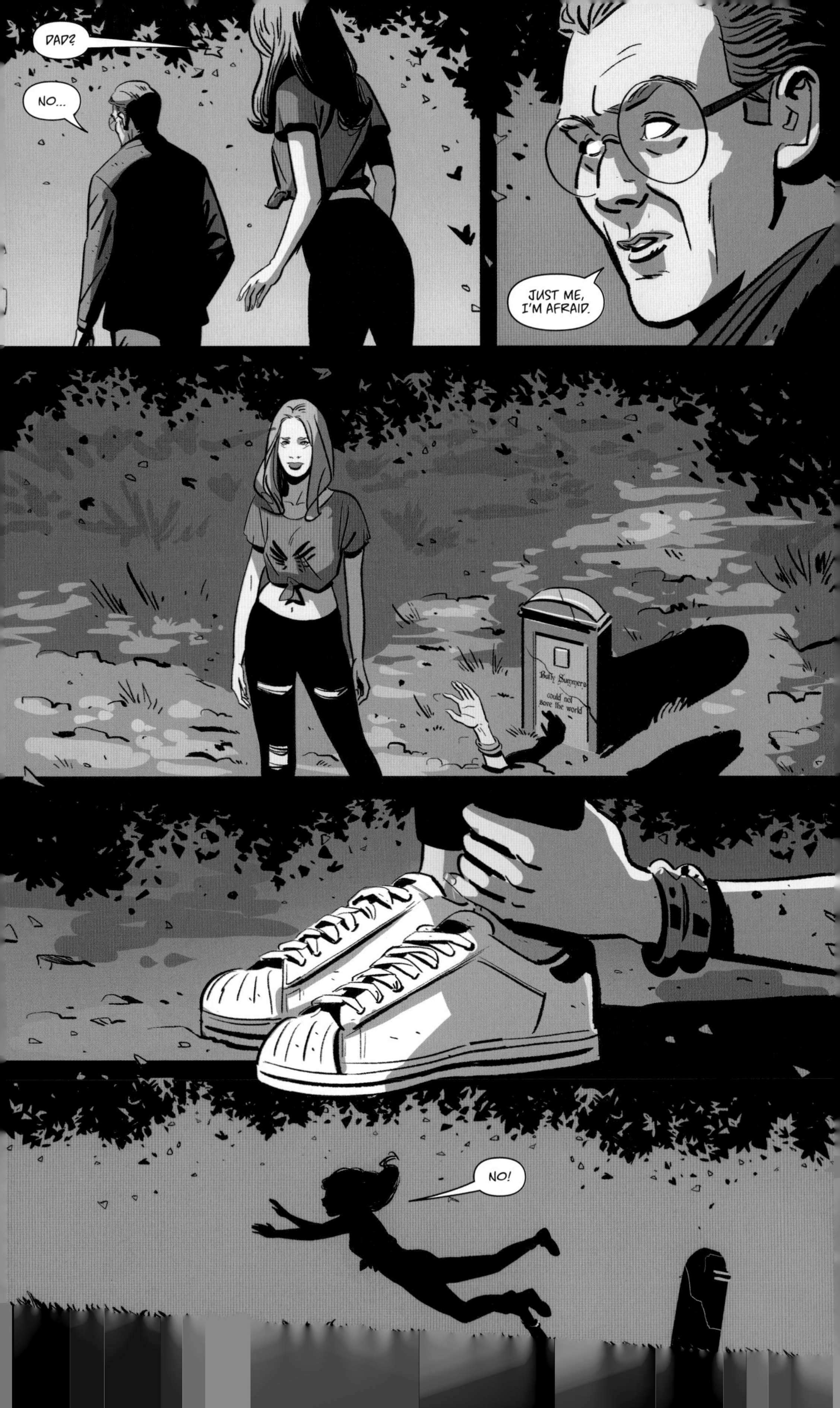
DAD?
NO...
JUST ME, I'M AFRAID.
Buffy Summers could not save the world
NO!

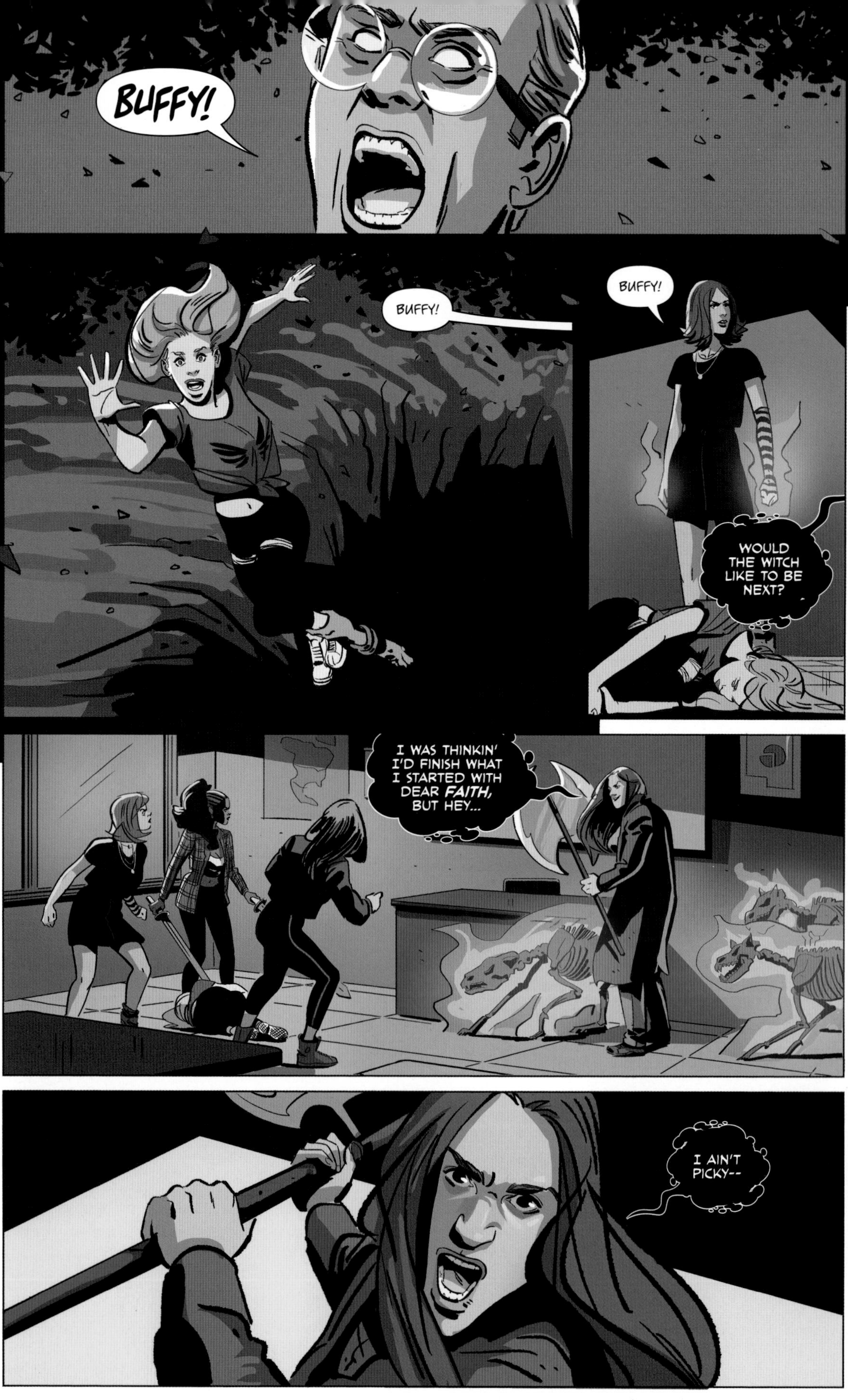
BUFFY!
BUFFY!
BUFFY!
WOULD THE WITCH LIKE TO BE NEXT?
I WAS THINKIN' I'D FINISH WHAT I STARTED WITH DEAR FAITH, BUT HEY...
I AIN'T PICKY--

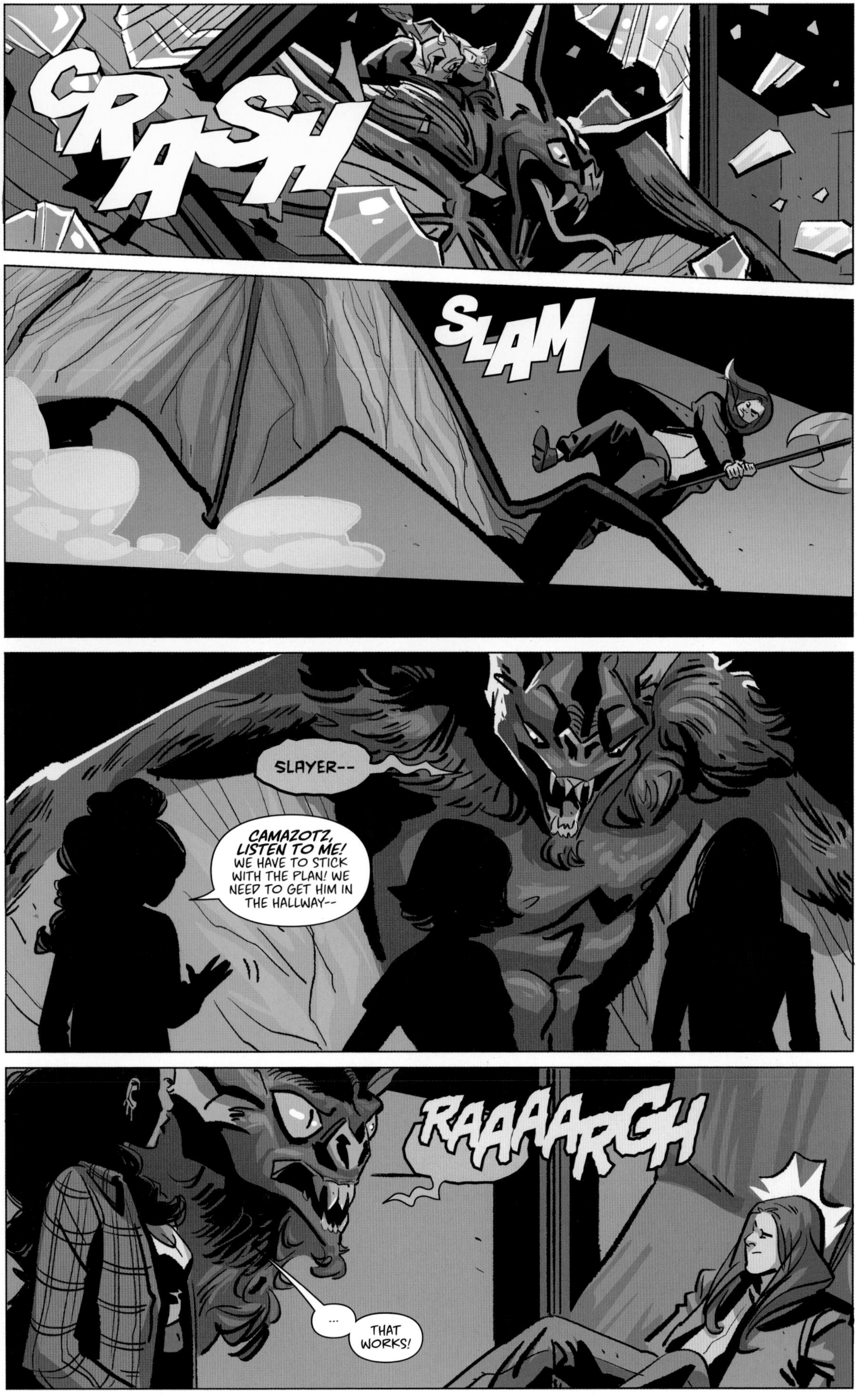
CRASH
SLAM
SLAYER--
CAMAZOTZ, LISTEN TO ME! WE HAVE TO STICK WITH THE PLAN! WE NEED TO GET HIM IN THE HALLWAY--
RAAAARGH
... THAT WORKS!

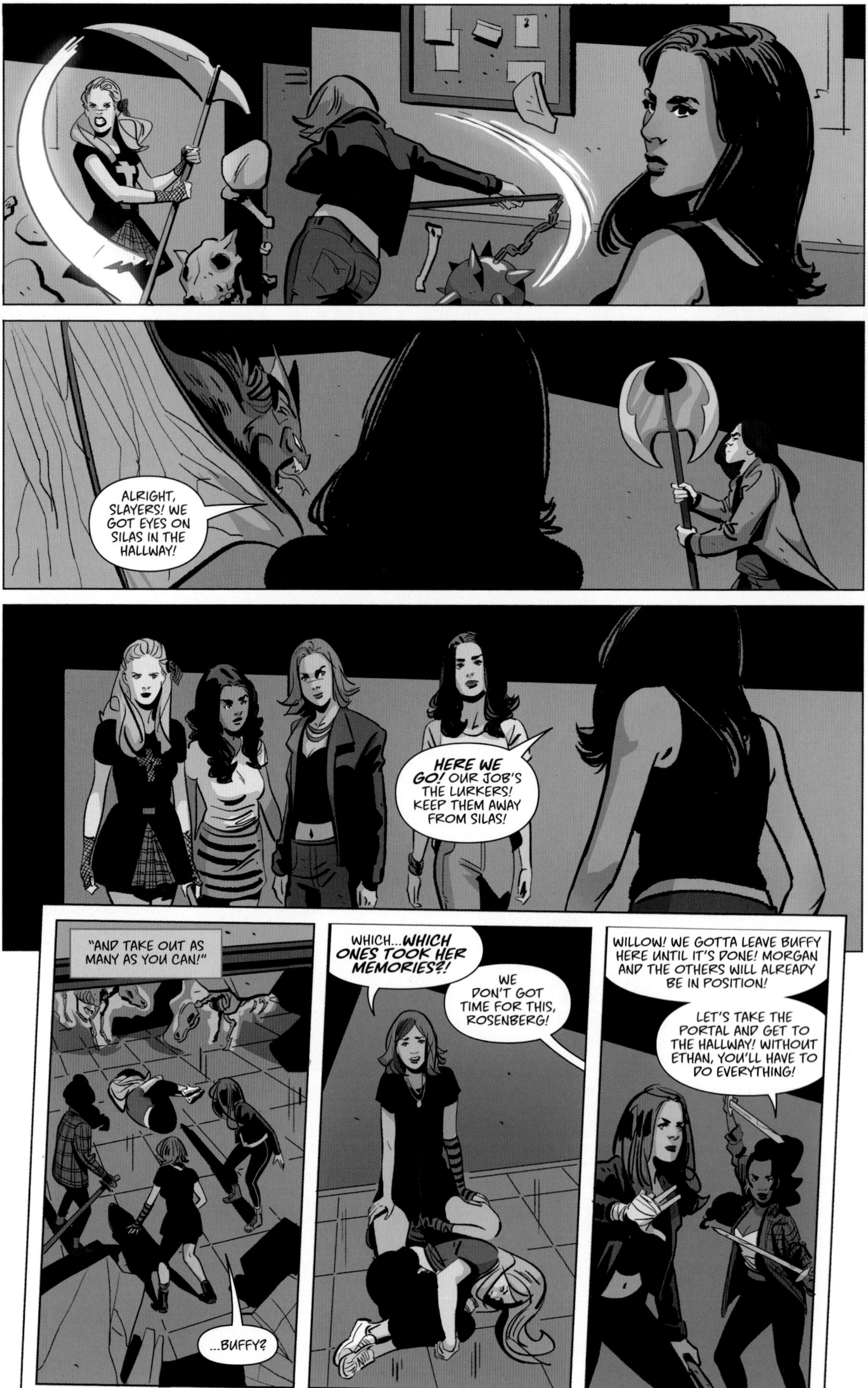
ALRIGHT, SLAYERS! WE GOT EYES ON SILAS IN THE HALLWAY!
HERE WE GO! OUR JOB'S THE LURKERS! KEEP THEM AWAY FROM SILAS!
"AND TAKE OUT AS MANY AS YOU CAN!"
...BUFFY?
WHICH...WHICH ONES TOOK HER MEMORIES?!
WE DON'T GOT TIME FOR THIS, ROSENBERG!
WILLOW! WE GOTTA LEAVE BUFFY HERE UNTIL IT'S DONE! MORGAN AND THE OTHERS WILL ALREADY BE IN POSITION!
LET'S TAKE THE PORTAL AND GET TO THE HALLWAY! WITHOUT ETHAN, YOU'LL HAVE TO DO EVERYTHING!

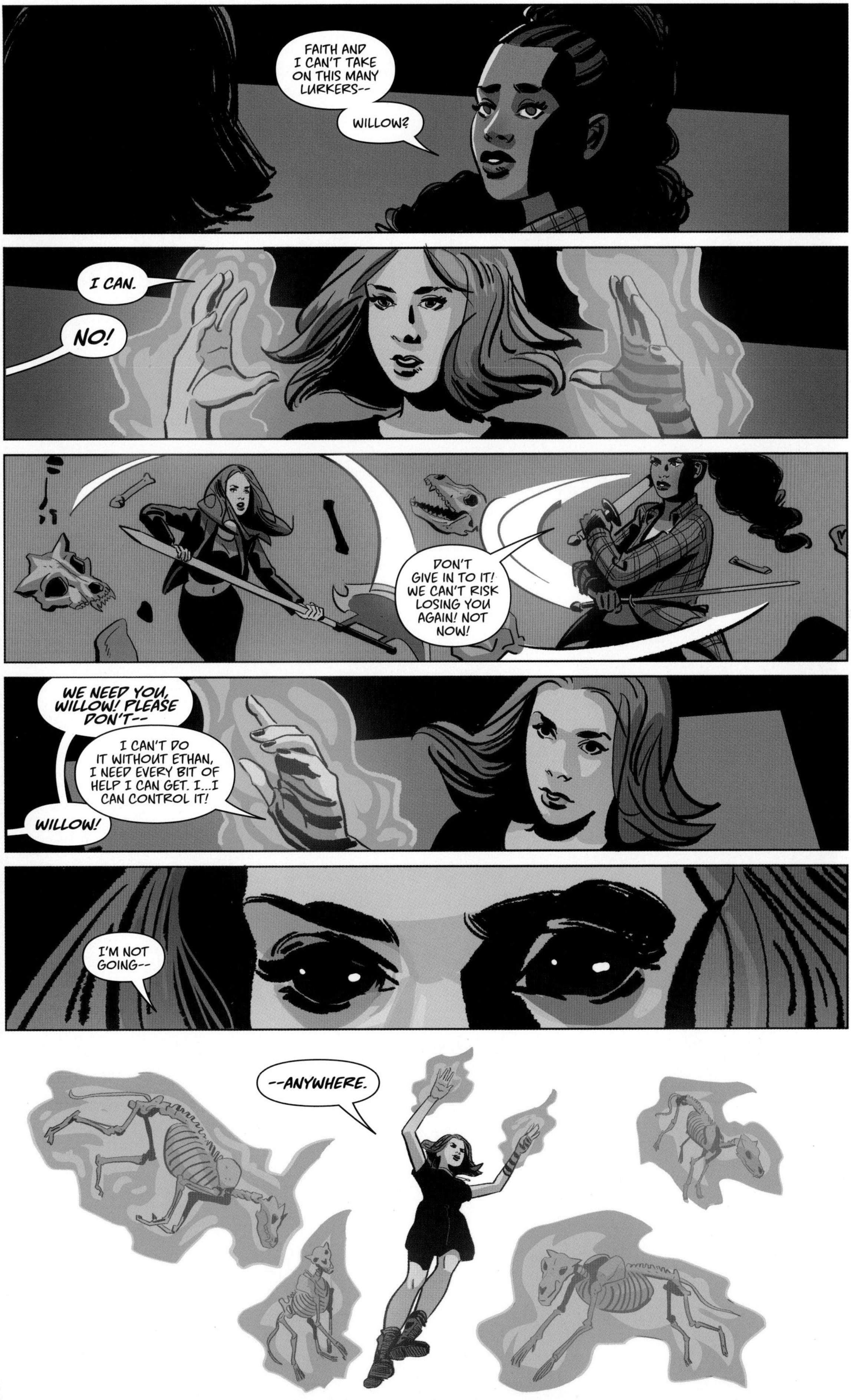
FAITH AND I CAN'T TAKE ON THIS MANY LURKERS--
WILLOW?
I CAN.
NO!
DON'T GIVE IN TO IT! WE CAN'T RISK LOSING YOU AGAIN! NOT NOW!
WE NEED YOU, WILLOW! PLEASE DON'T--
I CAN'T DO IT WITHOUT ETHAN, I NEED EVERY BIT OF HELP I CAN GET. I...I CAN CONTROL IT!
WILLOW!
I'M NOT GOING--
--ANYWHERE.

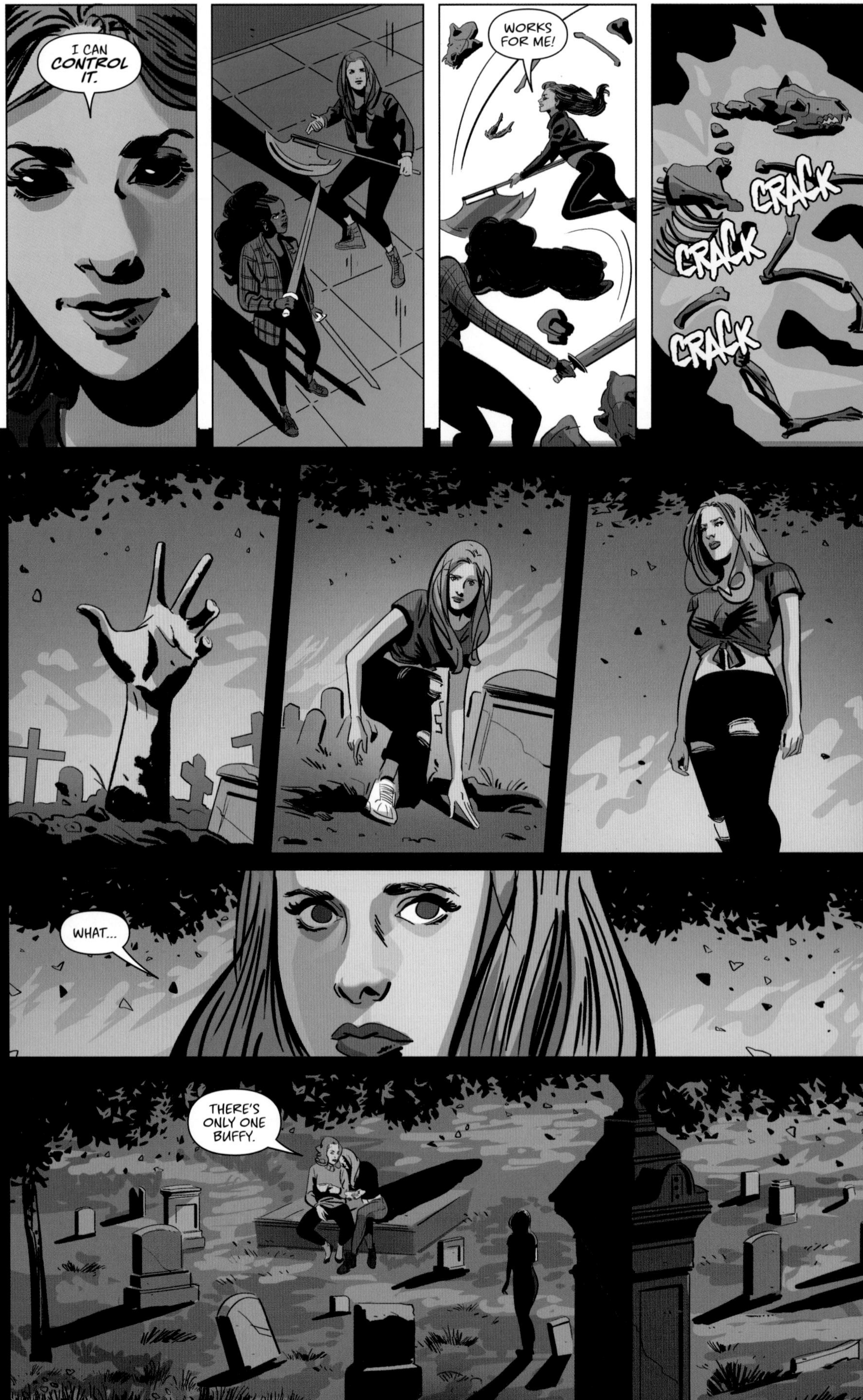
I CAN CONTROL IT.
WORKS FOR ME!
CRACK
CRACK
CRACK
WHAT...
THERE'S ONLY ONE BUFFY.

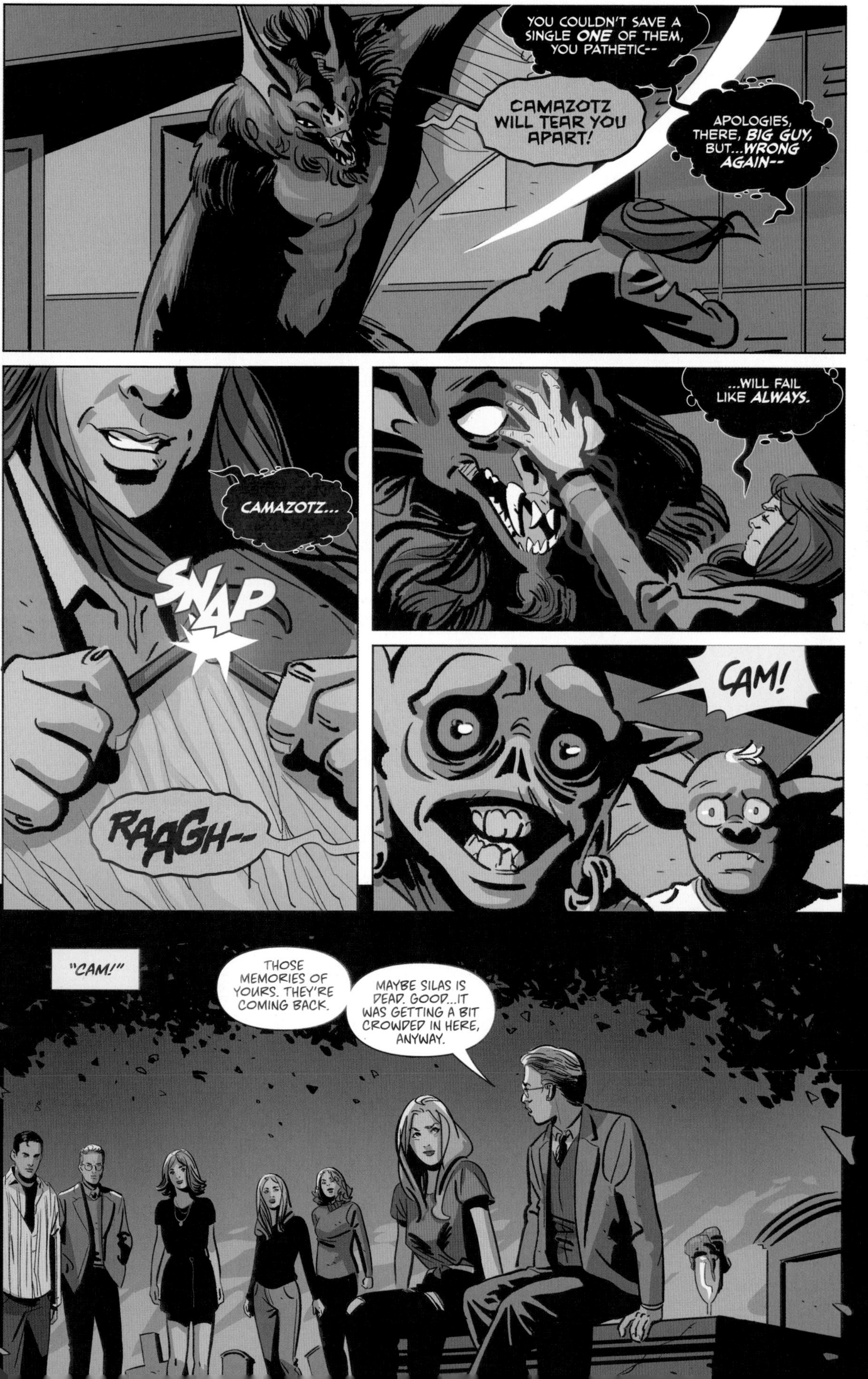
YOU COULDN'T SAVE A SINGLE ONE OF THEM, YOU PATHETIC--
CAMAZOTZ WILL TEAR YOU APART!
APOLOGIES, THERE, BIG GUY, BUT...WRONG AGAIN--
CAMAZOTZ...
SNAP
RAAGH--
...WILL FAIL LIKE ALWAYS.
CAM!
"CAM!"
THOSE MEMORIES OF YOURS. THEY'RE COMING BACK.
MAYBE SILAS IS DEAD. GOOD...IT WAS GETTING A BIT CROWDED IN HERE, ANYWAY.

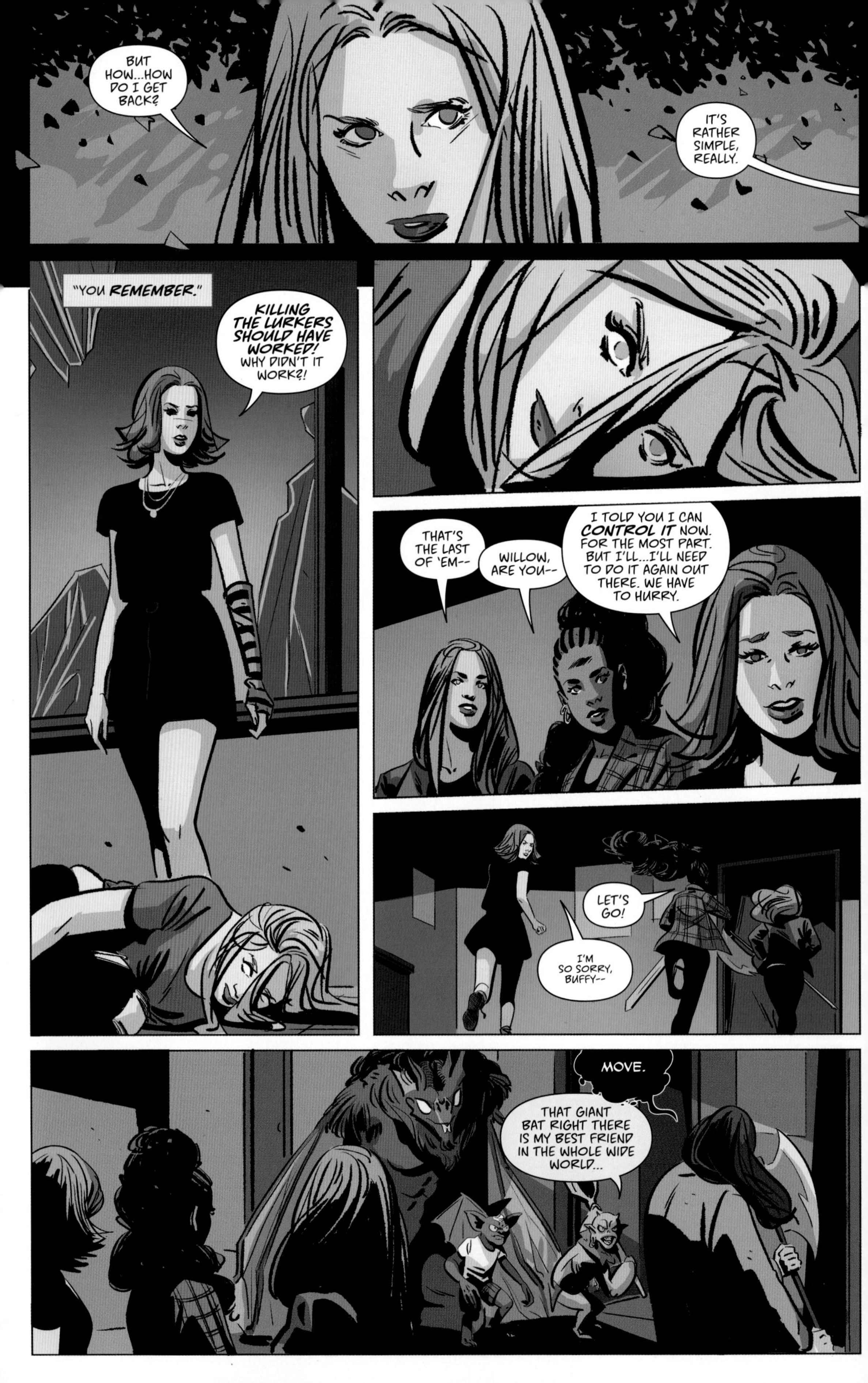
BUT HOW...HOW DO I GET BACK?
IT'S RATHER SIMPLE, REALLY.
"YOU REMEMBER."
KILLING THE LURKERS SHOULD HAVE WORKED! WHY DIDN'T IT WORK?!
THAT'S THE LAST OF 'EM--
WILLOW, ARE YOU--
I TOLD YOU I CAN CONTROL IT NOW. FOR THE MOST PART. BUT I'LL...I'LL NEED TO DO IT AGAIN OUT THERE. WE HAVE TO HURRY.
LET'S GO!
I'M SO SORRY, BUFFY--
MOVE.
THAT GIANT BAT RIGHT THERE IS MY BEST FRIEND IN THE WHOLE WIDE WORLD...

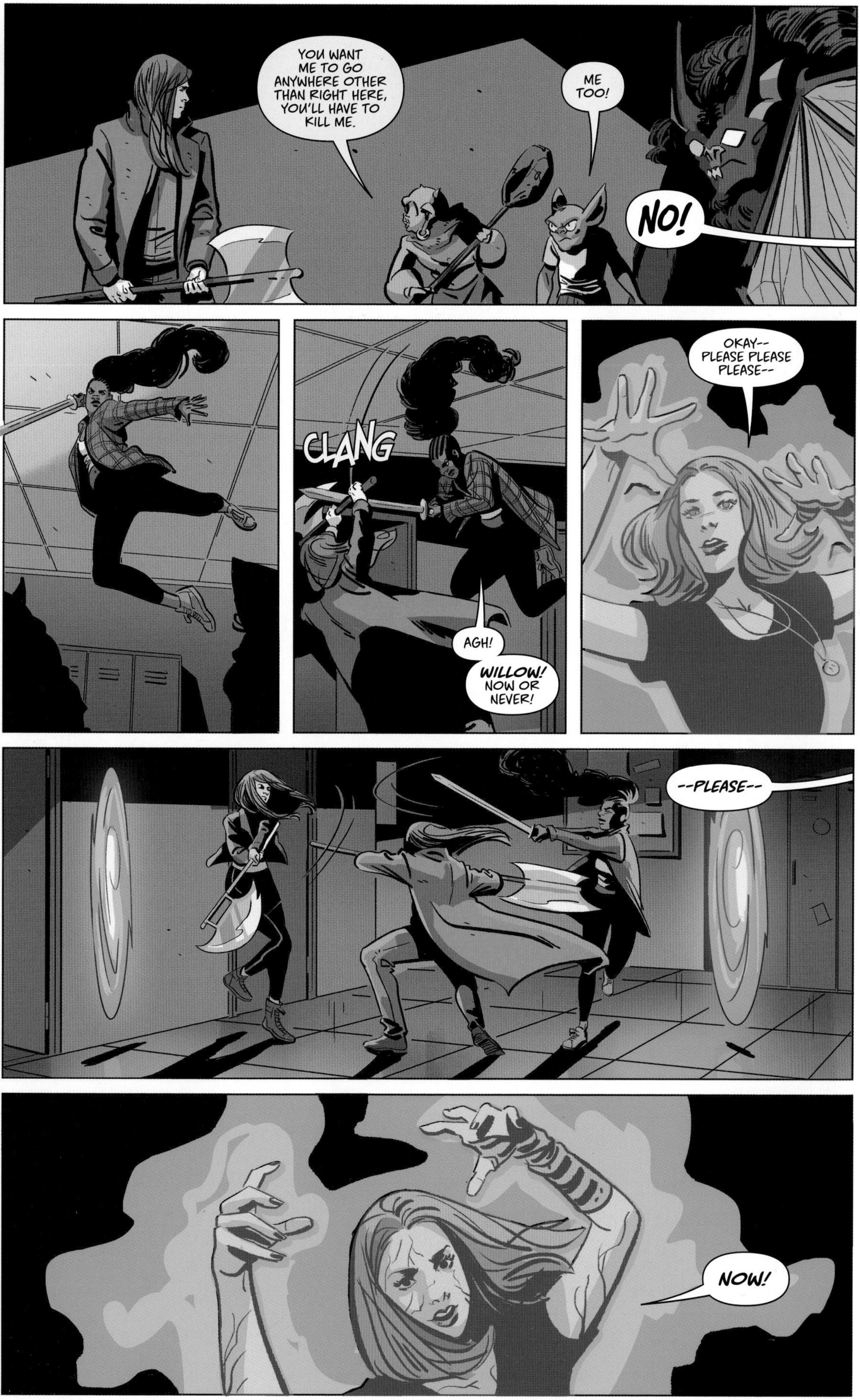
YOU WANT ME TO GO ANYWHERE OTHER THAN RIGHT HERE, YOU'LL HAVE TO KILL ME.
ME TOO!
NO!
CLANG
AGH!
WILLOW! NOW OR NEVER!
OKAY-- PLEASE PLEASE PLEASE--
--PLEASE--
NOW!

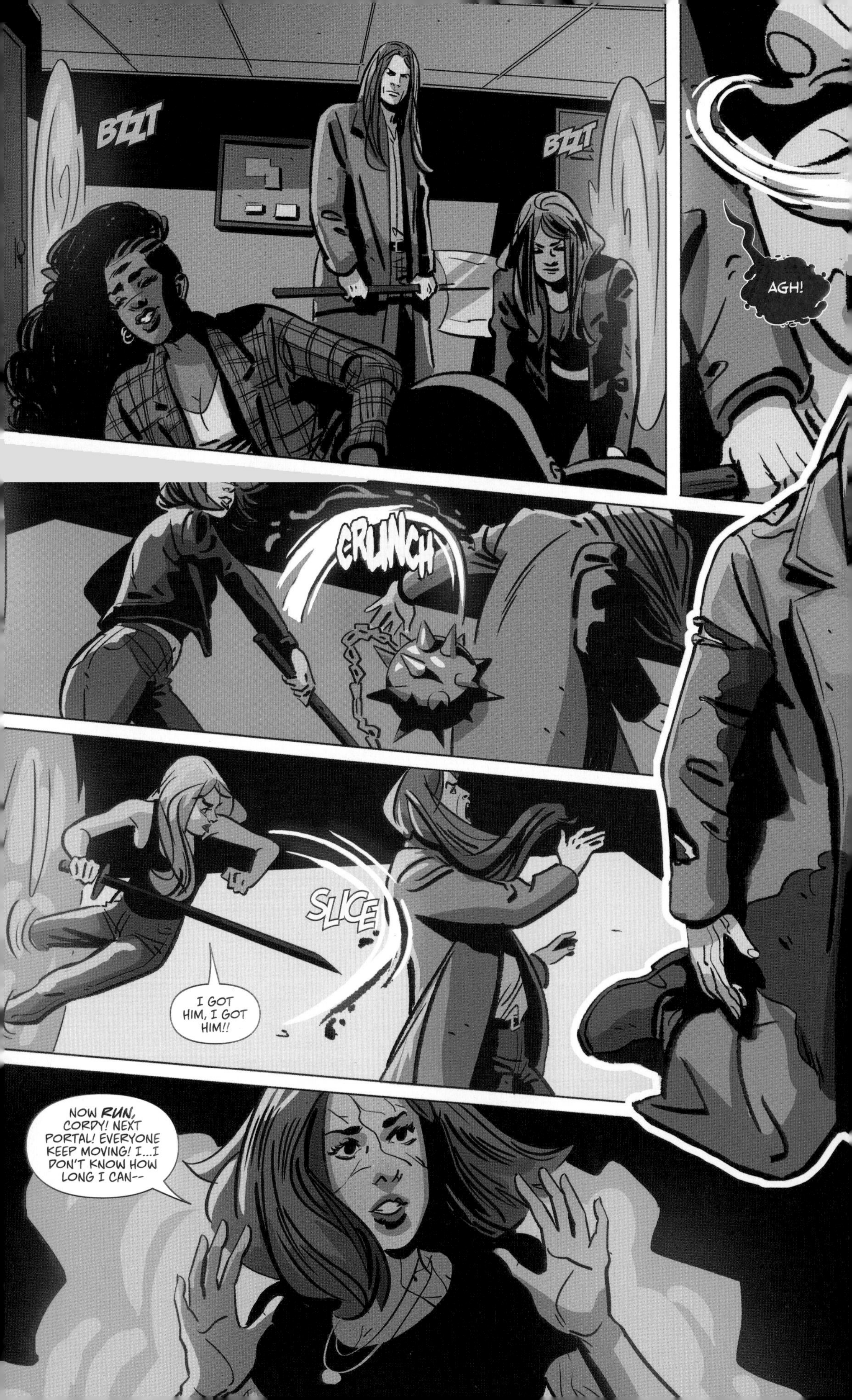
BZZT
BZZT
AGH!
CRUNCH
SLICE
I GOT HIM, I GOT HIM!!
NOW RUN, CORDY! NEXT PORTAL! EVERYONE KEEP MOVING! I...I DON'T KNOW HOW LONG I CAN--

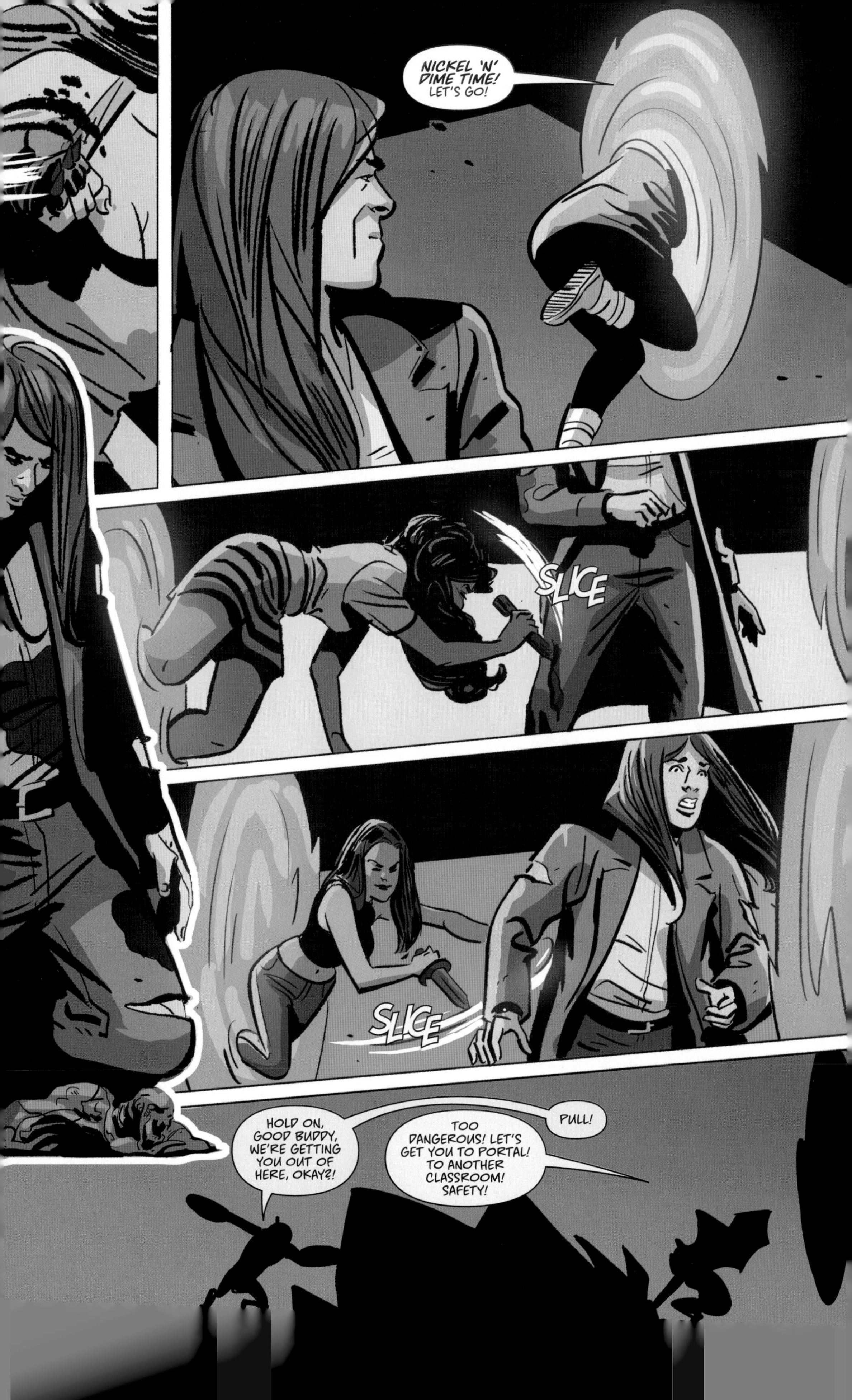
NICKEL 'N' DIME TIME! LET'S GO!
SLICE
SLICE
HOLD ON, GOOD BUDDY, WE'RE GETTING YOU OUT OF HERE, OKAY?!
PULL!
TOO DANGEROUS! LET'S GET YOU TO PORTAL! TO ANOTHER CLASSROOM! SAFETY!

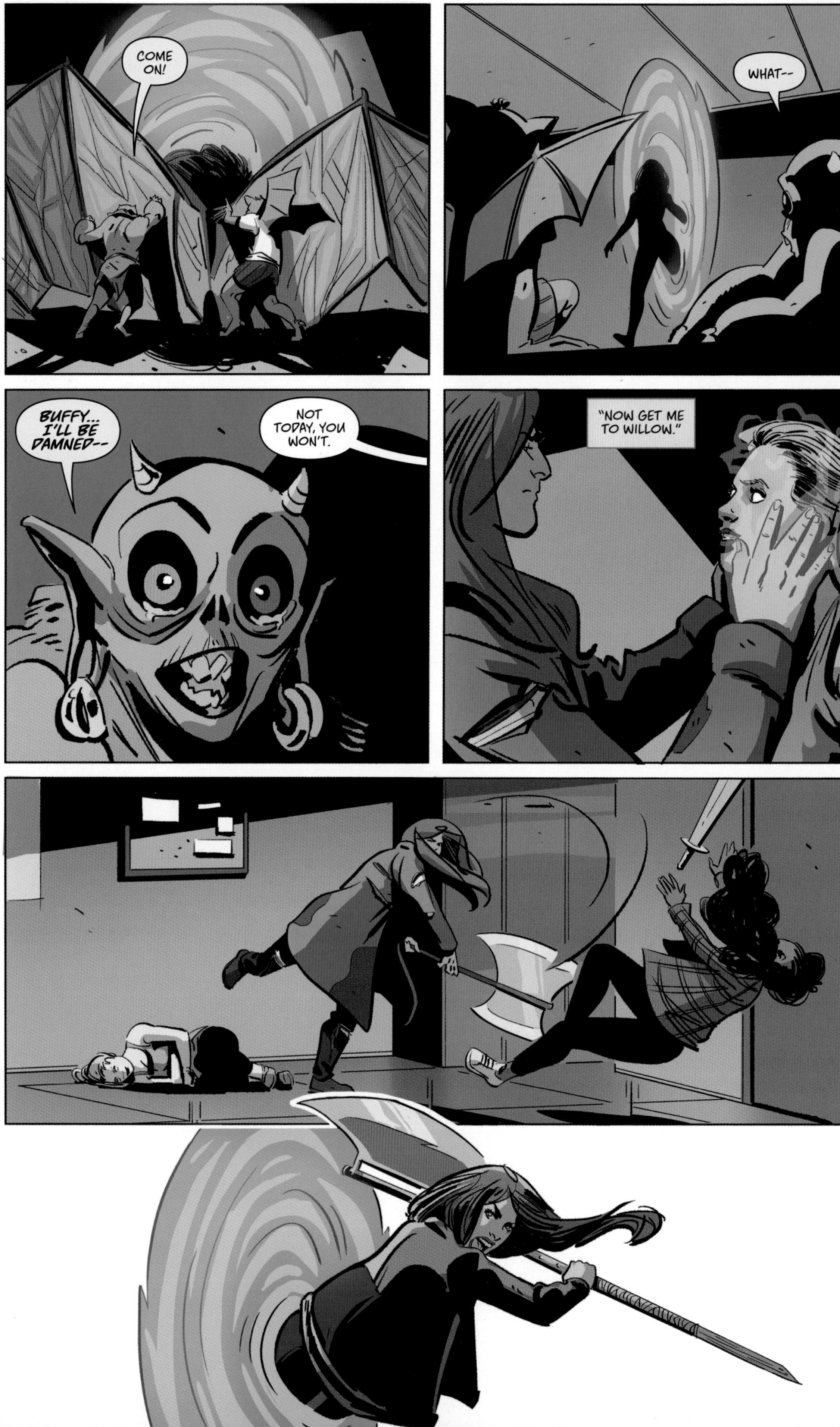
COME ON!
WHAT--
BUFFY... I'LL BE DAMNED--
NOT TODAY, YOU WON'T.
"NOW GET ME TO WILLOW."

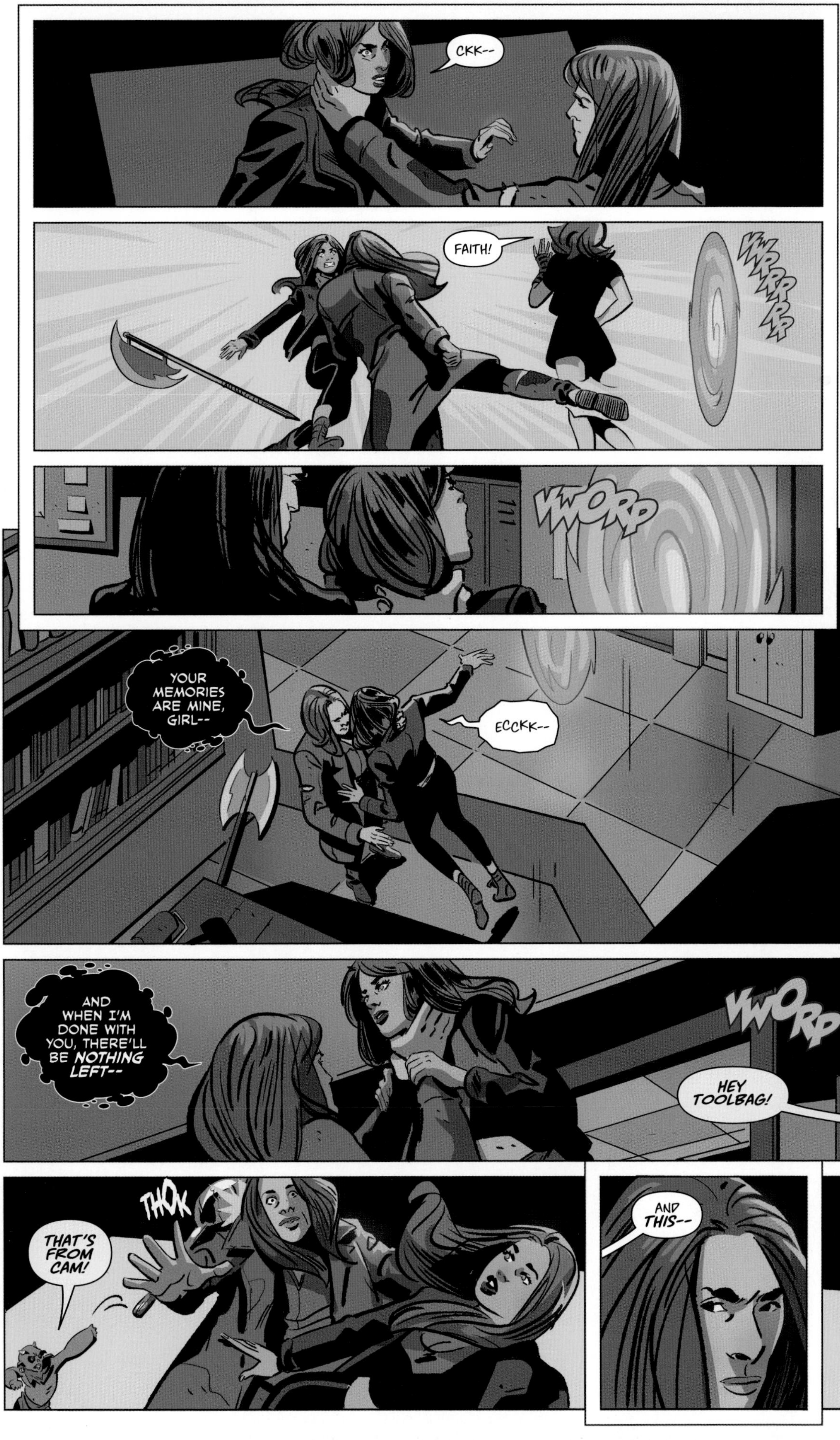
CKK--
FAITH!
VWRRRRR
VWORP
YOUR MEMORIES ARE MINE, GIRL--
ECCKK--
AND WHEN I'M DONE WITH YOU, THERE'LL BE NOTHING LEFT--
VWORP
HEY TOOLBAG!
THOK
THAT'S FROM CAM!
AND THIS--

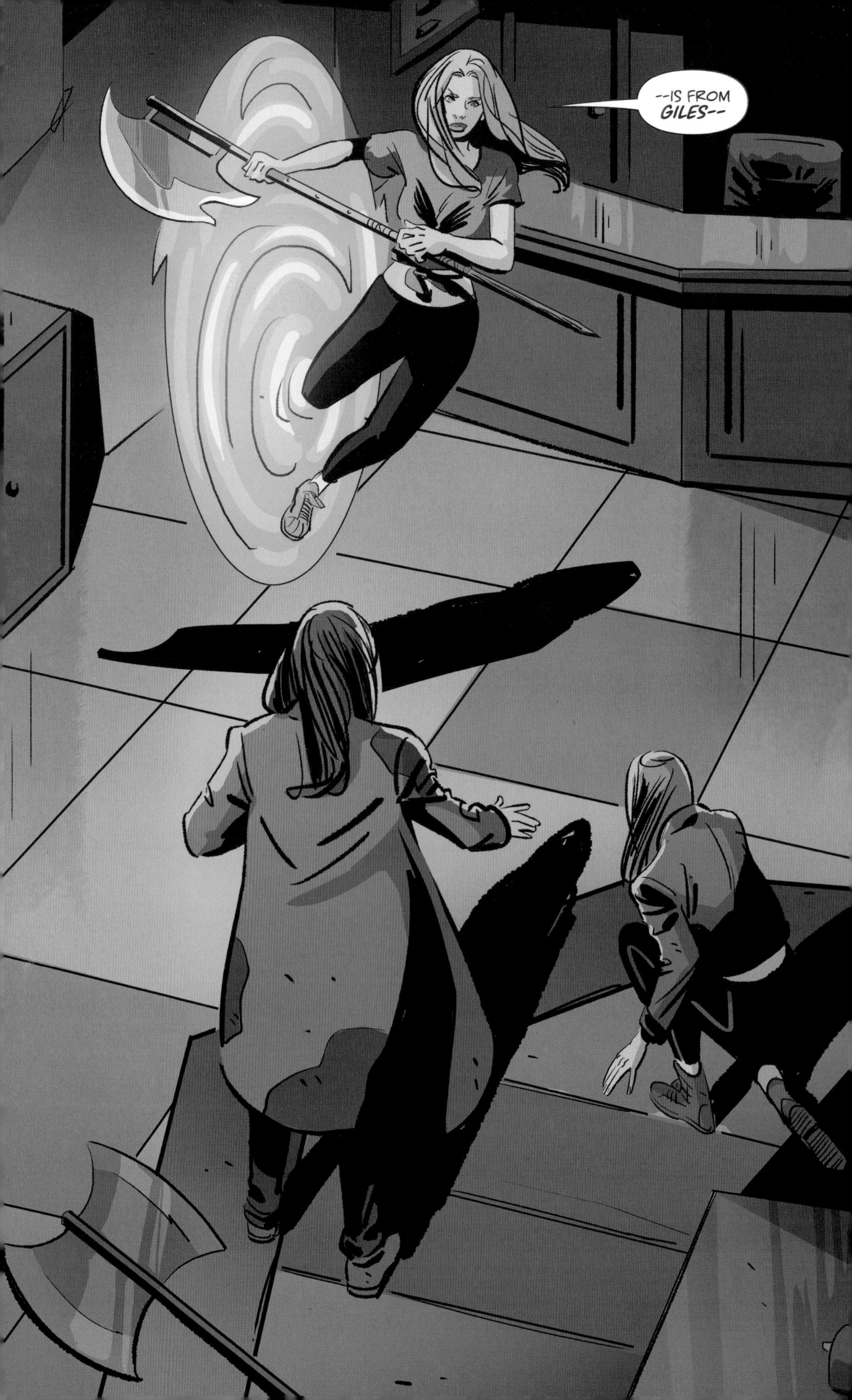
--IS FROM GILES--

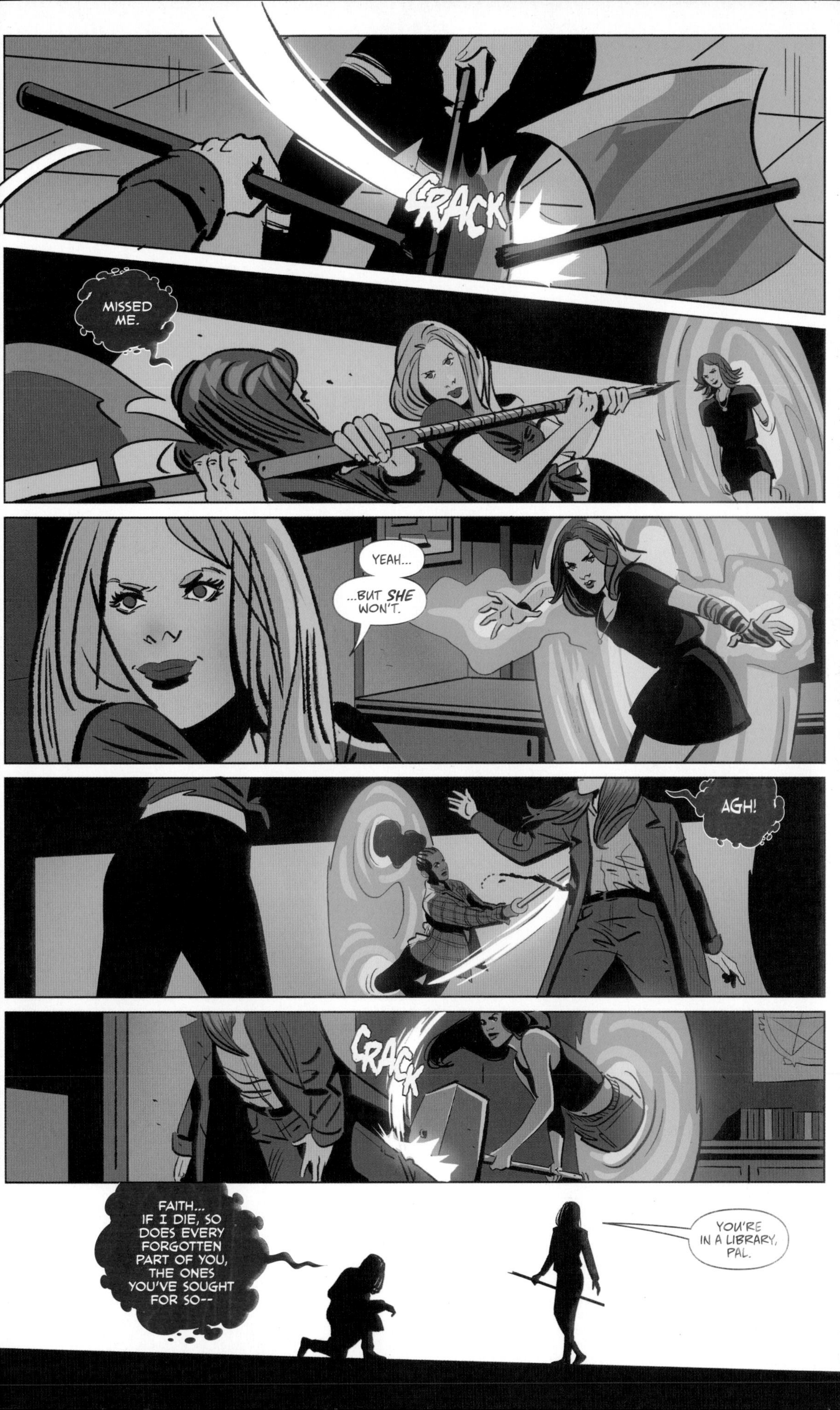
CRACK
MISSED ME.
YEAH...
...BUT SHE WON'T.
AGH!
CRACK
FAITH... IF I DIE, SO DOES EVERY FORGOTTEN PART OF YOU, THE ONES YOU'VE SOUGHT FOR SO--
YOU'RE IN A LIBRARY, PAL.

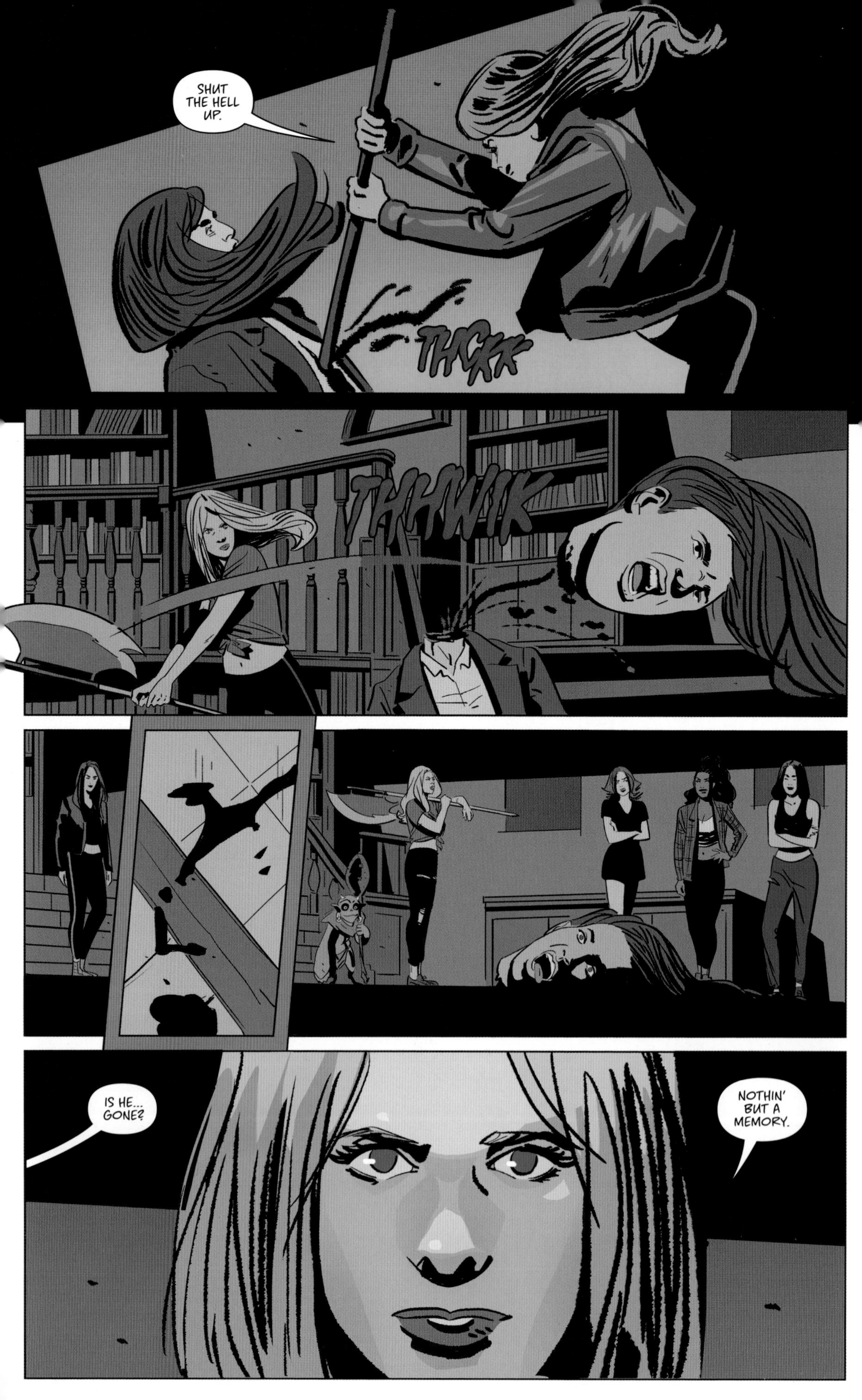
SHUT THE HELL UP.
THCKK
THHWIK
IS HE... GONE?
NOTHIN' BUT A MEMORY.

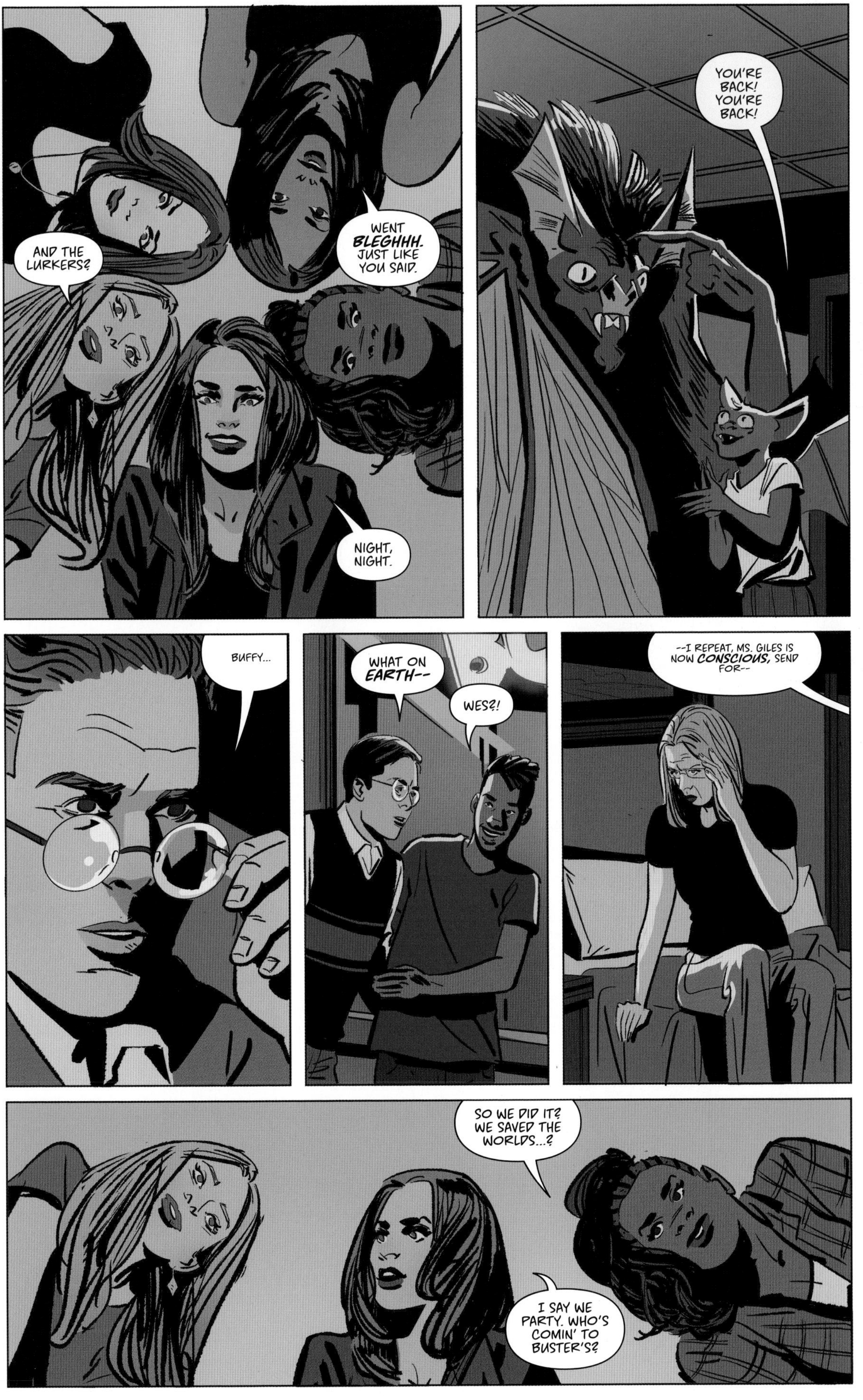
AND THE LURKERS?
WENT BLEGHHH. JUST LIKE YOU SAID.
NIGHT, NIGHT.
YOU'RE BACK! YOU'RE BACK!
BUFFY...
WHAT ON EARTH--
WES?!
--I REPEAT, MS. GILES IS NOW CONSCIOUS, SEND FOR--
SO WE DID IT? WE SAVED THE WORLDS...?
I SAY WE PARTY. WHO'S COMIN' TO BUSTER'S?

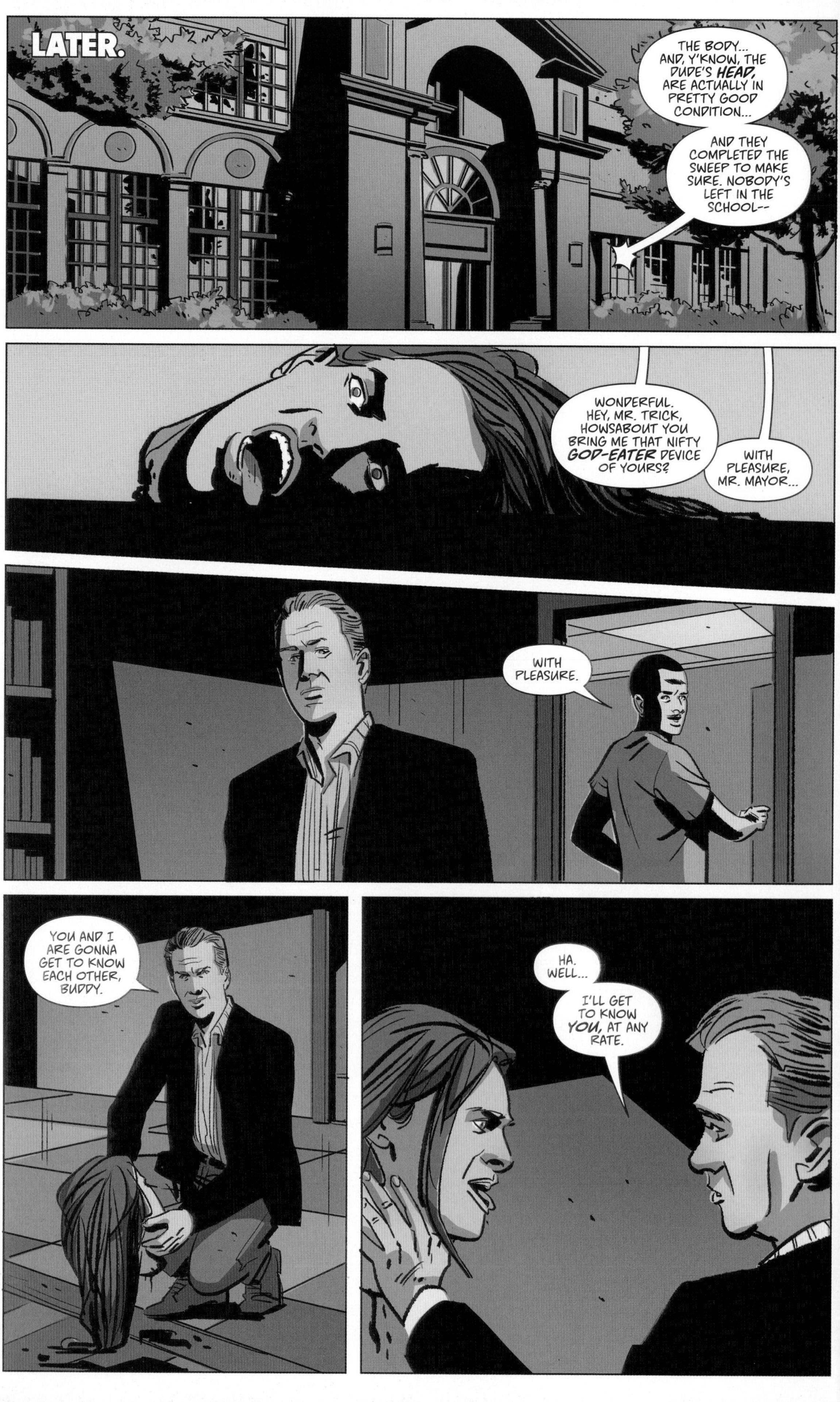
LATER.
THE BODY... AND, Y'KNOW, THE DUDE'S HEAD, ARE ACTUALLY IN PRETTY GOOD CONDITION...
AND THEY COMPLETED THE SWEEP TO MAKE SURE. NOBODY'S LEFT IN THE SCHOOL--
WONDERFUL. HEY, MR. TRICK, HOWSABOUT YOU BRING ME THAT NIFTY GOD-EATER DEVICE OF YOURS?
WITH PLEASURE, MR. MAYOR...
WITH PLEASURE.
YOU AND I ARE GONNA GET TO KNOW EACH OTHER, BUDDY.
HA. WELL...
I'LL GET TO KNOW YOU, AT ANY RATE.

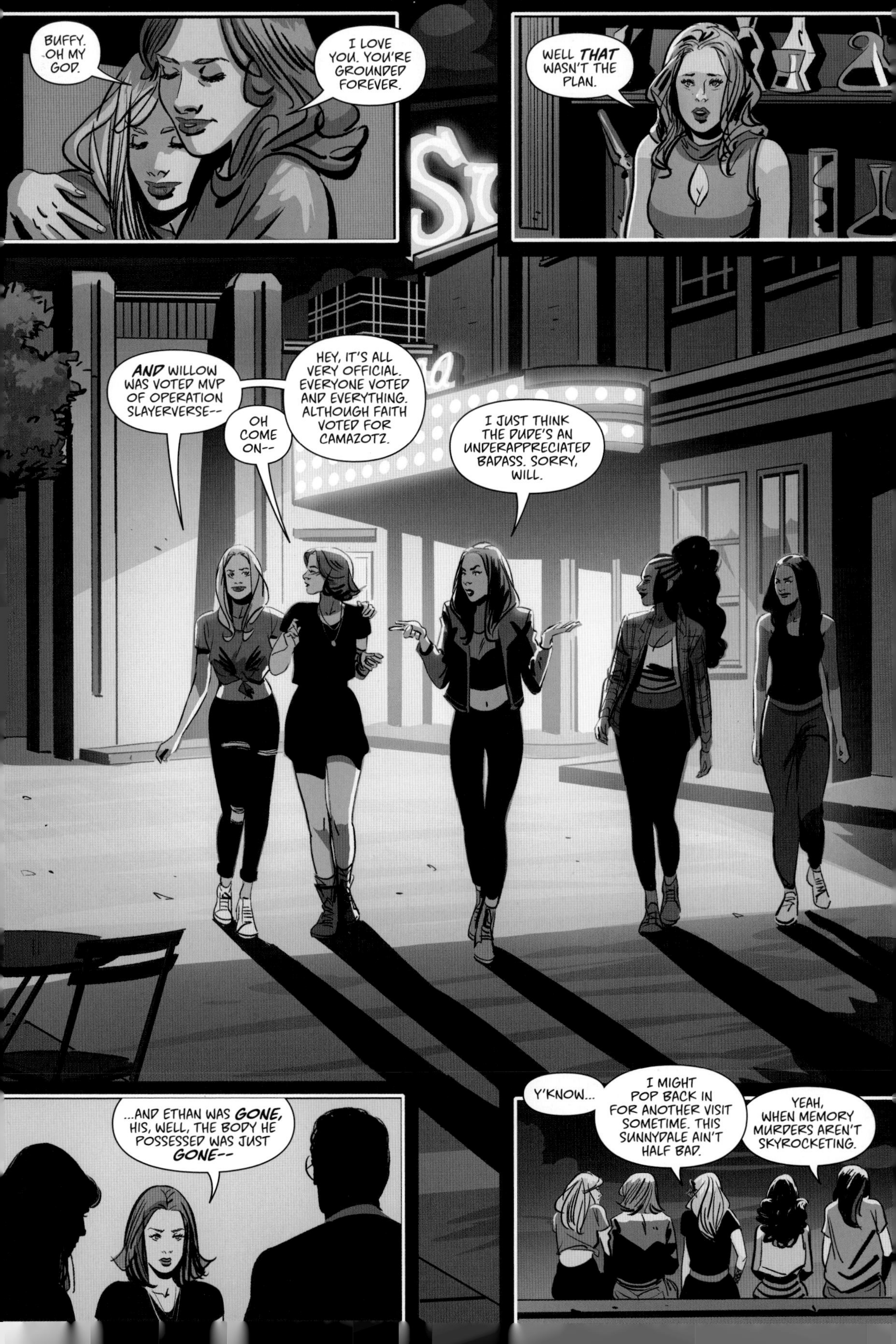
BUFFY. OH MY GOD.
I LOVE YOU. YOU'RE GROUNDED FOREVER.
WELL THAT WASN'T THE PLAN.
AND WILLOW WAS VOTED MVP OF OPERATION SLAYERVERSE--
HEY, IT'S ALL VERY OFFICIAL. EVERYONE VOTED AND EVERYTHING. ALTHOUGH FAITH VOTED FOR CAMAZOTZ.
OH COME ON--
I JUST THINK THE DUDE'S AN UNDERAPPRECIATED BADASS. SORRY, WILL.
...AND ETHAN WAS GONE, HIS, WELL, THE BODY HE POSSESSED WAS JUST GONE--
Y'KNOW...
I MIGHT POP BACK IN FOR ANOTHER VISIT SOMETIME. THIS SUNNYDALE AIN'T HALF BAD.
YEAH, WHEN MEMORY MURDERS AREN'T SKYROCKETING.

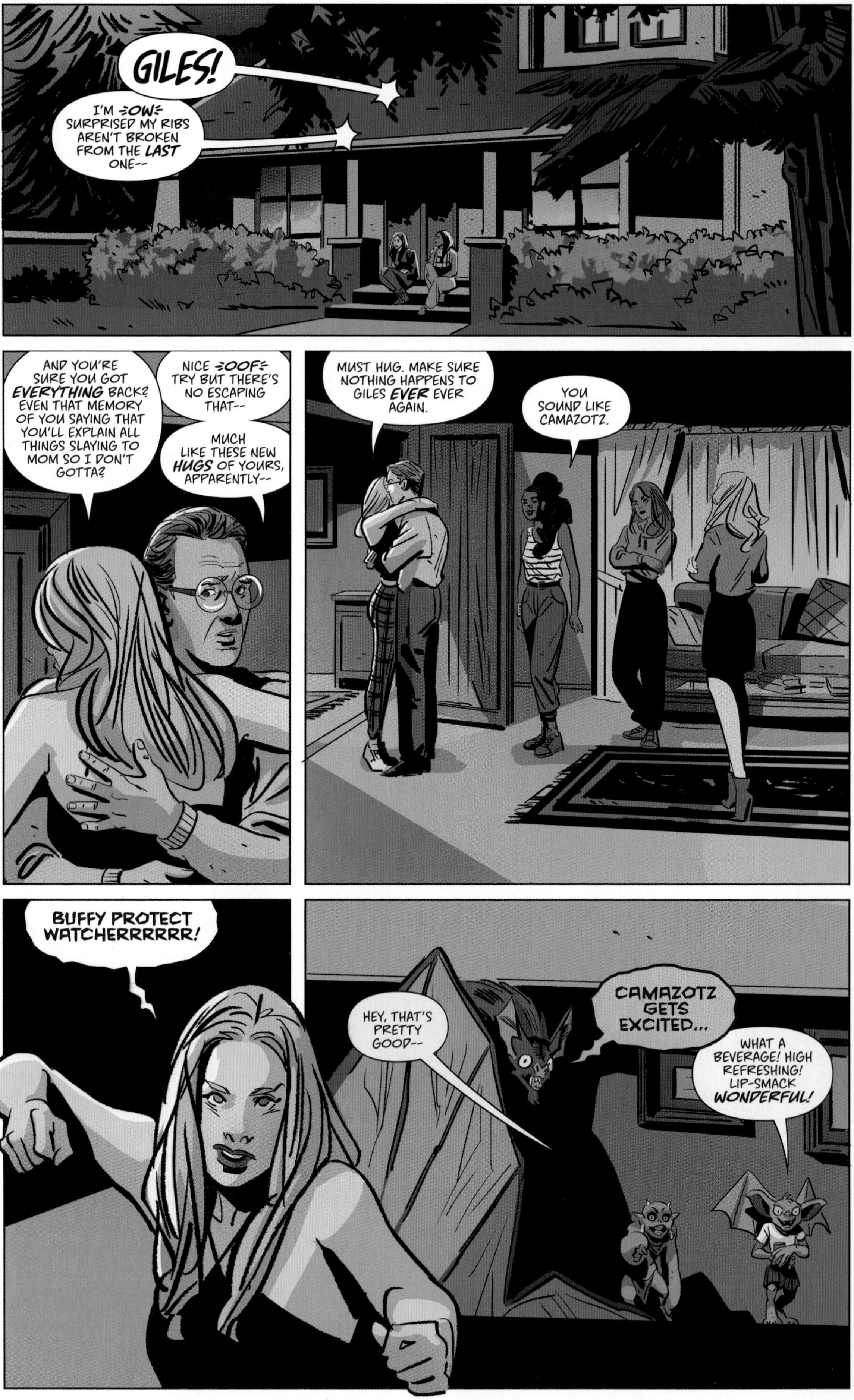
GILES!
I'M =OW= SURPRISED MY RIBS AREN'T BROKEN FROM THE LAST ONE--
AND YOU'RE SURE YOU GOT EVERYTHING BACK? EVEN THAT MEMORY OF YOU SAYING THAT YOU'LL EXPLAIN ALL THINGS SLAYING TO MOM SO I DON'T GOTTA?
NICE =OOF= TRY BUT THERE'S NO ESCAPING THAT--
MUCH LIKE THESE NEW HUGS OF YOURS, APPARENTLY--
MUST HUG. MAKE SURE NOTHING HAPPENS TO GILES EVER EVER AGAIN.
YOU SOUND LIKE CAMAZOTZ.
BUFFY PROTECT WATCHERRRRRR!
HEY, THAT'S PRETTY GOOD--
CAMAZOTZ GETS EXCITED...
WHAT A BEVERAGE! HIGH REFRESHING! LIP-SMACK WONDERFUL!

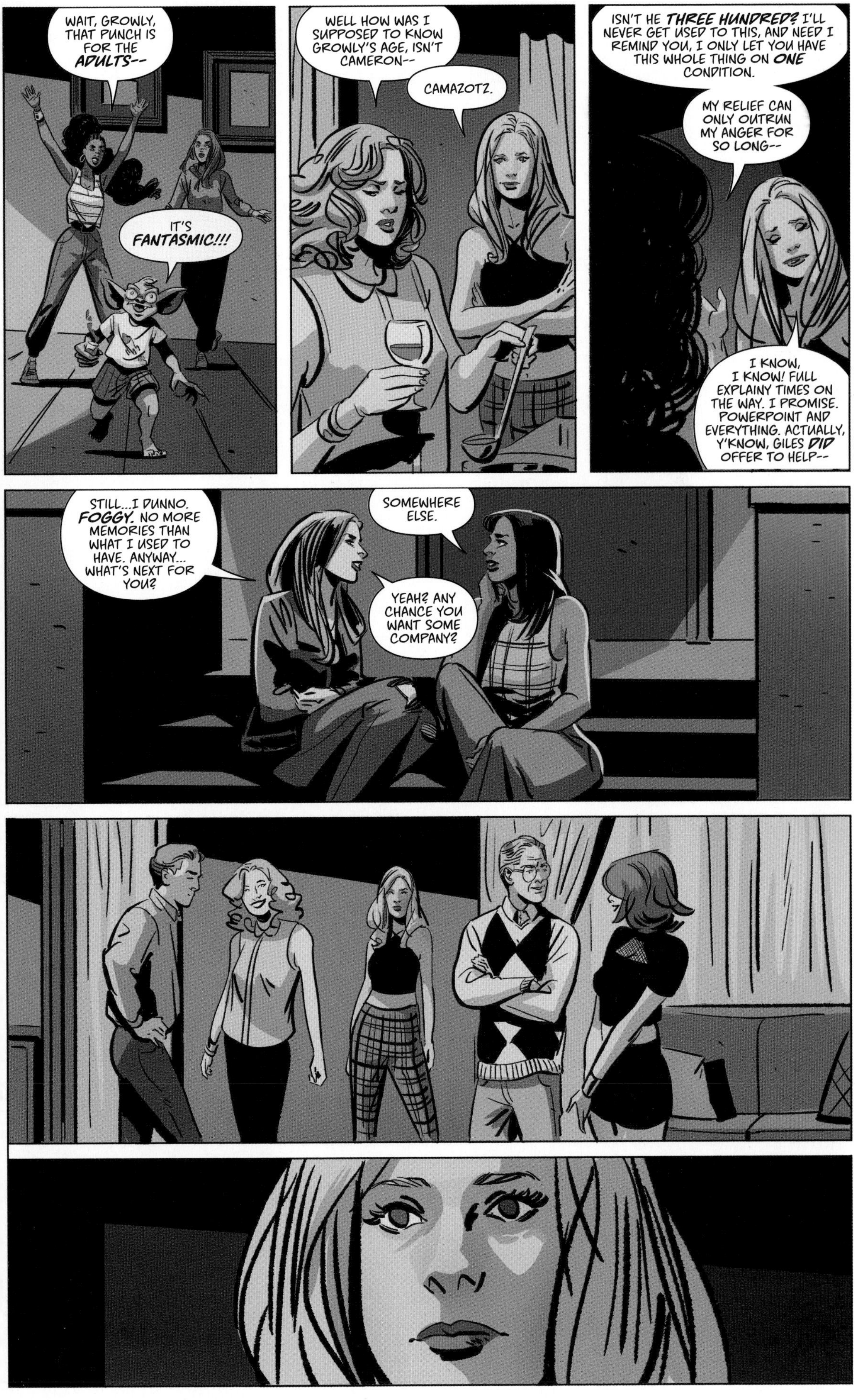
WAIT, GROWLY, THAT PUNCH IS FOR THE ADULTS--
IT'S FANTASMIC!!!
WELL HOW WAS I SUPPOSED TO KNOW GROWLY'S AGE, ISN'T CAMERON--
CAMAZOTZ.
ISN'T HE THREE HUNDRED? I'LL NEVER GET USED TO THIS, AND NEED I REMIND YOU, I ONLY LET YOU HAVE THIS WHOLE THING ON ONE CONDITION.
MY RELIEF CAN ONLY OUTRUN MY ANGER FOR SO LONG--
I KNOW, I KNOW! FULL EXPLAINY TIMES ON THE WAY. I PROMISE. POWERPOINT AND EVERYTHING. ACTUALLY, Y'KNOW, GILES DID OFFER TO HELP--
STILL...I DUNNO. FOGGY. NO MORE MEMORIES THAN WHAT I USED TO HAVE. ANYWAY... WHAT'S NEXT FOR YOU?
SOMEWHERE ELSE.
YEAH? ANY CHANCE YOU WANT SOME COMPANY?

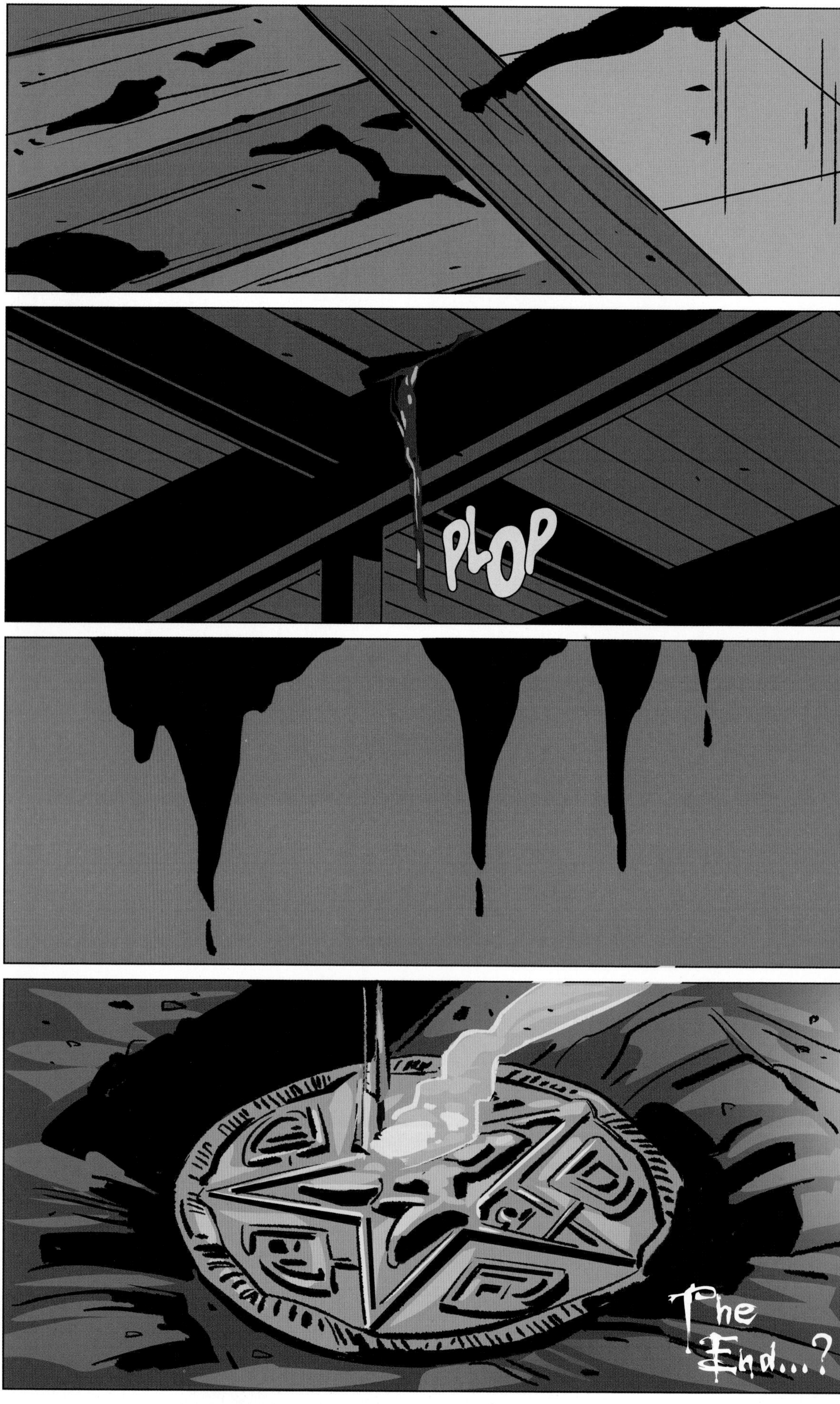
PLOP
The End...?

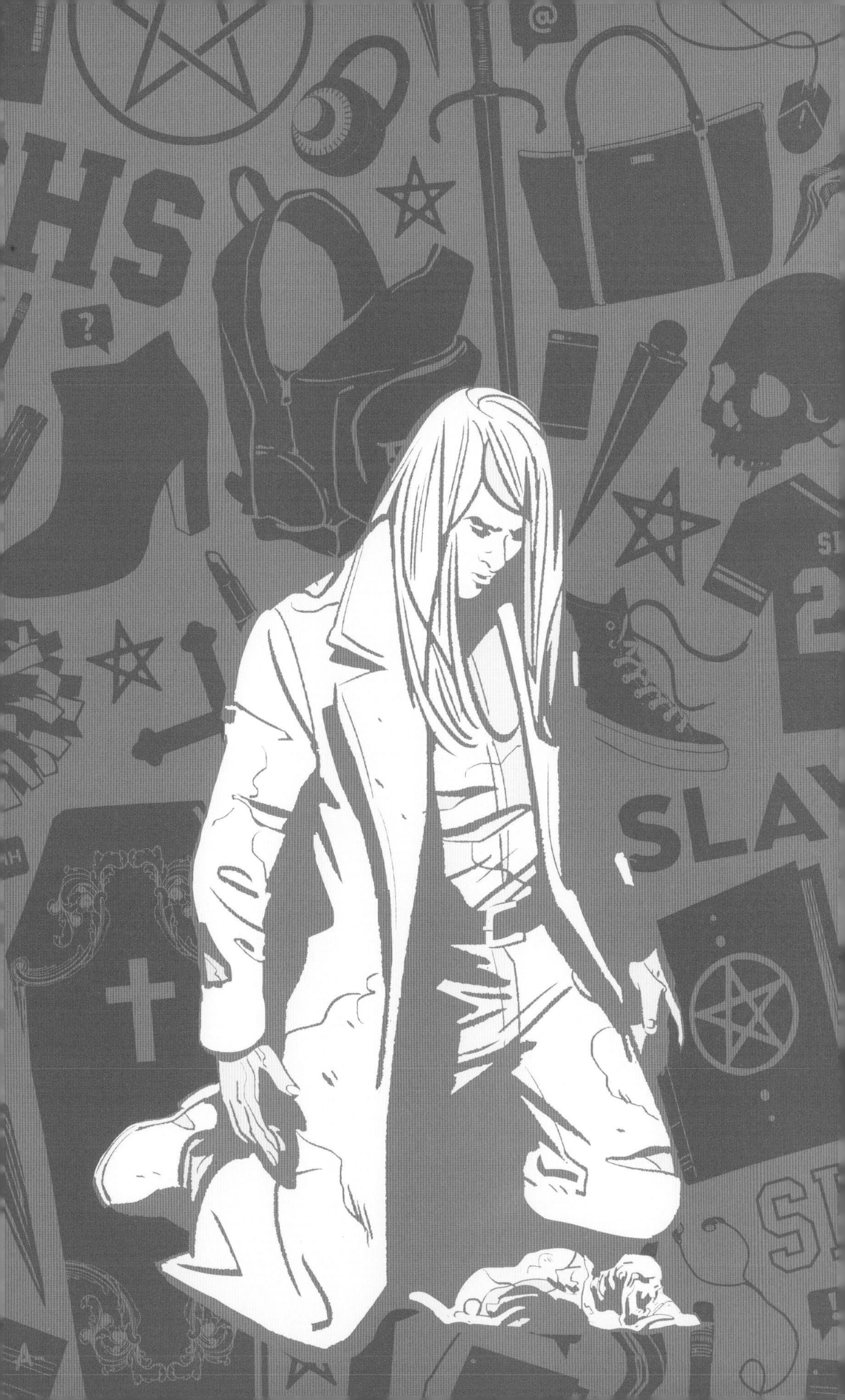

EPILOGUE

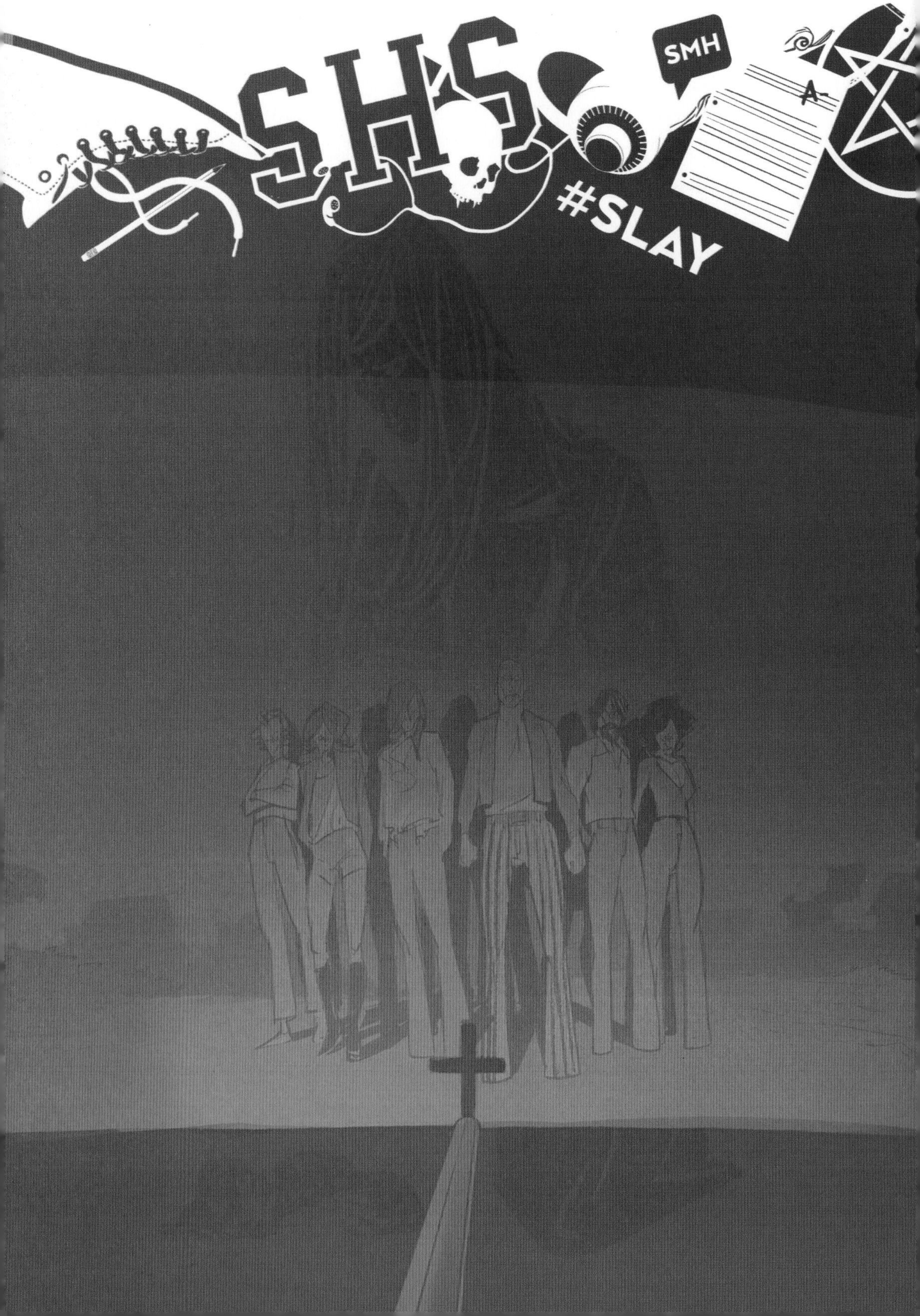
S.H.S
SMH
A-
#SLAY

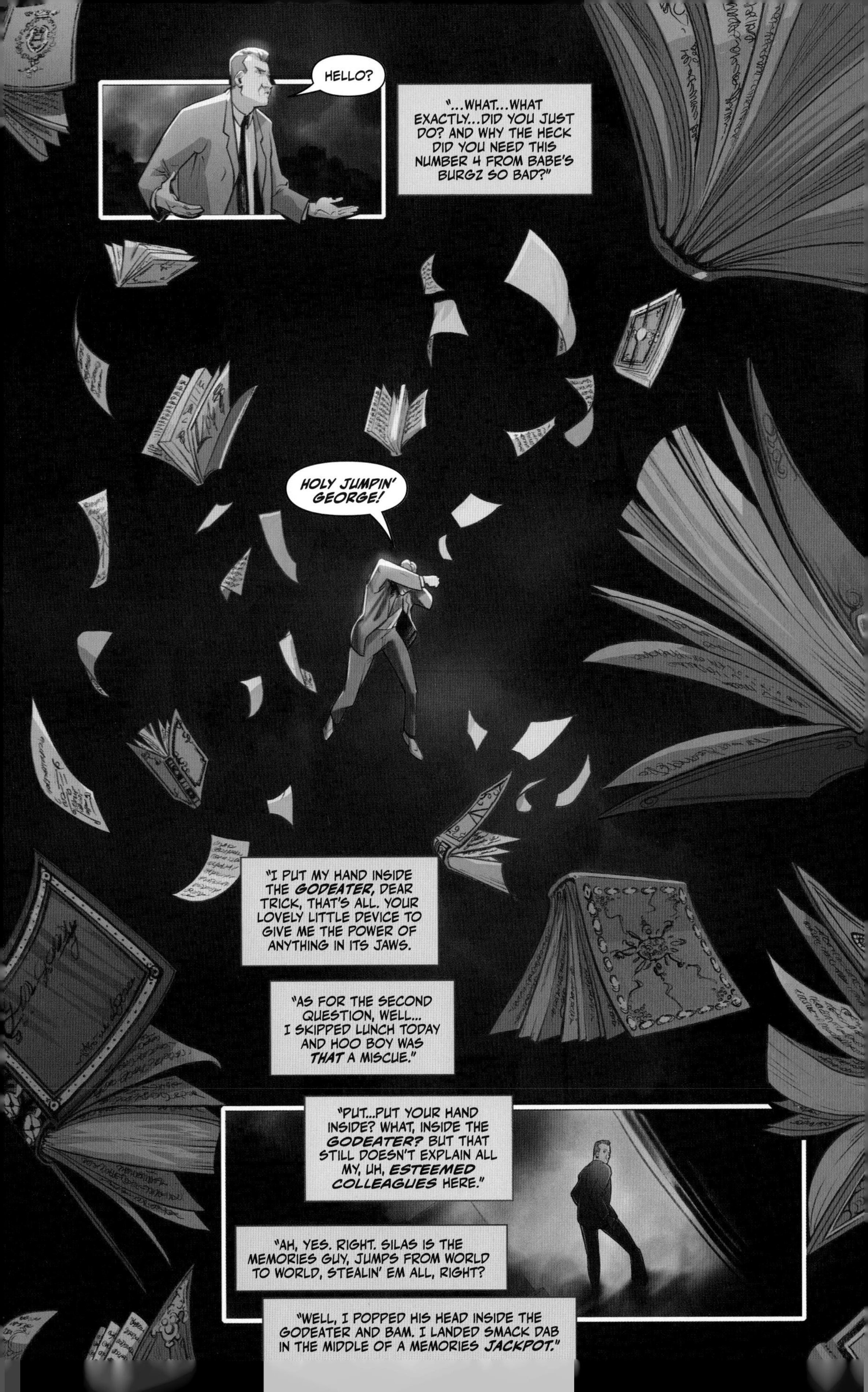
HELLO?
"...WHAT...WHAT EXACTLY...DID YOU JUST DO? AND WHY THE HECK DID YOU NEED THIS NUMBER 4 FROM BABE'S BURGZ SO BAD?"
HOLY JUMPIN' GEORGE!
"I PUT MY HAND INSIDE THE GODEATER, DEAR TRICK, THAT'S ALL. YOUR LOVELY LITTLE DEVICE TO GIVE ME THE POWER OF ANYTHING IN ITS JAWS.
"AS FOR THE SECOND QUESTION, WELL... I SKIPPED LUNCH TODAY AND HOO BOY WAS THAT A MISCUE."
"PUT...PUT YOUR HAND INSIDE? WHAT, INSIDE THE GODEATER? BUT THAT STILL DOESN'T EXPLAIN ALL MY, UH, ESTEEMED COLLEAGUES HERE."
"AH, YES. RIGHT. SILAS IS THE MEMORIES GUY, JUMPS FROM WORLD TO WORLD, STEALIN' EM ALL, RIGHT?
"WELL, I POPPED HIS HEAD INSIDE THE GODEATER AND BAM. I LANDED SMACK DAB IN THE MIDDLE OF A MEMORIES JACKPOT."

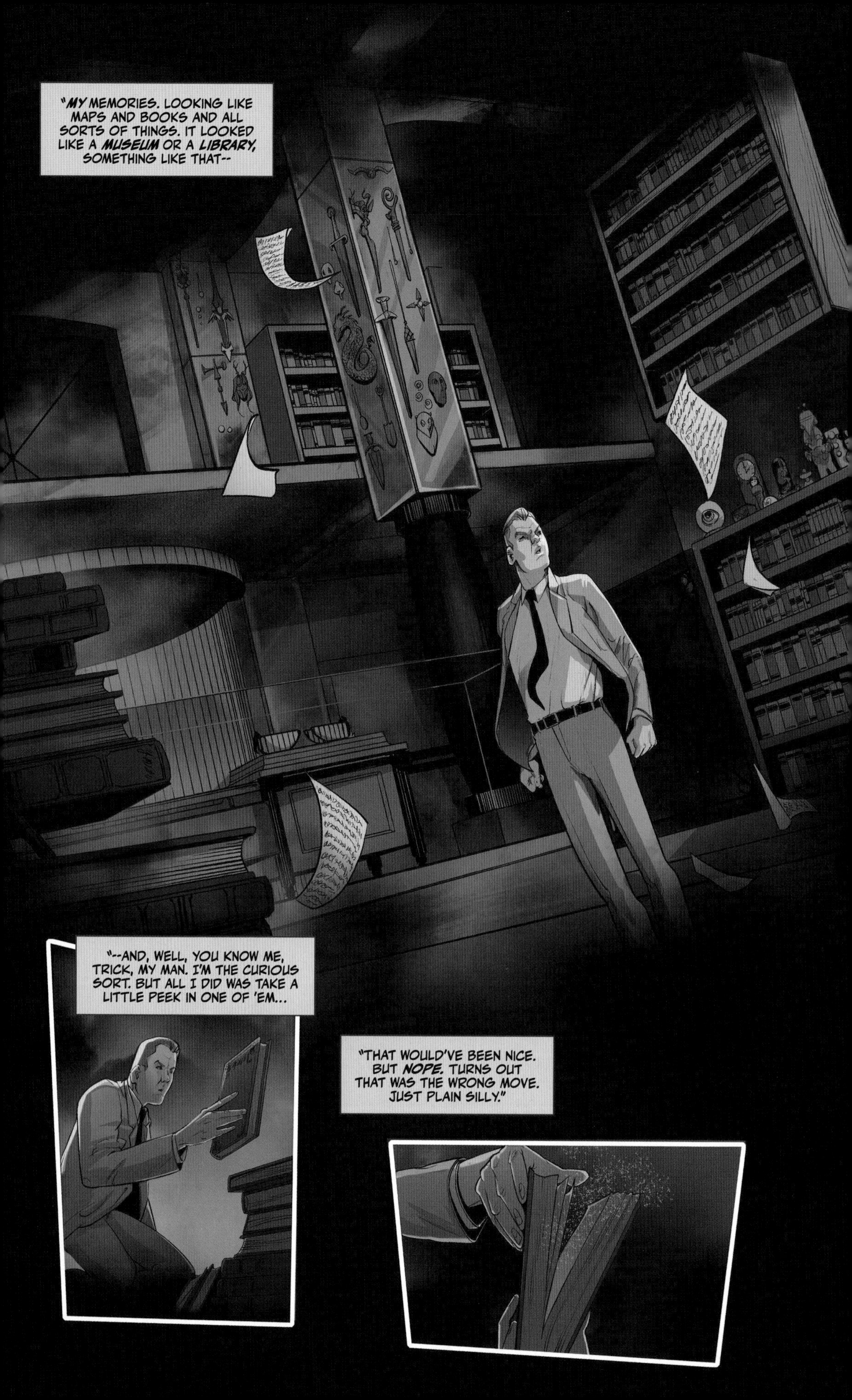

"MY MEMORIES. LOOKING LIKE MAPS AND BOOKS AND ALL SORTS OF THINGS. IT LOOKED LIKE A MUSEUM OR A LIBRARY, SOMETHING LIKE THAT--
"--AND, WELL, YOU KNOW ME, TRICK, MY MAN. I'M THE CURIOUS SORT. BUT ALL I DID WAS TAKE A LITTLE PEEK IN ONE OF 'EM...
"THAT WOULD'VE BEEN NICE. BUT NOPE. TURNS OUT THAT WAS THE WRONG MOVE. JUST PLAIN SILLY."

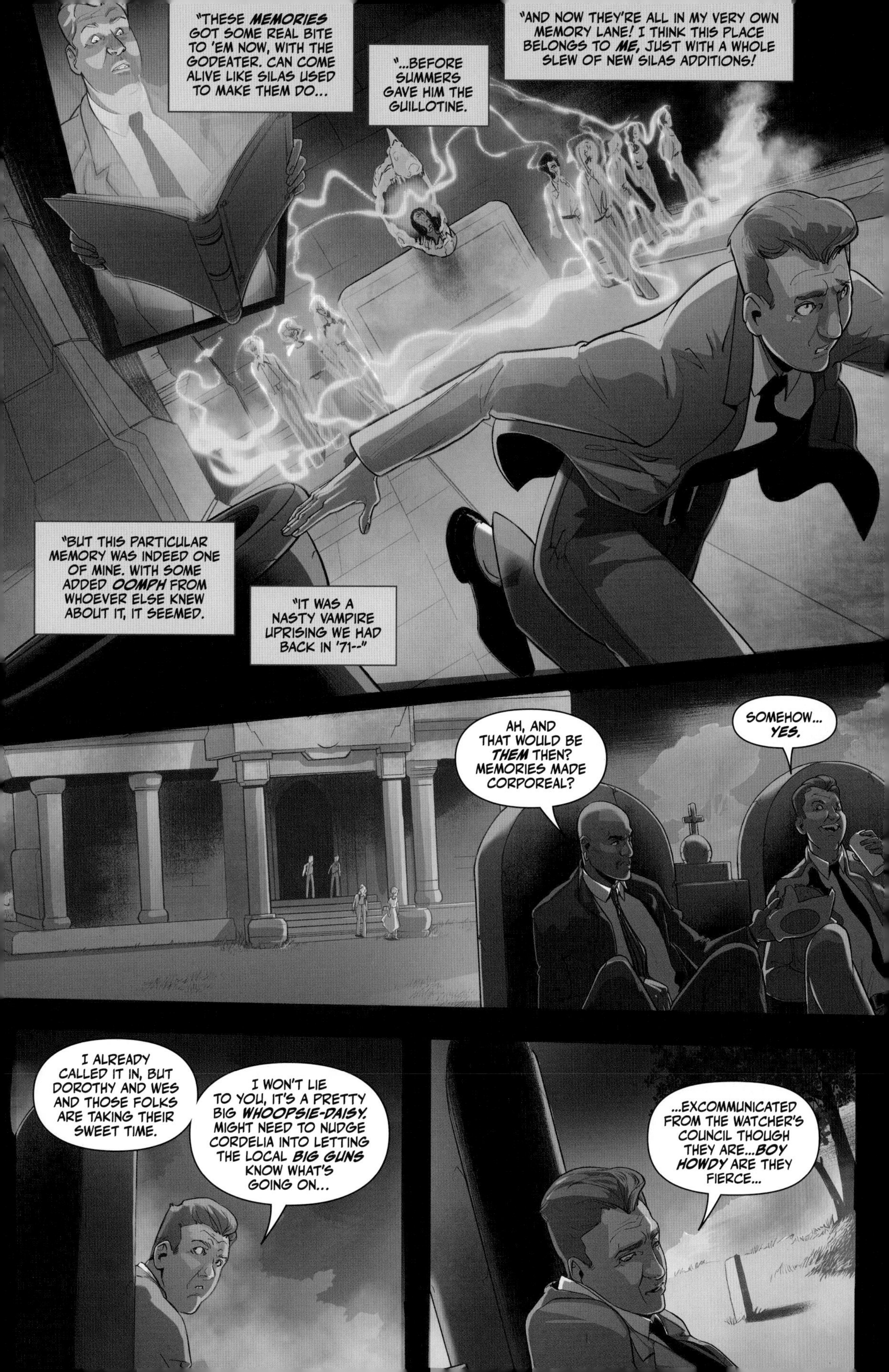
"THESE MEMORIES GOT SOME REAL BITE TO 'EM NOW, WITH THE GODEATER. CAN COME ALIVE LIKE SILAS USED TO MAKE THEM DO...
"...BEFORE SUMMERS GAVE HIM THE GUILLOTINE.
"AND NOW THEY'RE ALL IN MY VERY OWN MEMORY LANE! I THINK THIS PLACE BELONGS TO ME, JUST WITH A WHOLE SLEW OF NEW SILAS ADDITIONS!
"BUT THIS PARTICULAR MEMORY WAS INDEED ONE OF MINE. WITH SOME ADDED OOMPH FROM WHOEVER ELSE KNEW ABOUT IT, IT SEEMED.
"IT WAS A NASTY VAMPIRE UPRISING WE HAD BACK IN '71--"
AH, AND THAT WOULD BE THEM THEN? MEMORIES MADE CORPOREAL?
SOMEHOW... YES.
I ALREADY CALLED IT IN, BUT DOROTHY AND WES AND THOSE FOLKS ARE TAKING THEIR SWEET TIME.
I WON'T LIE TO YOU, IT'S A PRETTY BIG WHOOPSIE-DAISY. MIGHT NEED TO NUDGE CORDELIA INTO LETTING THE LOCAL BIG GUNS KNOW WHAT'S GOING ON...
...EXCOMMUNICATED FROM THE WATCHER'S COUNCIL THOUGH THEY ARE...BOY HOWDY ARE THEY FIERCE...

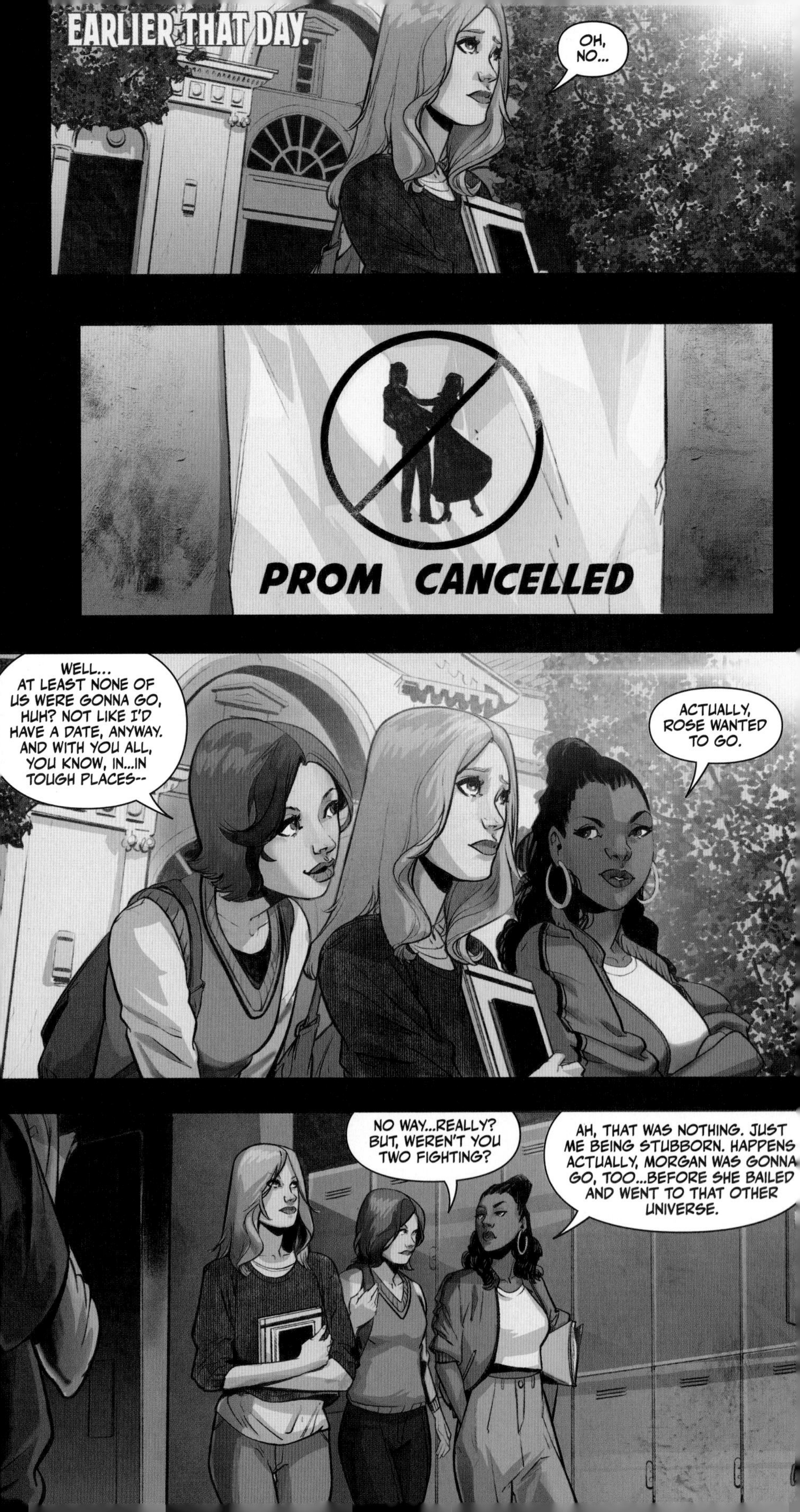
EARLIER THAT DAY.
OH, NO...
PROM CANCELLED
WELL... AT LEAST NONE OF US WERE GONNA GO, HUH? NOT LIKE I'D HAVE A DATE, ANYWAY. AND WITH YOU ALL, YOU KNOW, IN...IN TOUGH PLACES--
ACTUALLY, ROSE WANTED TO GO.
NO WAY...REALLY? BUT, WEREN'T YOU TWO FIGHTING?
AH, THAT WAS NOTHING. JUST ME BEING STUBBORN. HAPPENS ACTUALLY, MORGAN WAS GONNA GO, TOO...BEFORE SHE BAILED AND WENT TO THAT OTHER UNIVERSE.

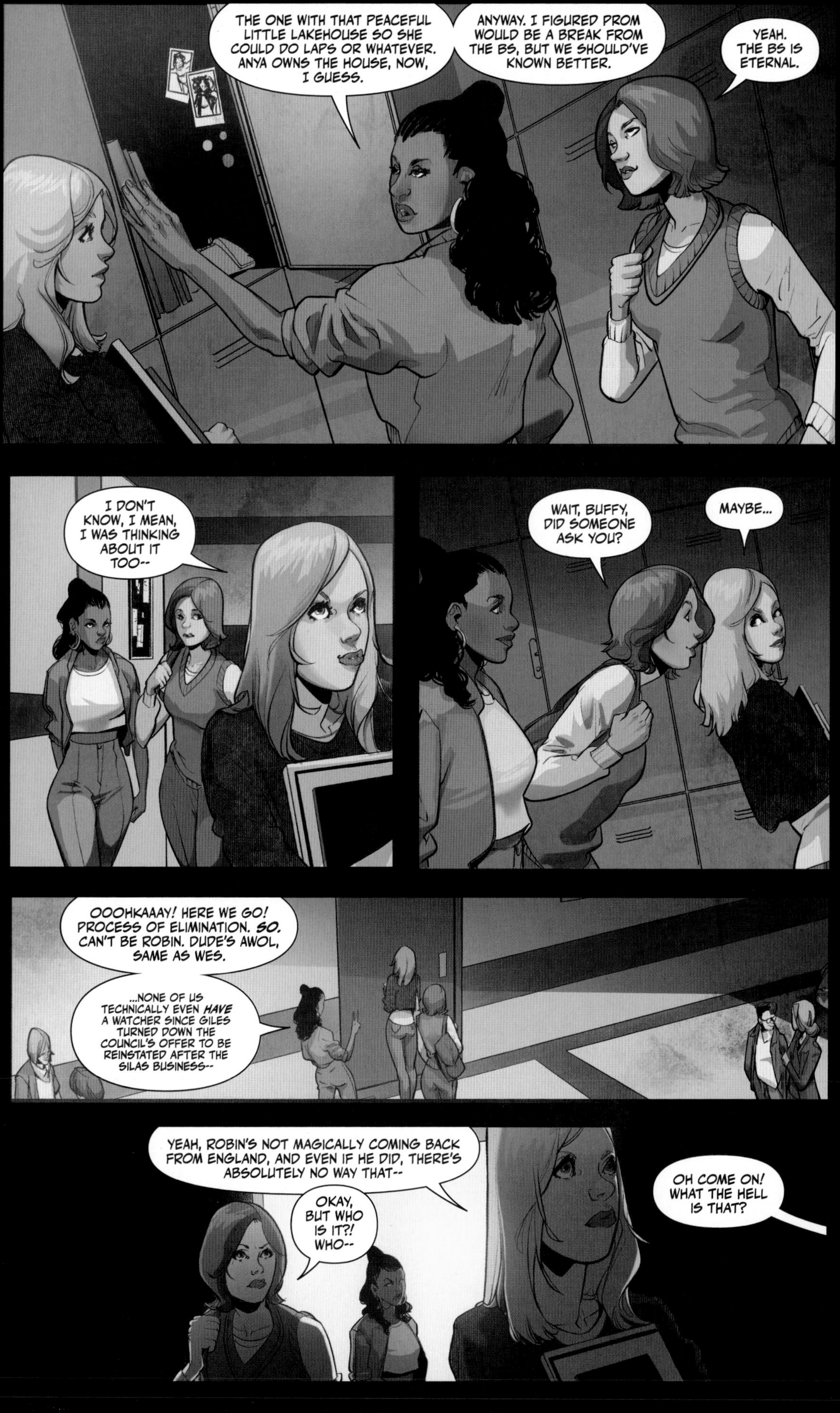
THE ONE WITH THAT PEACEFUL LITTLE LAKEHOUSE SO SHE COULD DO LAPS OR WHATEVER. ANYA OWNS THE HOUSE, NOW, I GUESS.
ANYWAY. I FIGURED PROM WOULD BE A BREAK FROM THE BS, BUT WE SHOULD'VE KNOWN BETTER.
YEAH. THE BS IS ETERNAL.
I DON'T KNOW, I MEAN, I WAS THINKING ABOUT IT TOO--
WAIT, BUFFY, DID SOMEONE ASK YOU?
MAYBE...
OOOHKAAAY! HERE WE GO! PROCESS OF ELIMINATION. *SO.* CAN'T BE ROBIN. DUDE'S AWOL, SAME AS WES.
...NONE OF US TECHNICALLY EVEN *HAVE* A WATCHER SINCE GILES TURNED DOWN THE COUNCIL'S OFFER TO BE REINSTATED AFTER THE SILAS BUSINESS--
YEAH, ROBIN'S NOT MAGICALLY COMING BACK FROM ENGLAND, AND EVEN IF HE DID, THERE'S ABSOLUTELY NO WAY THAT--
OKAY, BUT WHO IS IT?! WHO--
OH COME ON! WHAT THE HELL IS THAT?

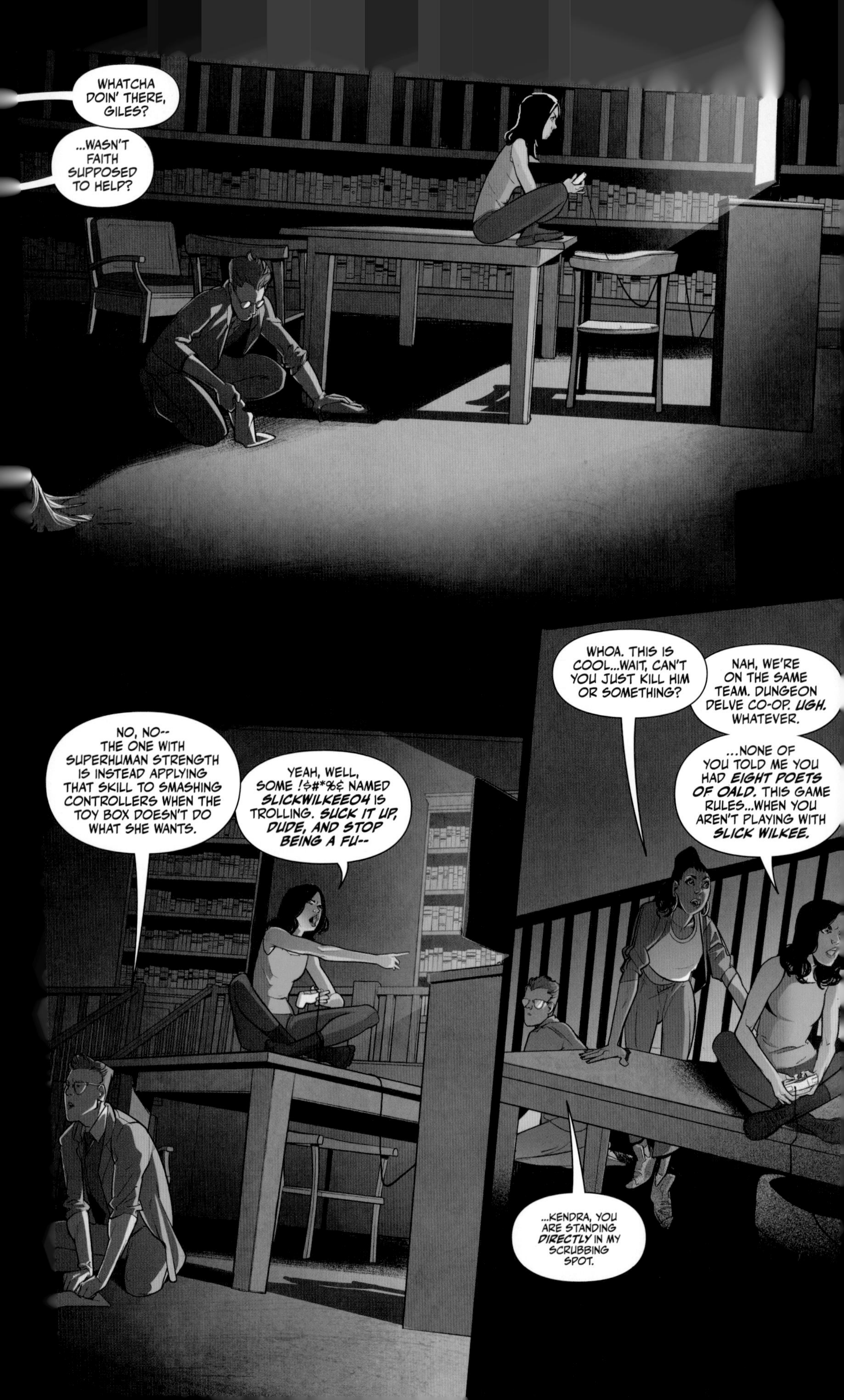
WHATCHA DOIN' THERE, GILES?
...WASN'T FAITH SUPPOSED TO HELP?
NO, NO-- THE ONE WITH SUPERHUMAN STRENGTH IS INSTEAD APPLYING THAT SKILL TO SMASHING CONTROLLERS WHEN THE TOY BOX DOESN'T DO WHAT SHE WANTS.
YEAH, WELL, SOME !$#*%& NAMED SLICKWILKEE04 IS TROLLING. SUCK IT UP, DUDE, AND STOP BEING A FU--
WHOA. THIS IS COOL...WAIT, CAN'T YOU JUST KILL HIM OR SOMETHING?
NAH, WE'RE ON THE SAME TEAM. DUNGEON DELVE CO-OP. UGH. WHATEVER.
...NONE OF YOU TOLD ME YOU HAD EIGHT POETS OF OALD. THIS GAME RULES...WHEN YOU AREN'T PLAYING WITH SLICK WILKEE.
...KENDRA, YOU ARE STANDING DIRECTLY IN MY SCRUBBING SPOT.

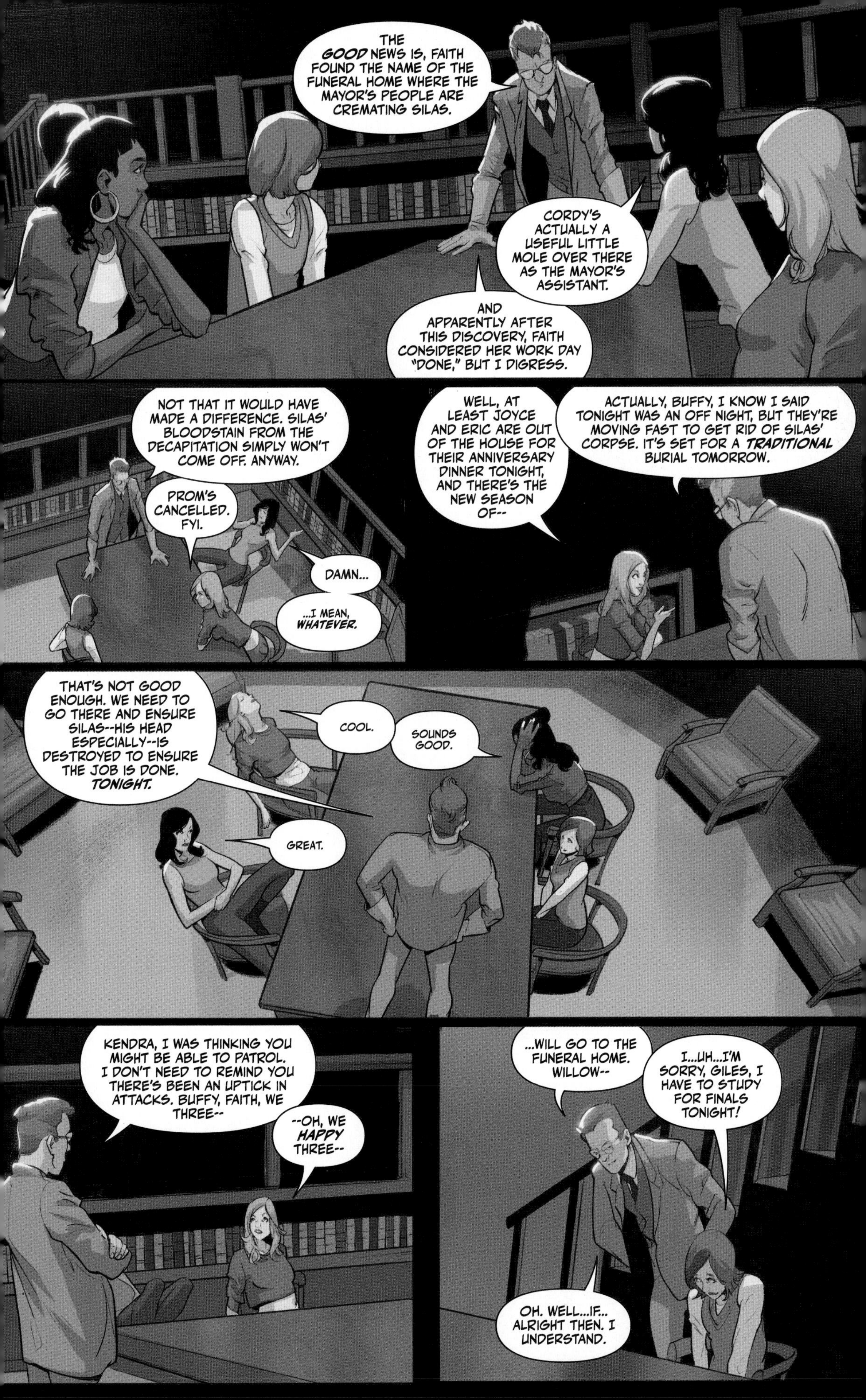
THE GOOD NEWS IS, FAITH FOUND THE NAME OF THE FUNERAL HOME WHERE THE MAYOR'S PEOPLE ARE CREMATING SILAS.
CORDY'S ACTUALLY A USEFUL LITTLE MOLE OVER THERE AS THE MAYOR'S ASSISTANT.
AND APPARENTLY AFTER THIS DISCOVERY, FAITH CONSIDERED HER WORK DAY "DONE," BUT I DIGRESS.
NOT THAT IT WOULD HAVE MADE A DIFFERENCE. SILAS' BLOODSTAIN FROM THE DECAPITATION SIMPLY WON'T COME OFF. ANYWAY.
PROM'S CANCELLED. FYI.
DAMN...
...I MEAN, WHATEVER.
WELL, AT LEAST JOYCE AND ERIC ARE OUT OF THE HOUSE FOR THEIR ANNIVERSARY DINNER TONIGHT, AND THERE'S THE NEW SEASON OF--
ACTUALLY, BUFFY, I KNOW I SAID TONIGHT WAS AN OFF NIGHT, BUT THEY'RE MOVING FAST TO GET RID OF SILAS' CORPSE. IT'S SET FOR A TRADITIONAL BURIAL TOMORROW.
THAT'S NOT GOOD ENOUGH. WE NEED TO GO THERE AND ENSURE SILAS--HIS HEAD ESPECIALLY--IS DESTROYED TO ENSURE THE JOB IS DONE. TONIGHT.
COOL.
SOUNDS GOOD.
GREAT.
KENDRA, I WAS THINKING YOU MIGHT BE ABLE TO PATROL. I DON'T NEED TO REMIND YOU THERE'S BEEN AN UPTICK IN ATTACKS. BUFFY, FAITH, WE THREE--
--OH, WE HAPPY THREE--
...WILL GO TO THE FUNERAL HOME. WILLOW--
I...UH...I'M SORRY, GILES, I HAVE TO STUDY FOR FINALS TONIGHT!
OH. WELL...IF... ALRIGHT THEN. I UNDERSTAND.

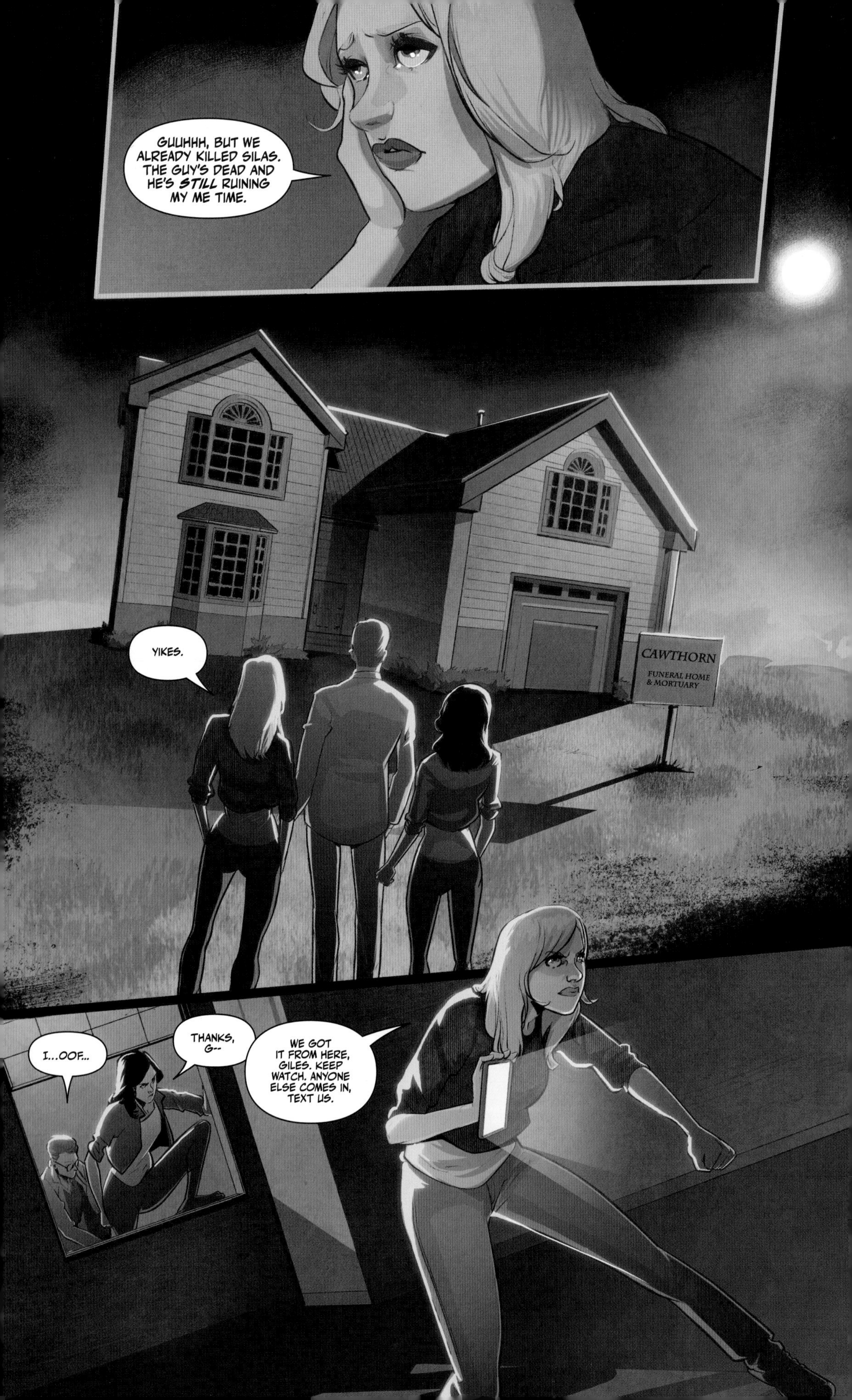
GUUHHH, BUT WE ALREADY KILLED SILAS. THE GUY'S DEAD AND HE'S STILL RUINING MY ME TIME.
YIKES.
CAWTHORN
FUNERAL HOME & MORTUARY
I...OOF...
THANKS, G--
WE GOT IT FROM HERE, GILES. KEEP WATCH. ANYONE ELSE COMES IN, TEXT US.

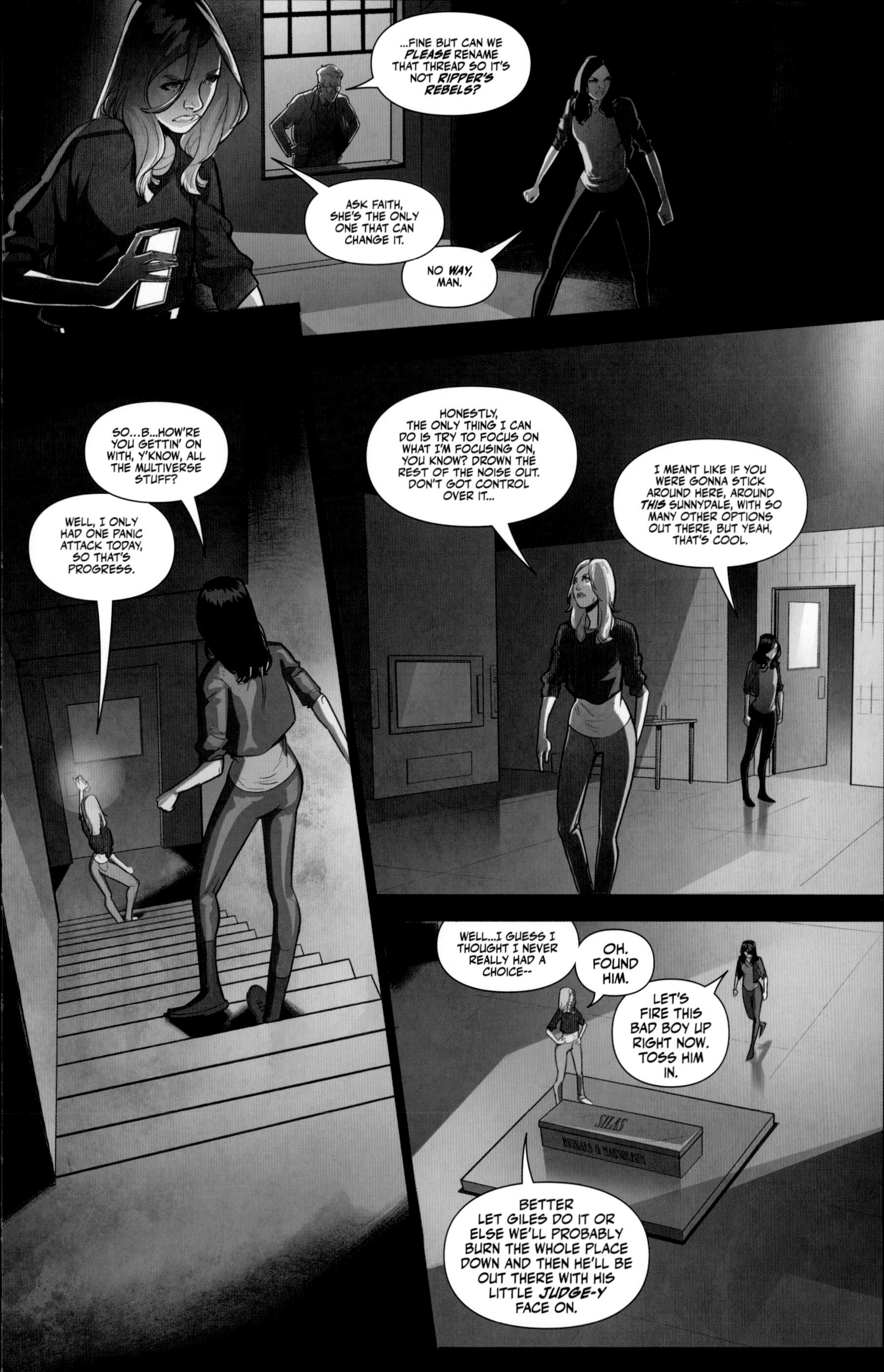
...FINE BUT CAN WE PLEASE RENAME THAT THREAD SO IT'S NOT RIPPER'S REBELS?
ASK FAITH, SHE'S THE ONLY ONE THAT CAN CHANGE IT.
NO WAY, MAN.
SO...B...HOW'RE YOU GETTIN' ON WITH, Y'KNOW, ALL THE MULTIVERSE STUFF?
WELL, I ONLY HAD ONE PANIC ATTACK TODAY, SO THAT'S PROGRESS.
HONESTLY, THE ONLY THING I CAN DO IS TRY TO FOCUS ON WHAT I'M FOCUSING ON, YOU KNOW? DROWN THE REST OF THE NOISE OUT. DON'T GOT CONTROL OVER IT...
I MEANT LIKE IF YOU WERE GONNA STICK AROUND HERE, AROUND THIS SUNNYDALE, WITH SO MANY OTHER OPTIONS OUT THERE, BUT YEAH, THAT'S COOL.
WELL...I GUESS I THOUGHT I NEVER REALLY HAD A CHOICE--
OH. FOUND HIM.
LET'S FIRE THIS BAD BOY UP RIGHT NOW. TOSS HIM IN.
SILAS
BETTER LET GILES DO IT OR ELSE WE'LL PROBABLY BURN THE WHOLE PLACE DOWN AND THEN HE'LL BE OUT THERE WITH HIS LITTLE JUDGE-Y FACE ON.

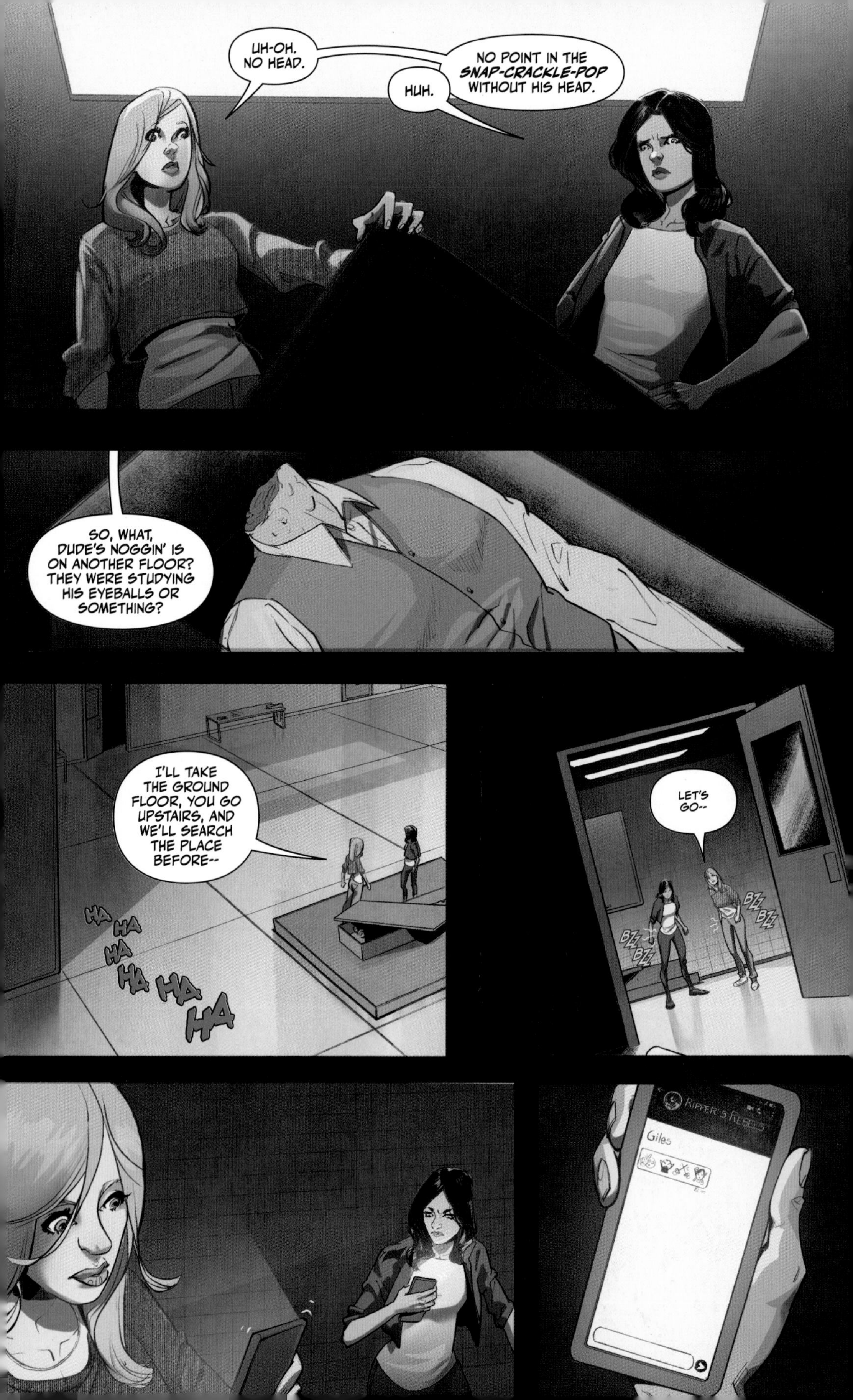
UH-OH. NO HEAD.
NO POINT IN THE SNAP-CRACKLE-POP WITHOUT HIS HEAD.
HUH.
SO, WHAT, DUDE'S NOGGIN' IS ON ANOTHER FLOOR? THEY WERE STUDYING HIS EYEBALLS OR SOMETHING?
I'LL TAKE THE GROUND FLOOR, YOU GO UPSTAIRS, AND WE'LL SEARCH THE PLACE BEFORE--
HA HA HA HA HA HA HA
LET'S GO--
BZZ BZZ
BZZ BZZ
RIPPER'S REBELS
Giles

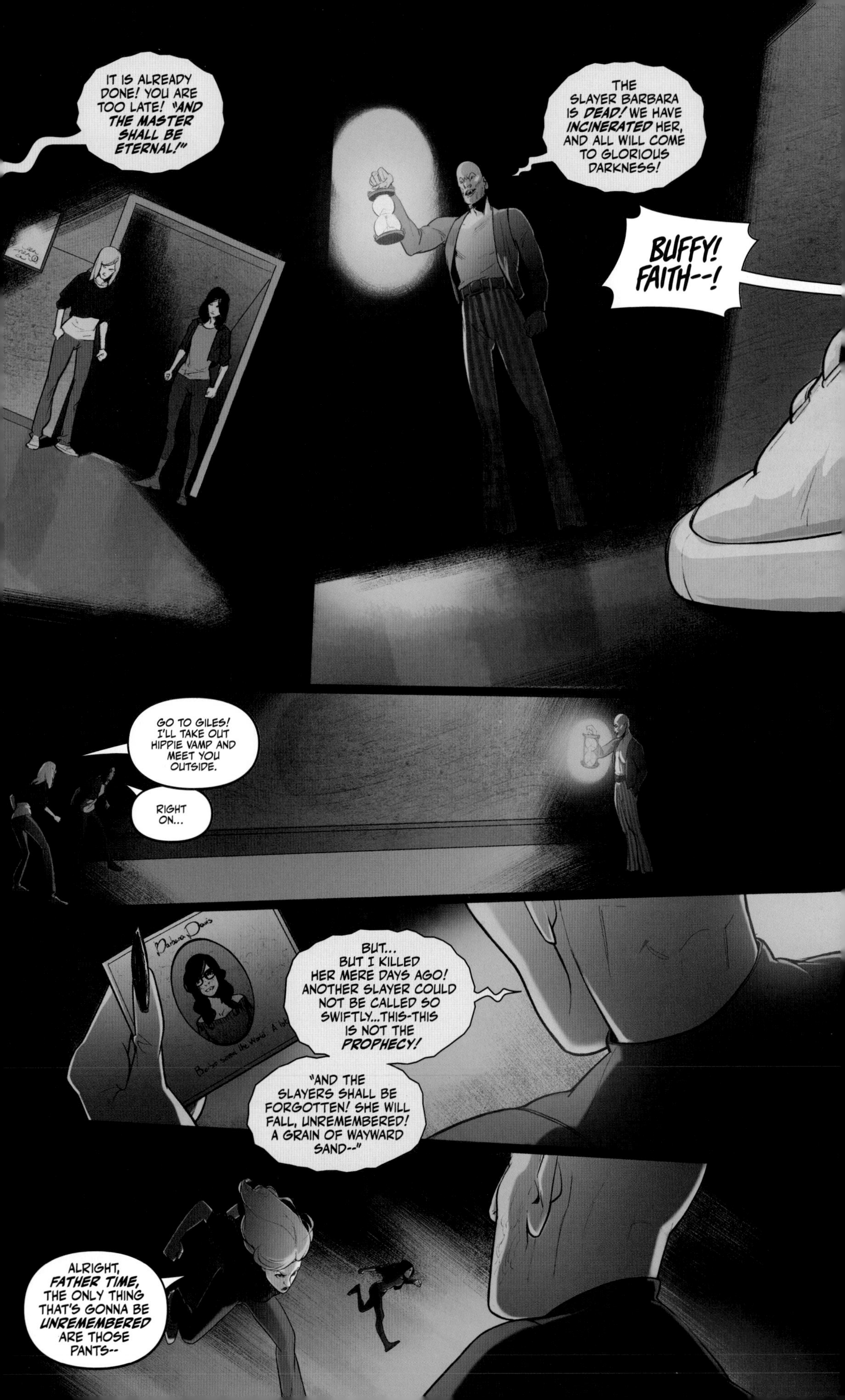
IT IS ALREADY DONE! YOU ARE TOO LATE! "AND THE MASTER SHALL BE ETERNAL!"
THE SLAYER BARBARA IS DEAD! WE HAVE INCINERATED HER, AND ALL WILL COME TO GLORIOUS DARKNESS!
BUFFY! FAITH--!
GO TO GILES! I'LL TAKE OUT HIPPIE VAMP AND MEET YOU OUTSIDE.
RIGHT ON...
BUT... BUT I KILLED HER MERE DAYS AGO! ANOTHER SLAYER COULD NOT BE CALLED SO SWIFTLY...THIS-THIS IS NOT THE PROPHECY!
"AND THE SLAYERS SHALL BE FORGOTTEN! SHE WILL FALL, UNREMEMBERED! A GRAIN OF WAYWARD SAND--"
ALRIGHT, FATHER TIME, THE ONLY THING THAT'S GONNA BE UNREMEMBERED ARE THOSE PANTS--

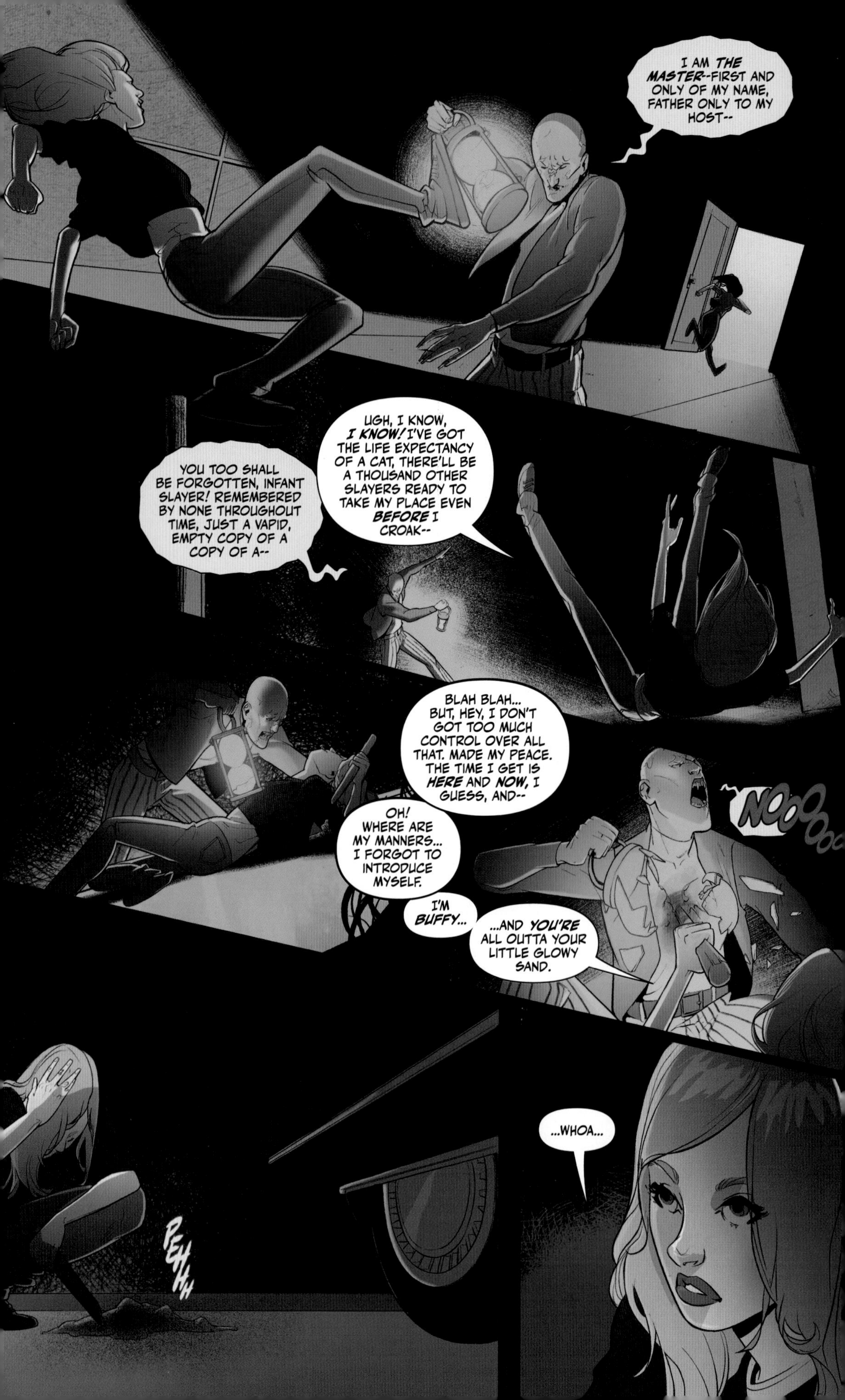

I AM **THE MASTER**--FIRST AND ONLY OF MY NAME, FATHER ONLY TO MY HOST--
YOU TOO SHALL BE FORGOTTEN, INFANT SLAYER! REMEMBERED BY NONE THROUGHOUT TIME, JUST A VAPID, EMPTY COPY OF A COPY OF A--
UGH, I KNOW, ***I KNOW!*** I'VE GOT THE LIFE EXPECTANCY OF A CAT, THERE'LL BE A THOUSAND OTHER SLAYERS READY TO TAKE MY PLACE EVEN ***BEFORE*** I CROAK--
BLAH BLAH... BUT, HEY, I DON'T GOT TOO MUCH CONTROL OVER ALL THAT. MADE MY PEACE. THE TIME I GET IS ***HERE*** AND ***NOW,*** I GUESS, AND--
OH! WHERE ARE MY MANNERS... I FORGOT TO INTRODUCE MYSELF.
I'M ***BUFFY***...
...AND ***YOU'RE*** ALL OUTTA YOUR LITTLE GLOWY SAND.
NOOOOOO
PEHHH
...WHOA...

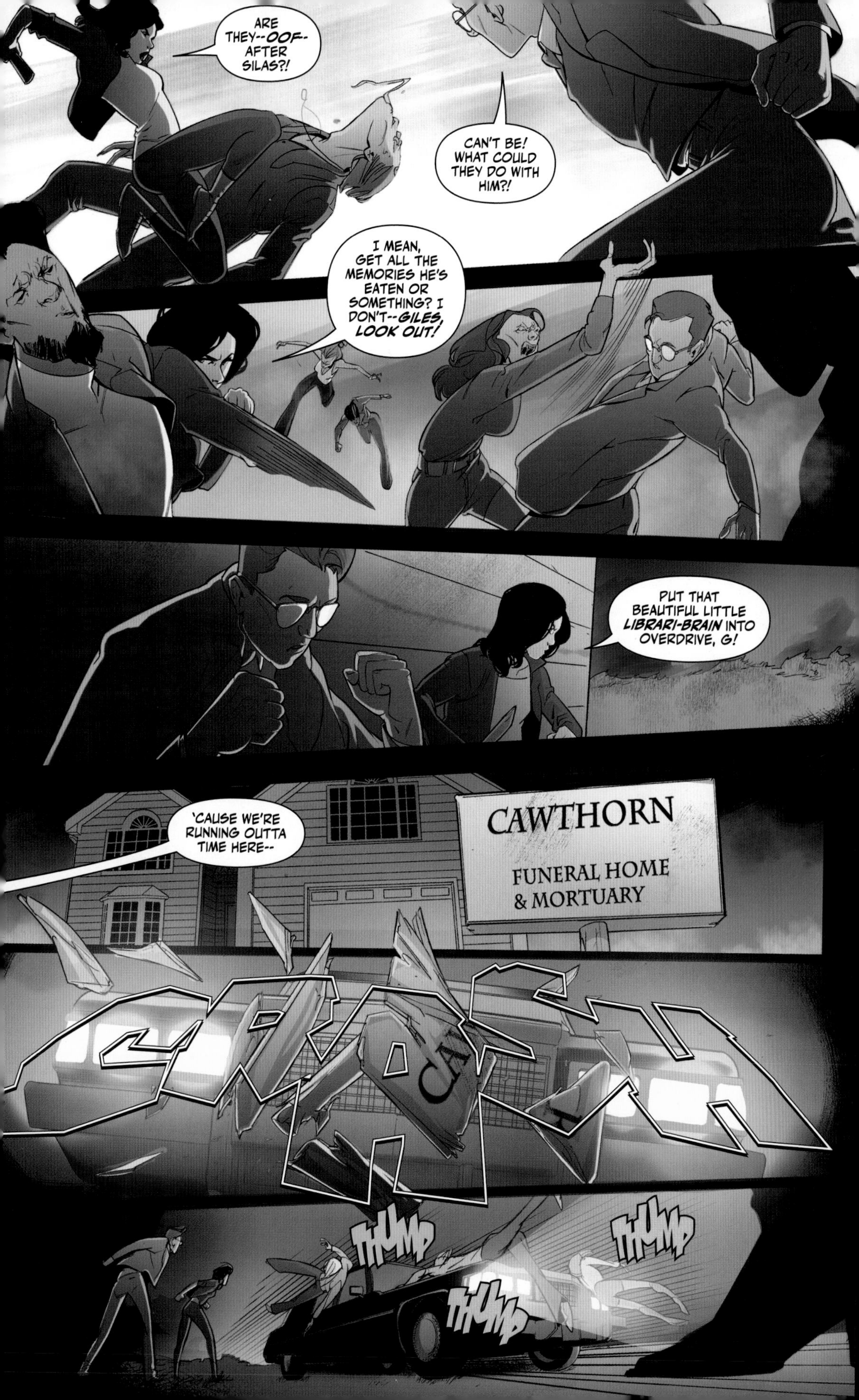
ARE THEY--OOF-- AFTER SILAS?!
CAN'T BE! WHAT COULD THEY DO WITH HIM?!
I MEAN, GET ALL THE MEMORIES HE'S EATEN OR SOMETHING? I DON'T--GILES, LOOK OUT!
PUT THAT BEAUTIFUL LITTLE LIBRARI-BRAIN INTO OVERDRIVE, G!
'CAUSE WE'RE RUNNING OUTTA TIME HERE--
CAWTHORN
FUNERAL HOME
& MORTUARY
CRASH
THUMP
THUMP
THUMP

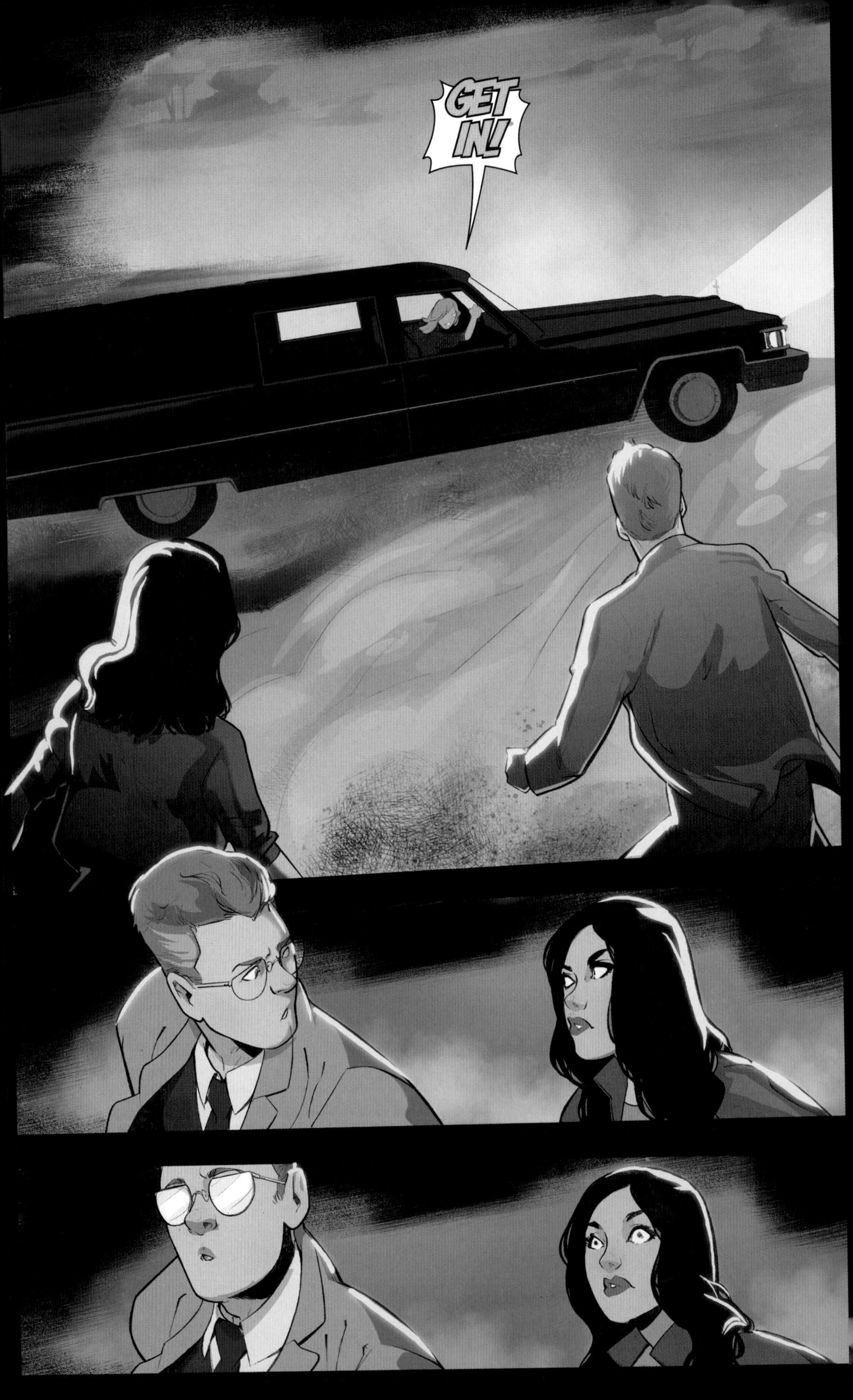
GET IN!

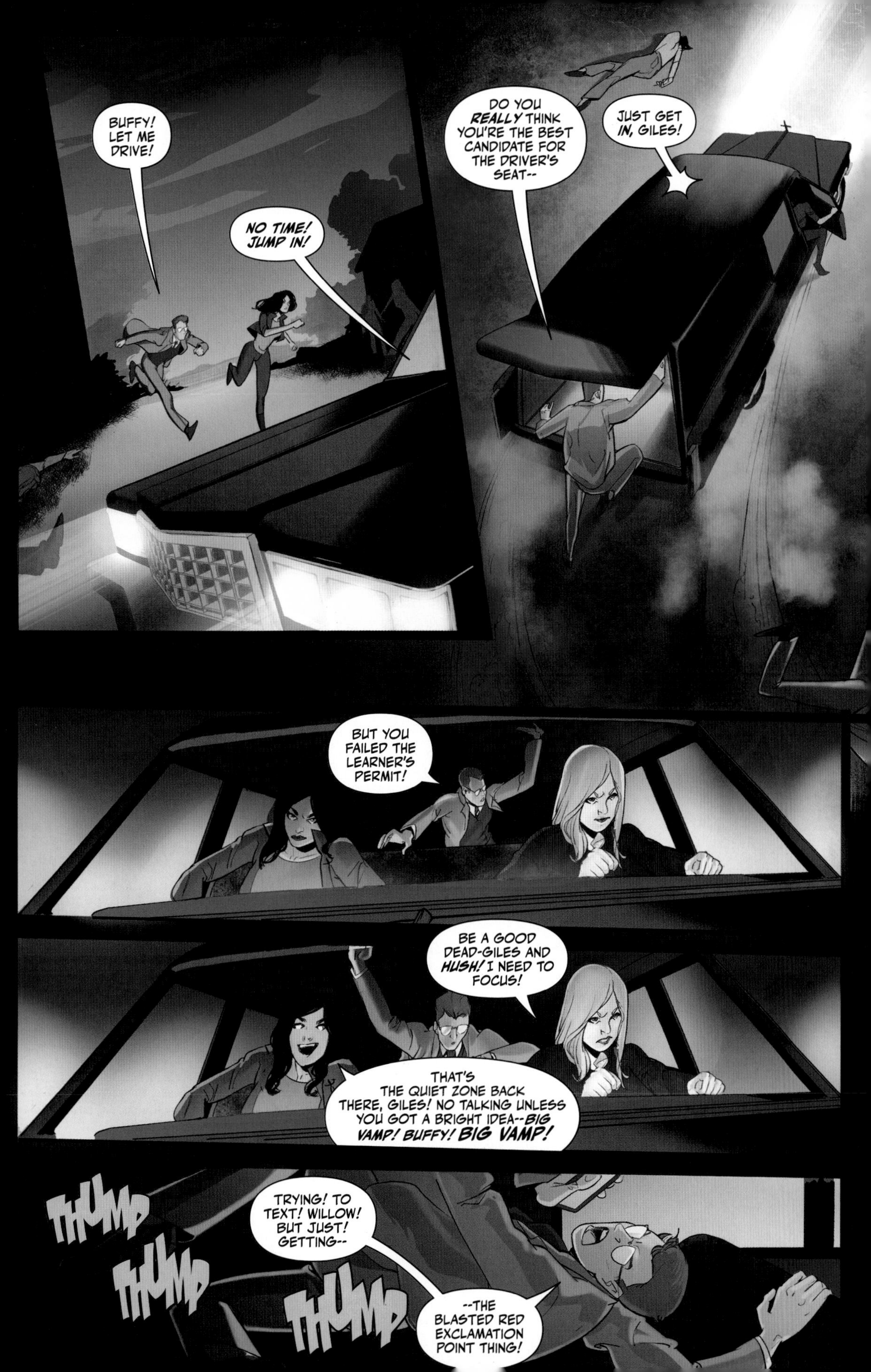
BUFFY! LET ME DRIVE!
NO TIME! JUMP IN!
DO YOU REALLY THINK YOU'RE THE BEST CANDIDATE FOR THE DRIVER'S SEAT--
JUST GET IN, GILES!
BUT YOU FAILED THE LEARNER'S PERMIT!
BE A GOOD DEAD-GILES AND HUSH! I NEED TO FOCUS!
THAT'S THE QUIET ZONE BACK THERE, GILES! NO TALKING UNLESS YOU GOT A BRIGHT IDEA--BIG VAMP! BUFFY! BIG VAMP!
THUMP
THUMP
THUMP
TRYING! TO TEXT! WILLOW! BUT JUST! GETTING--
--THE BLASTED RED EXCLAMATION POINT THING!

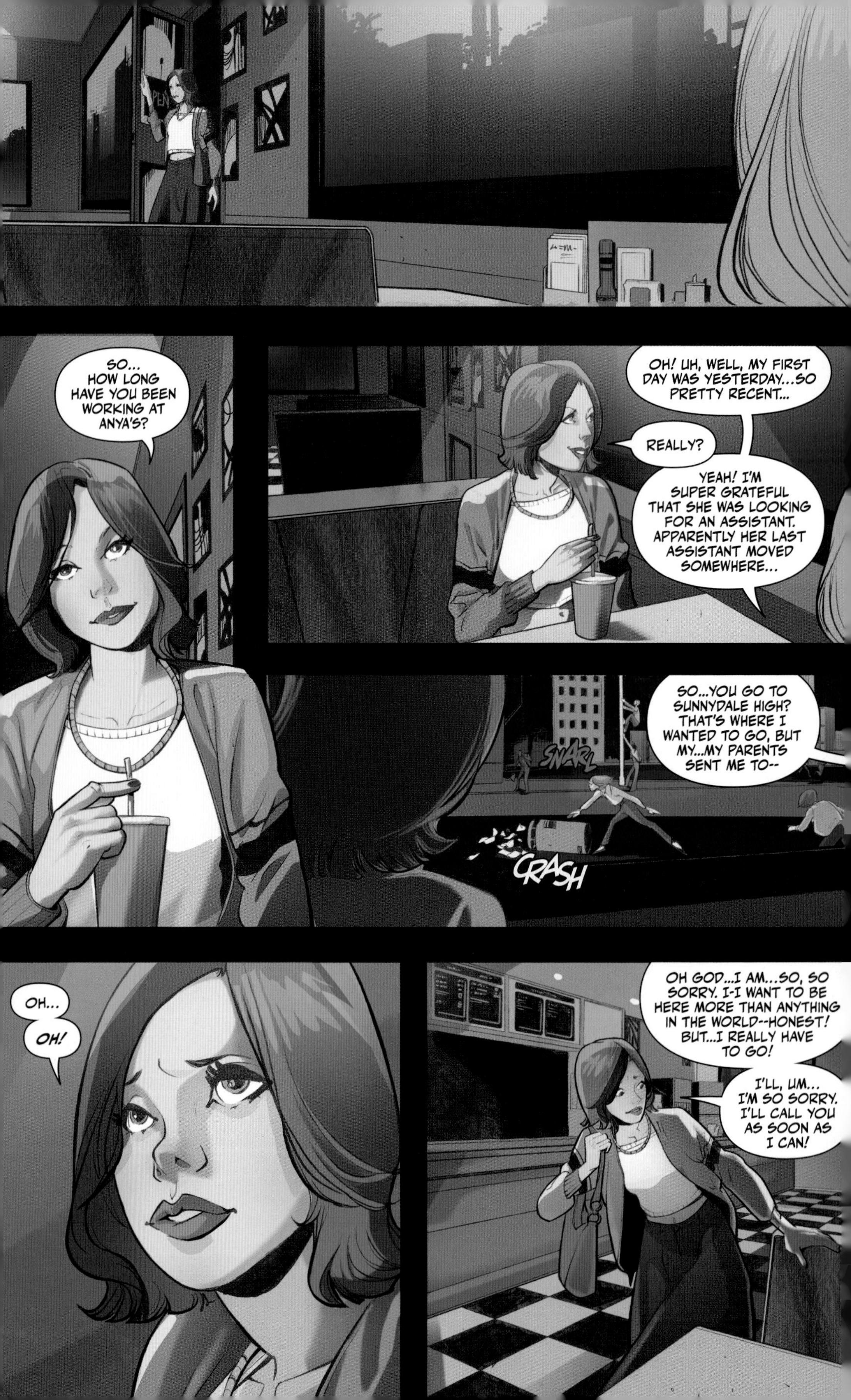
SO... HOW LONG HAVE YOU BEEN WORKING AT ANYA'S?
OH! UH, WELL, MY FIRST DAY WAS YESTERDAY...SO PRETTY RECENT...
REALLY?
YEAH! I'M SUPER GRATEFUL THAT SHE WAS LOOKING FOR AN ASSISTANT. APPARENTLY HER LAST ASSISTANT MOVED SOMEWHERE...
SO...YOU GO TO SUNNYDALE HIGH? THAT'S WHERE I WANTED TO GO, BUT MY...MY PARENTS SENT ME TO--
SNARL
CRASH
OH...
OH!
OH GOD...I AM...SO, SO SORRY. I-I WANT TO BE HERE MORE THAN ANYTHING IN THE WORLD--HONEST! BUT...I REALLY HAVE TO GO!
I'LL, UM... I'M SO SORRY. I'LL CALL YOU AS SOON AS I CAN!

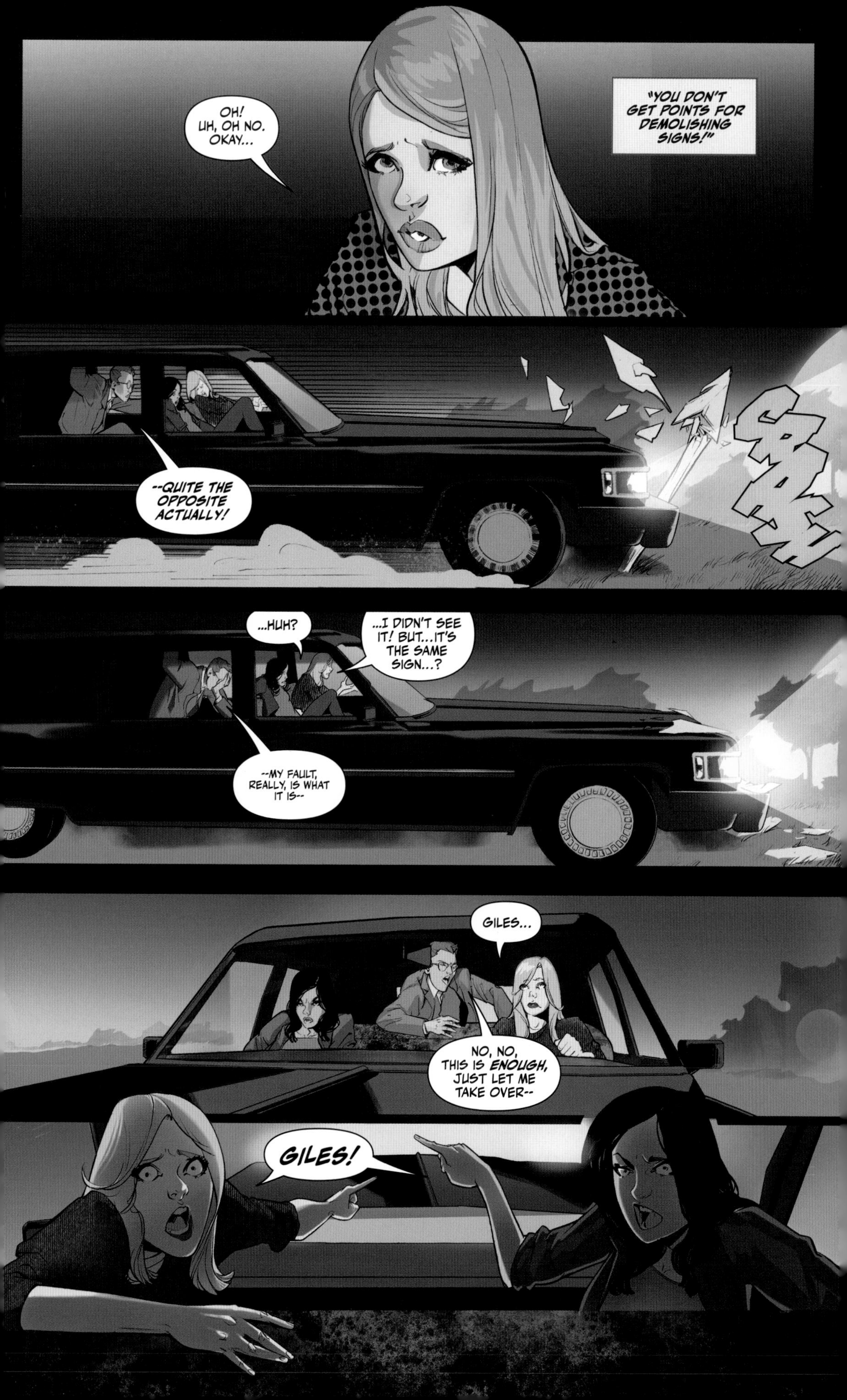
OH! UH, OH NO. OKAY...
"YOU DON'T GET POINTS FOR DEMOLISHING SIGNS!"
--QUITE THE OPPOSITE ACTUALLY!
...HUH?
...I DIDN'T SEE IT! BUT...IT'S THE SAME SIGN...?
--MY FAULT, REALLY, IS WHAT IT IS--
GILES...
NO, NO, THIS IS ENOUGH, JUST LET ME TAKE OVER--
GILES!

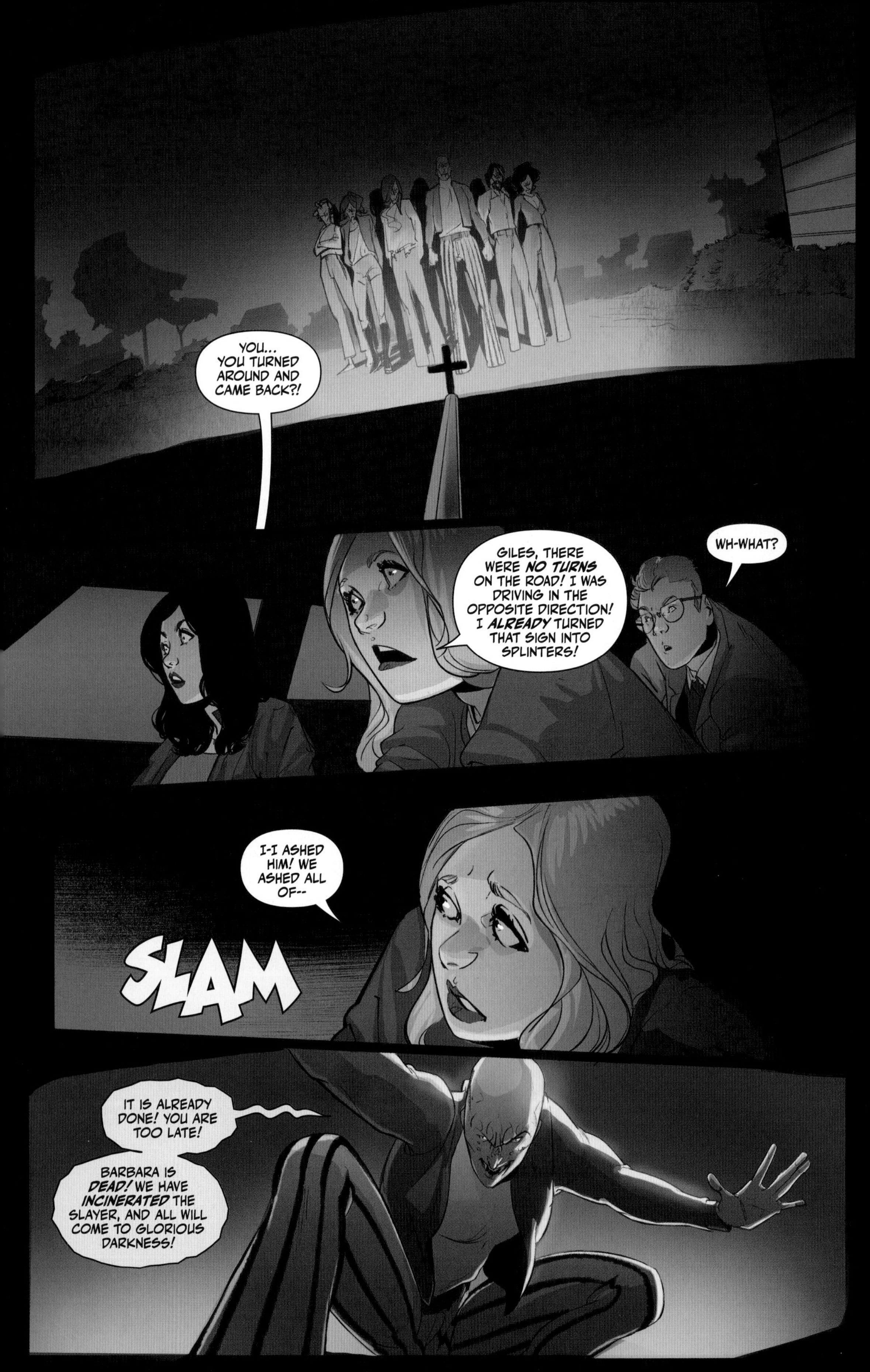

YOU... YOU TURNED AROUND AND CAME BACK?!
GILES, THERE WERE NO TURNS ON THE ROAD! I WAS DRIVING IN THE OPPOSITE DIRECTION! I ALREADY TURNED THAT SIGN INTO SPLINTERS!
WH-WHAT?
I-I ASHED HIM! WE ASHED ALL OF--
SLAM
IT IS ALREADY DONE! YOU ARE TOO LATE!
BARBARA IS DEAD! WE HAVE INCINERATED THE SLAYER, AND ALL WILL COME TO GLORIOUS DARKNESS!

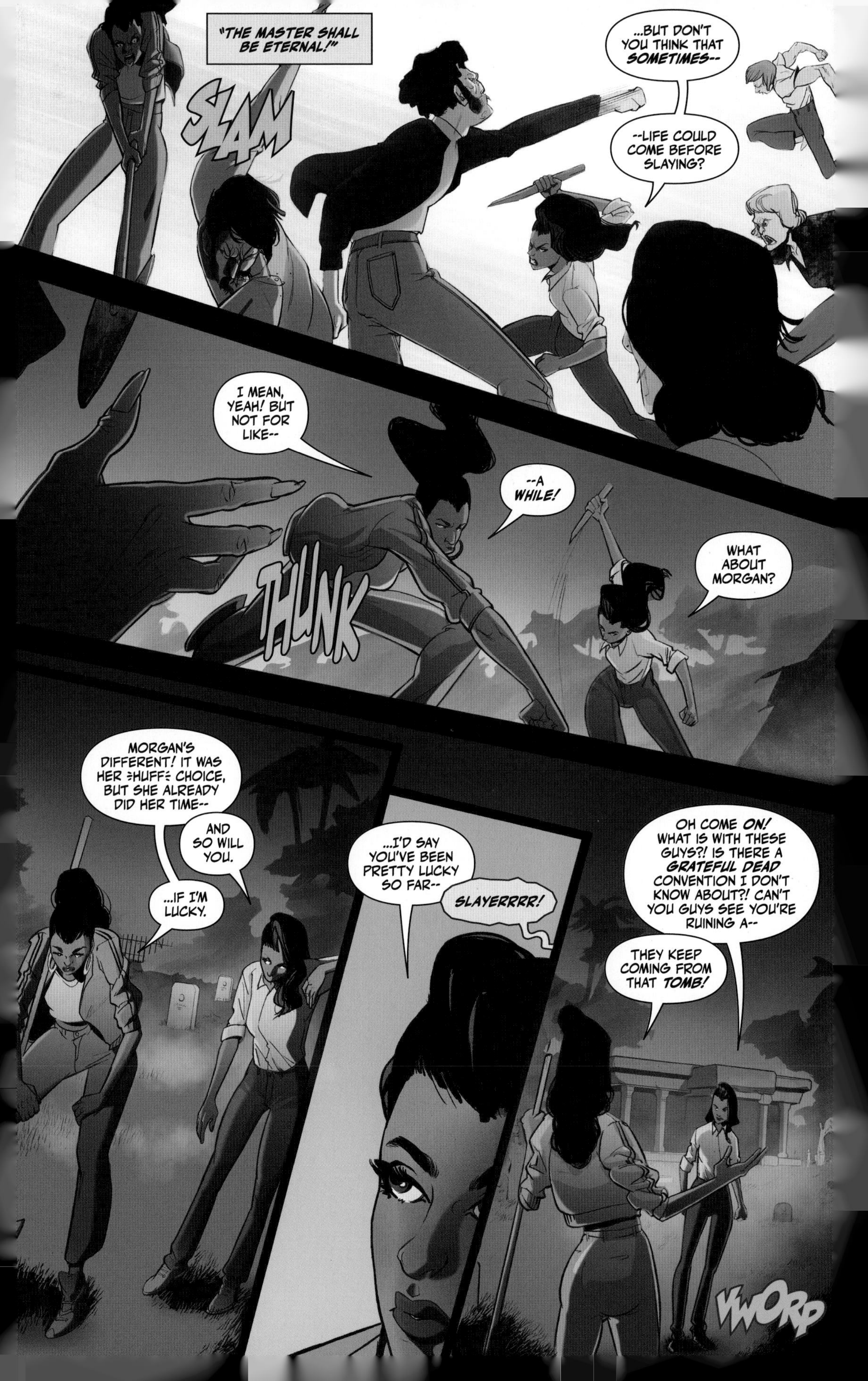
"THE MASTER SHALL BE ETERNAL!"
...BUT DON'T YOU THINK THAT SOMETIMES--
SLAM
--LIFE COULD COME BEFORE SLAYING?
I MEAN, YEAH! BUT NOT FOR LIKE--
--A WHILE!
THUNK
WHAT ABOUT MORGAN?
MORGAN'S DIFFERENT! IT WAS HER =HUFF= CHOICE, BUT SHE ALREADY DID HER TIME--
AND SO WILL YOU.
...IF I'M LUCKY.
...I'D SAY YOU'VE BEEN PRETTY LUCKY SO FAR--
SLAYERRRR!
OH COME ON! WHAT IS WITH THESE GUYS?! IS THERE A GRATEFUL DEAD CONVENTION I DON'T KNOW ABOUT?! CAN'T YOU GUYS SEE YOU'RE RUINING A--
THEY KEEP COMING FROM THAT TOMB!
VWORP

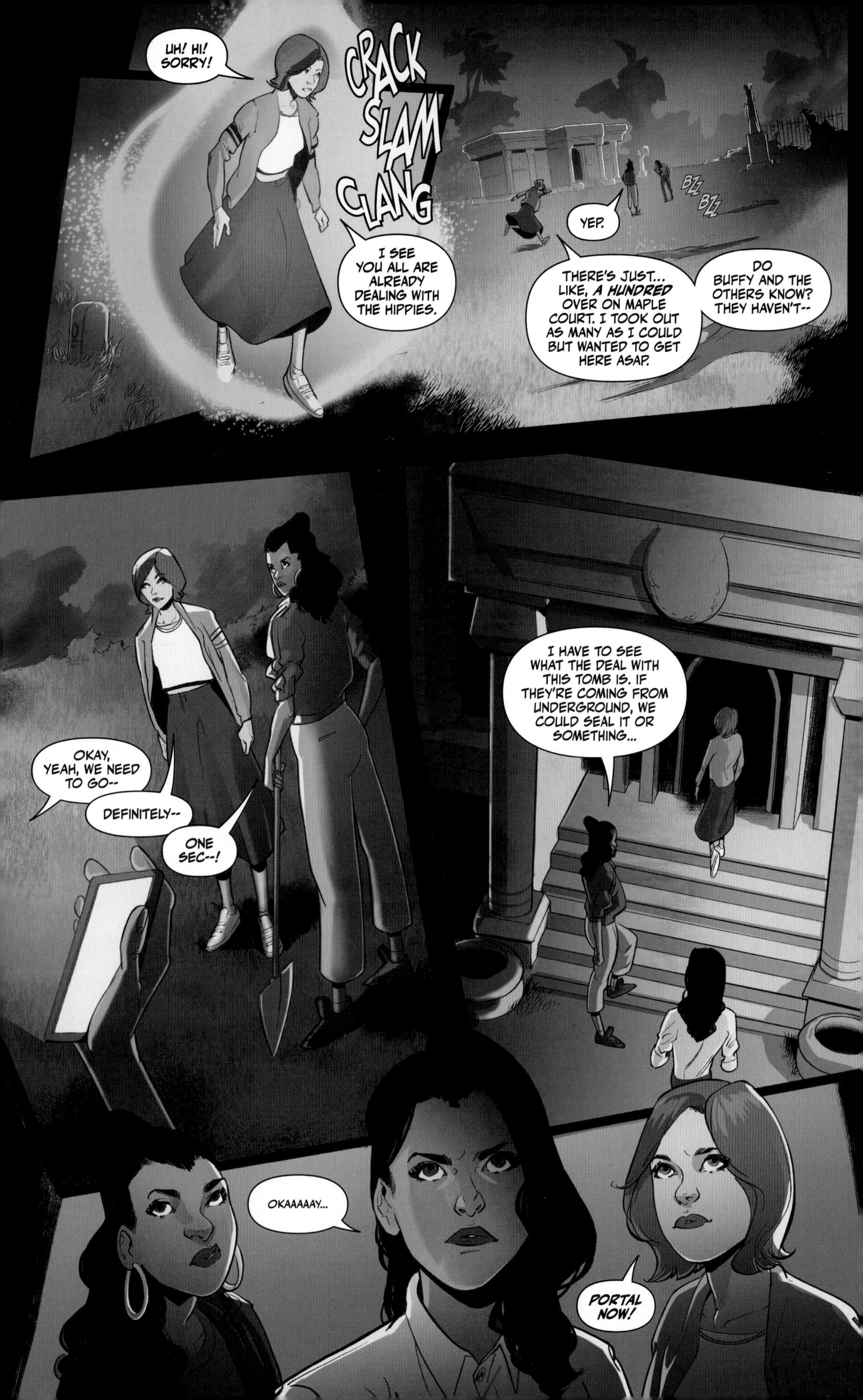
UH! HI! SORRY!
CRACK
SLAM
CLANG
I SEE YOU ALL ARE ALREADY DEALING WITH THE HIPPIES.
BZZ BZZ
YEP.
THERE'S JUST... LIKE, A HUNDRED OVER ON MAPLE COURT. I TOOK OUT AS MANY AS I COULD BUT WANTED TO GET HERE ASAP.
DO BUFFY AND THE OTHERS KNOW? THEY HAVEN'T--
OKAY, YEAH, WE NEED TO GO--
DEFINITELY--
ONE SEC--!
I HAVE TO SEE WHAT THE DEAL WITH THIS TOMB IS. IF THEY'RE COMING FROM UNDERGROUND, WE COULD SEAL IT OR SOMETHING...
OKAAAAAY...
PORTAL NOW!

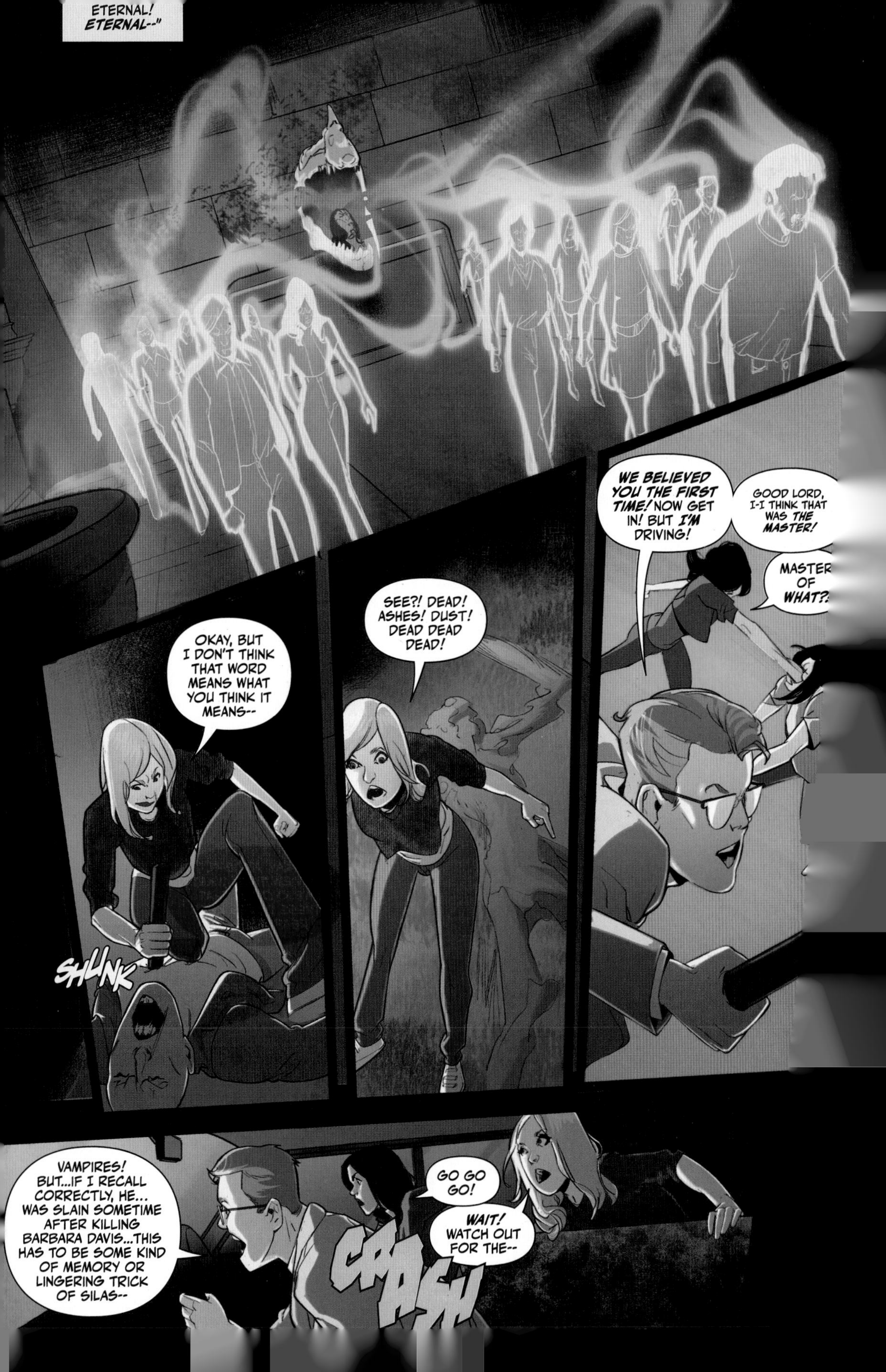
ETERNAL! ETERNAL--"
WE BELIEVED YOU THE FIRST TIME! NOW GET IN! BUT I'M DRIVING!
GOOD LORD, I-I THINK THAT WAS THE MASTER!
MASTER OF WHAT?!
OKAY, BUT I DON'T THINK THAT WORD MEANS WHAT YOU THINK IT MEANS--
SHUNK
SEE?! DEAD! ASHES! DUST! DEAD DEAD DEAD!
VAMPIRES! BUT...IF I RECALL CORRECTLY, HE... WAS SLAIN SOMETIME AFTER KILLING BARBARA DAVIS...THIS HAS TO BE SOME KIND OF MEMORY OR LINGERING TRICK OF SILAS--
GO GO GO!
WAIT! WATCH OUT FOR THE--
CRASH

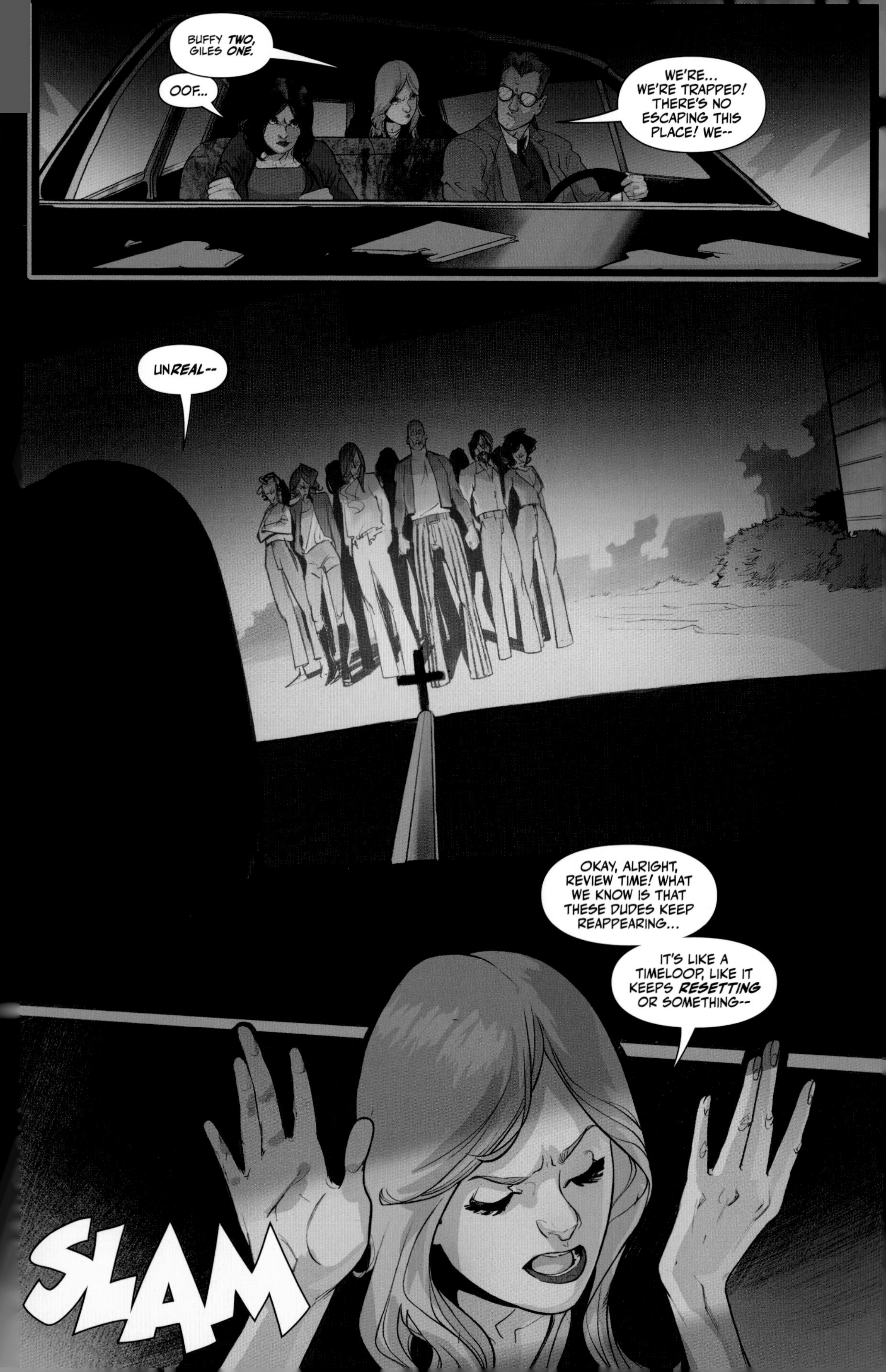
BUFFY TWO, GILES ONE.
OOF...
WE'RE... WE'RE TRAPPED! THERE'S NO ESCAPING THIS PLACE! WE--
UNREAL--
OKAY, ALRIGHT, REVIEW TIME! WHAT WE KNOW IS THAT THESE DUDES KEEP REAPPEARING...
IT'S LIKE A TIMELOOP, LIKE IT KEEPS RESETTING OR SOMETHING--
SLAM

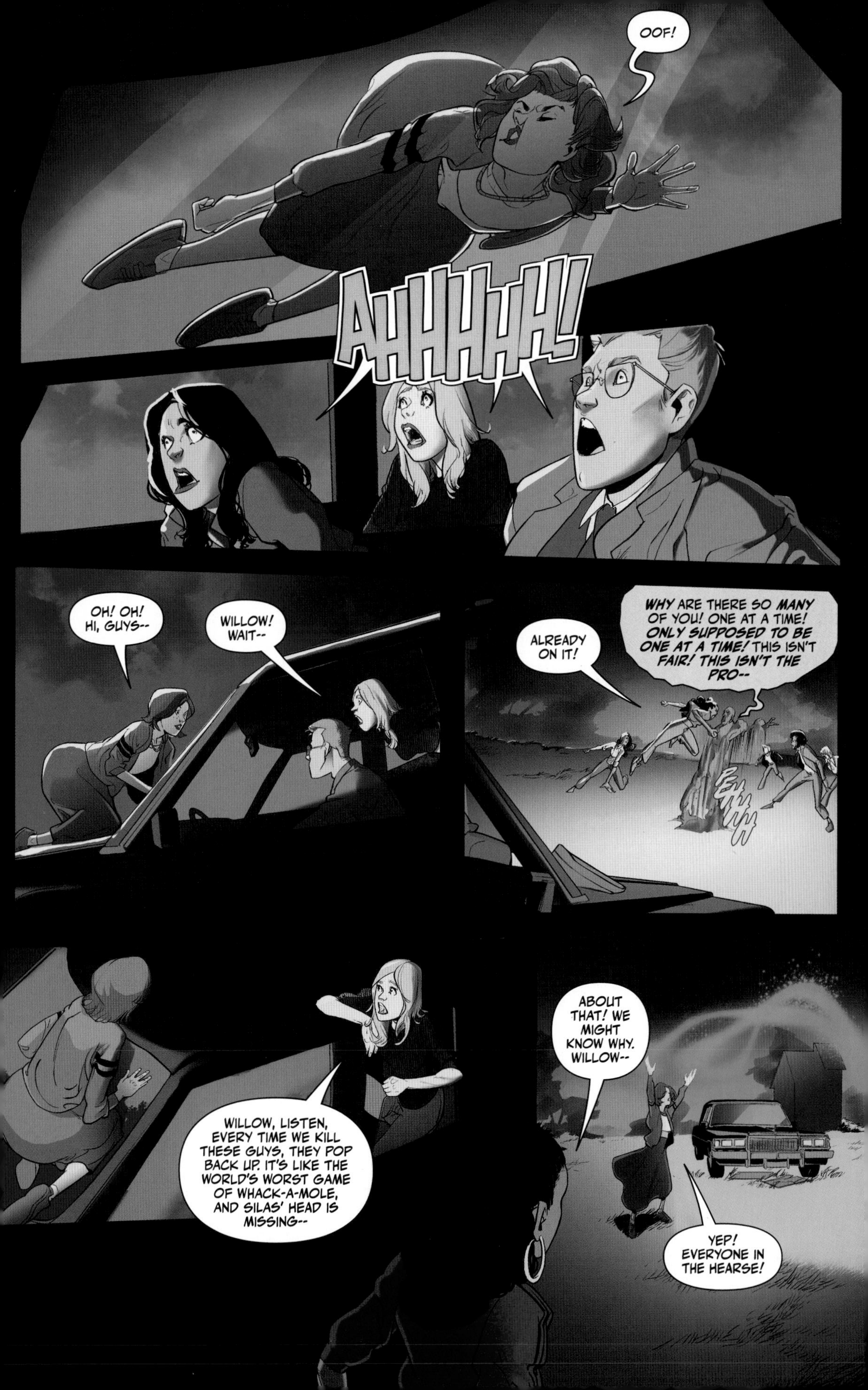
OOF!
AHHHHH!
OH! OH! HI, GUYS--
WILLOW! WAIT--
ALREADY ON IT!
WHY ARE THERE SO MANY OF YOU! ONE AT A TIME! ONLY SUPPOSED TO BE ONE AT A TIME! THIS ISN'T FAIR! THIS ISN'T THE PRO--
EHHHH
WILLOW, LISTEN, EVERY TIME WE KILL THESE GUYS, THEY POP BACK UP. IT'S LIKE THE WORLD'S WORST GAME OF WHACK-A-MOLE, AND SILAS' HEAD IS MISSING--
ABOUT THAT! WE MIGHT KNOW WHY. WILLOW--
YEP! EVERYONE IN THE HEARSE!

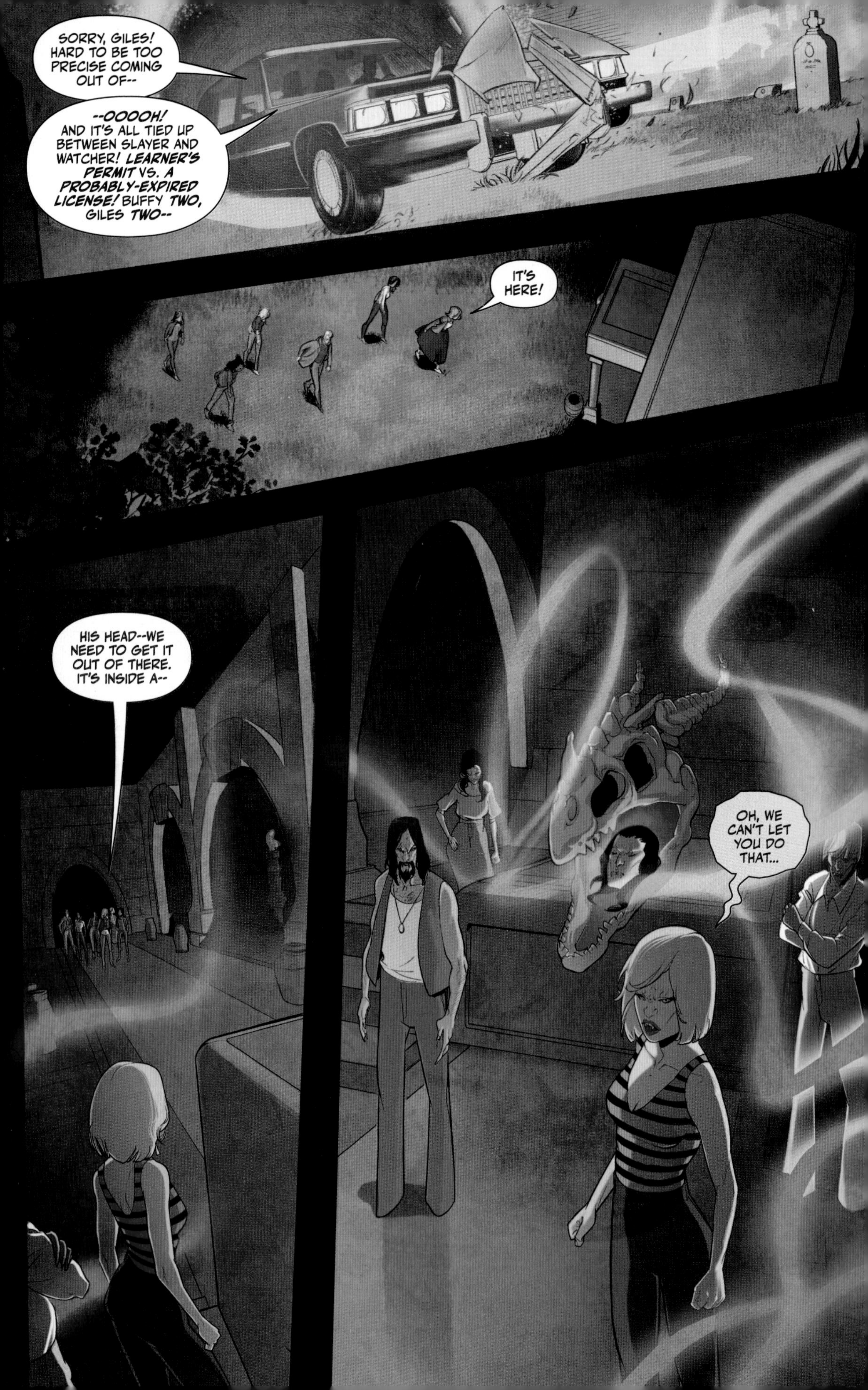
SORRY, GILES! HARD TO BE TOO PRECISE COMING OUT OF--
--OOOOH! AND IT'S ALL TIED UP BETWEEN SLAYER AND WATCHER! LEARNER'S PERMIT VS. A PROBABLY-EXPIRED LICENSE! BUFFY TWO, GILES TWO--
IT'S HERE!
HIS HEAD--WE NEED TO GET IT OUT OF THERE. IT'S INSIDE A--
OH, WE CAN'T LET YOU DO THAT...

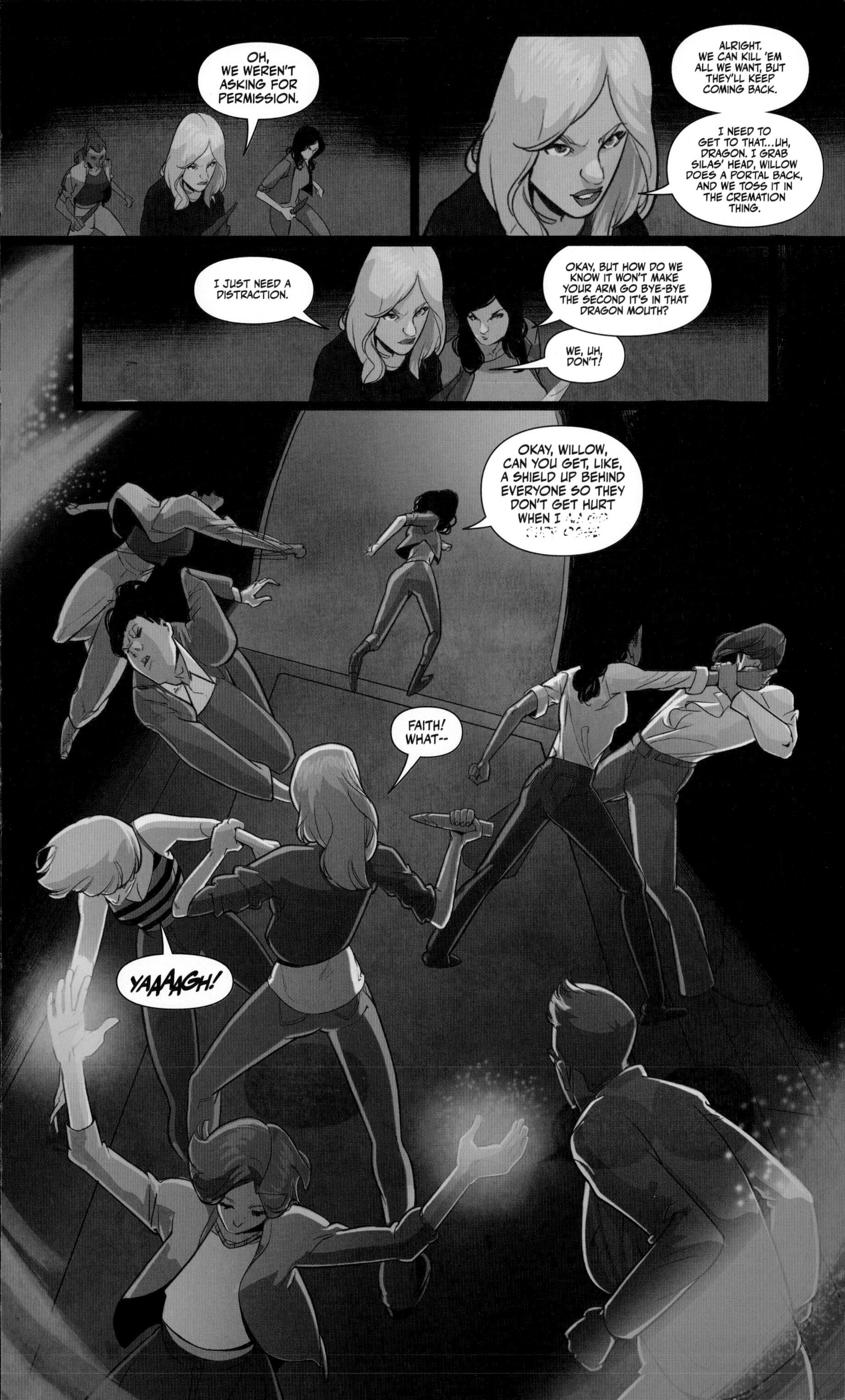

OH, WE WEREN'T ASKING FOR PERMISSION.
ALRIGHT. WE CAN KILL 'EM ALL WE WANT, BUT THEY'LL KEEP COMING BACK.
I NEED TO GET TO THAT...UH, DRAGON. I GRAB SILAS' HEAD, WILLOW DOES A PORTAL BACK, AND WE TOSS IT IN THE CREMATION THING.
I JUST NEED A DISTRACTION.
OKAY, BUT HOW DO WE KNOW IT WON'T MAKE YOUR ARM GO BYE-BYE THE SECOND IT'S IN THAT DRAGON MOUTH?
WE, UH, DON'T!
OKAY, WILLOW, CAN YOU GET, LIKE, A SHIELD UP BEHIND EVERYONE SO THEY DON'T GET HURT WHEN I
FAITH! WHAT--
YAAAAGH!

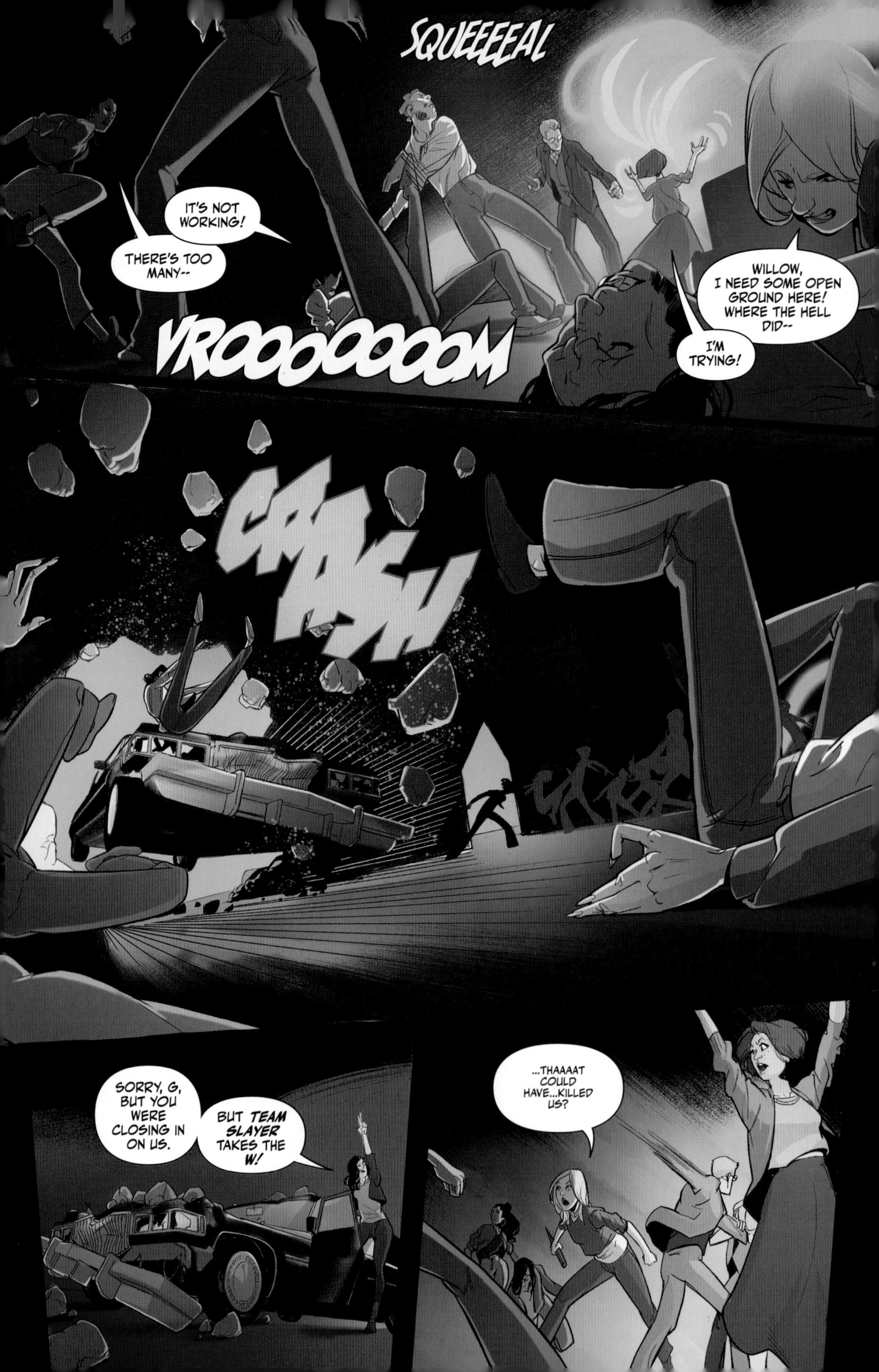
SQUEEEEAL
IT'S NOT WORKING!
THERE'S TOO MANY--
WILLOW, I NEED SOME OPEN GROUND HERE! WHERE THE HELL DID--
I'M TRYING!
VROOOOOOOM
CRASH
SORRY, G, BUT YOU WERE CLOSING IN ON US.
BUT *TEAM SLAYER* TAKES THE *W!*
...THAAAAT COULD HAVE...KILLED US?

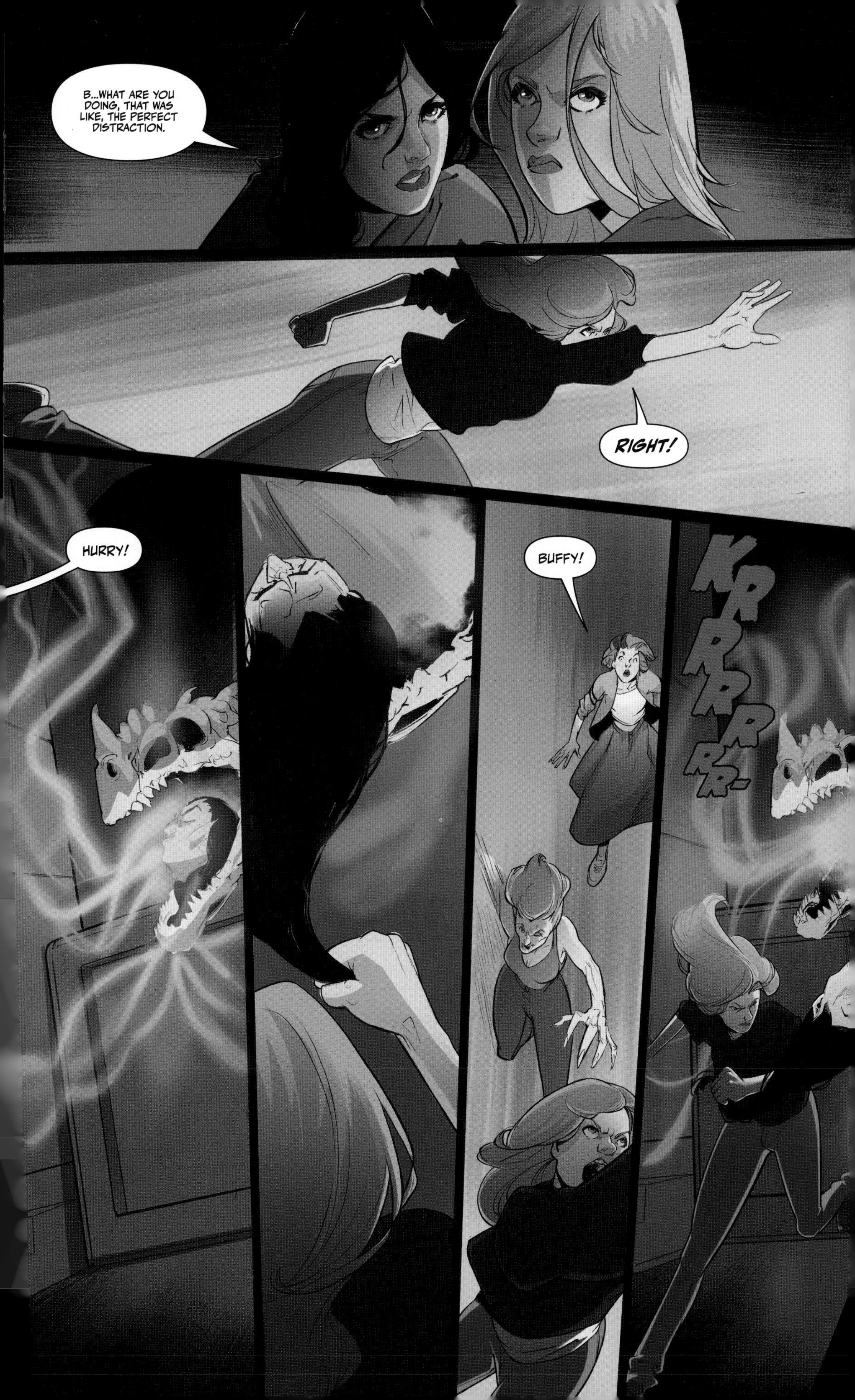
B...WHAT ARE YOU DOING, THAT WAS LIKE, THE PERFECT DISTRACTION.
RIGHT!
HURRY!
BUFFY!
KRRRRRRR-

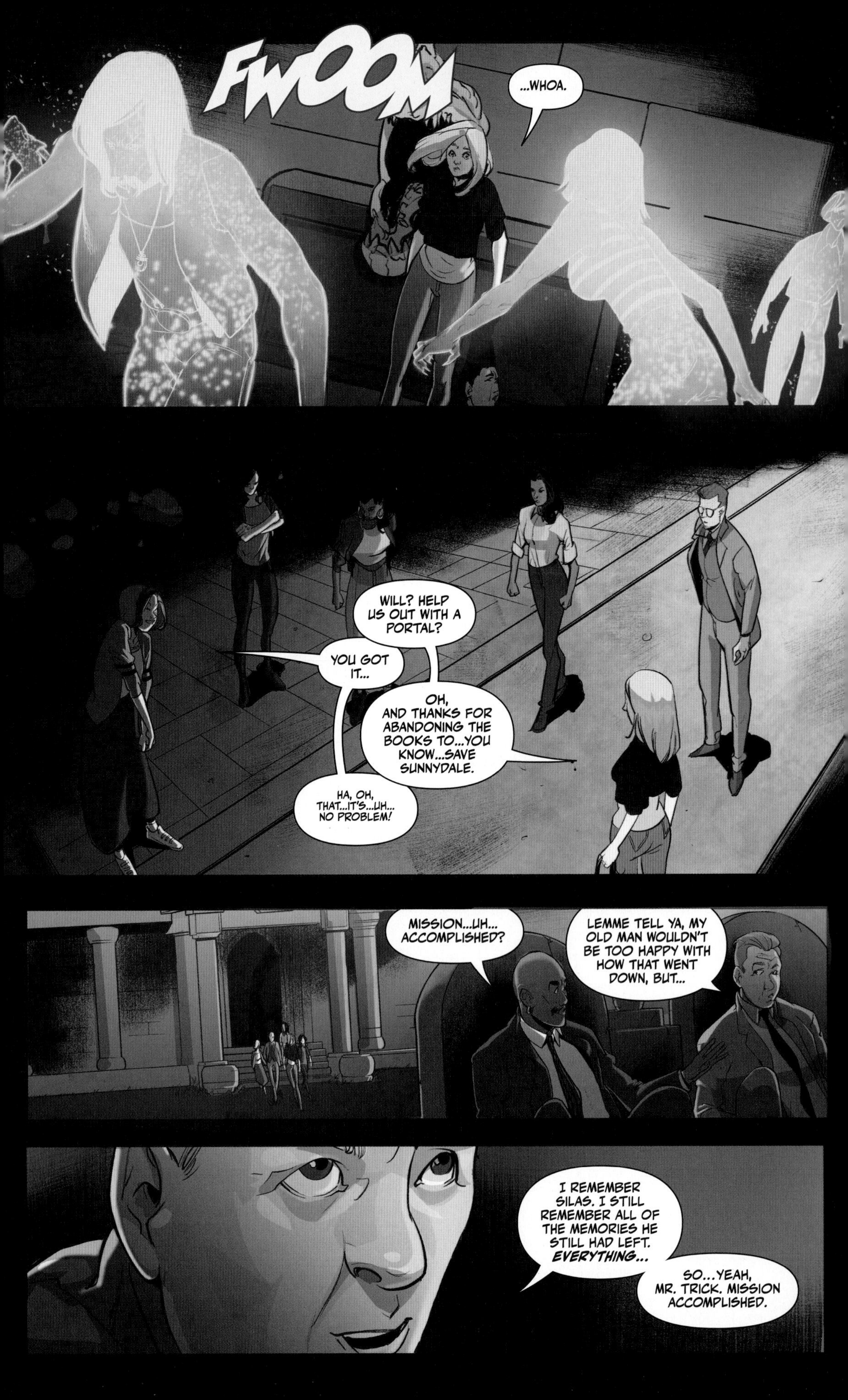
FWOOM
...WHOA.
WILL? HELP US OUT WITH A PORTAL?
YOU GOT IT...
OH, AND THANKS FOR ABANDONING THE BOOKS TO...YOU KNOW...SAVE SUNNYDALE.
HA, OH, THAT...IT'S...UH... NO PROBLEM!
MISSION...UH... ACCOMPLISHED?
LEMME TELL YA, MY OLD MAN WOULDN'T BE TOO HAPPY WITH HOW THAT WENT DOWN, BUT...
I REMEMBER SILAS. I STILL REMEMBER ALL OF THE MEMORIES HE STILL HAD LEFT. *EVERYTHING...*
SO...YEAH, MR. TRICK. MISSION ACCOMPLISHED.

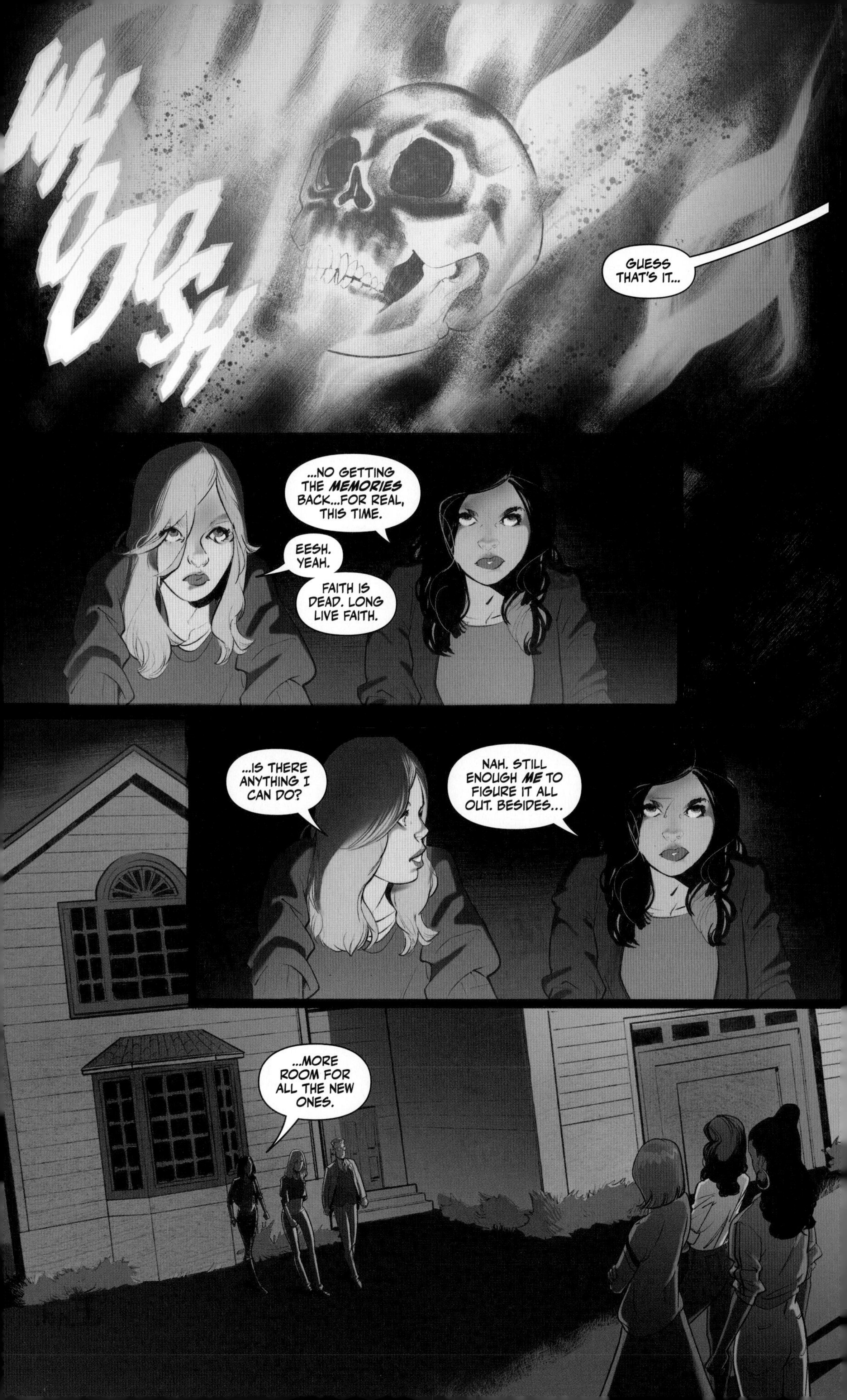
WHOOSH
GUESS THAT'S IT...
...NO GETTING THE MEMORIES BACK...FOR REAL, THIS TIME.
EESH. YEAH.
FAITH IS DEAD. LONG LIVE FAITH.
...IS THERE ANYTHING I CAN DO?
NAH. STILL ENOUGH ME TO FIGURE IT ALL OUT. BESIDES...
...MORE ROOM FOR ALL THE NEW ONES.

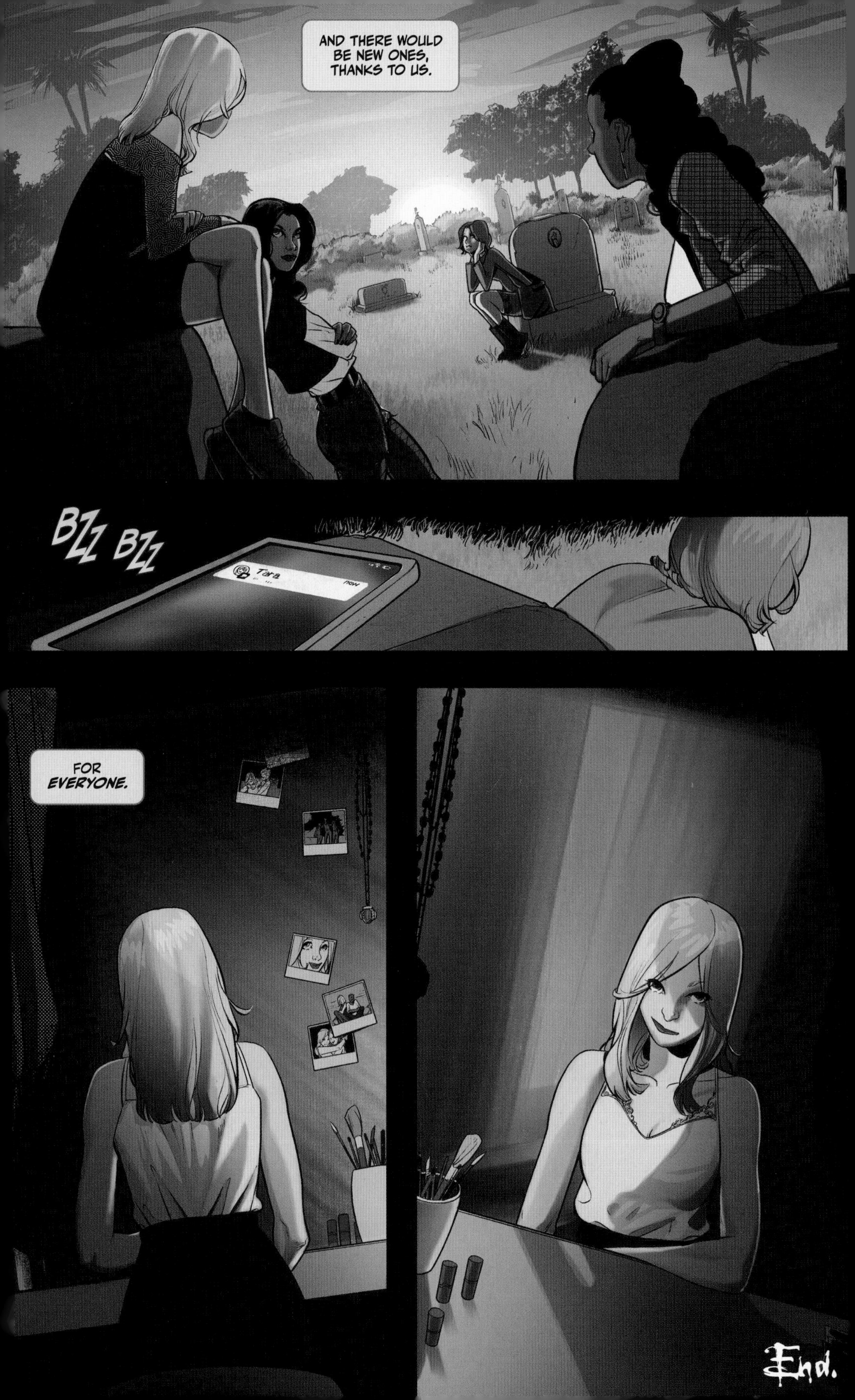
AND THERE WOULD BE NEW ONES, THANKS TO US.
BZZ BZZ
Tara
now
FOR EVERYONE.
End.

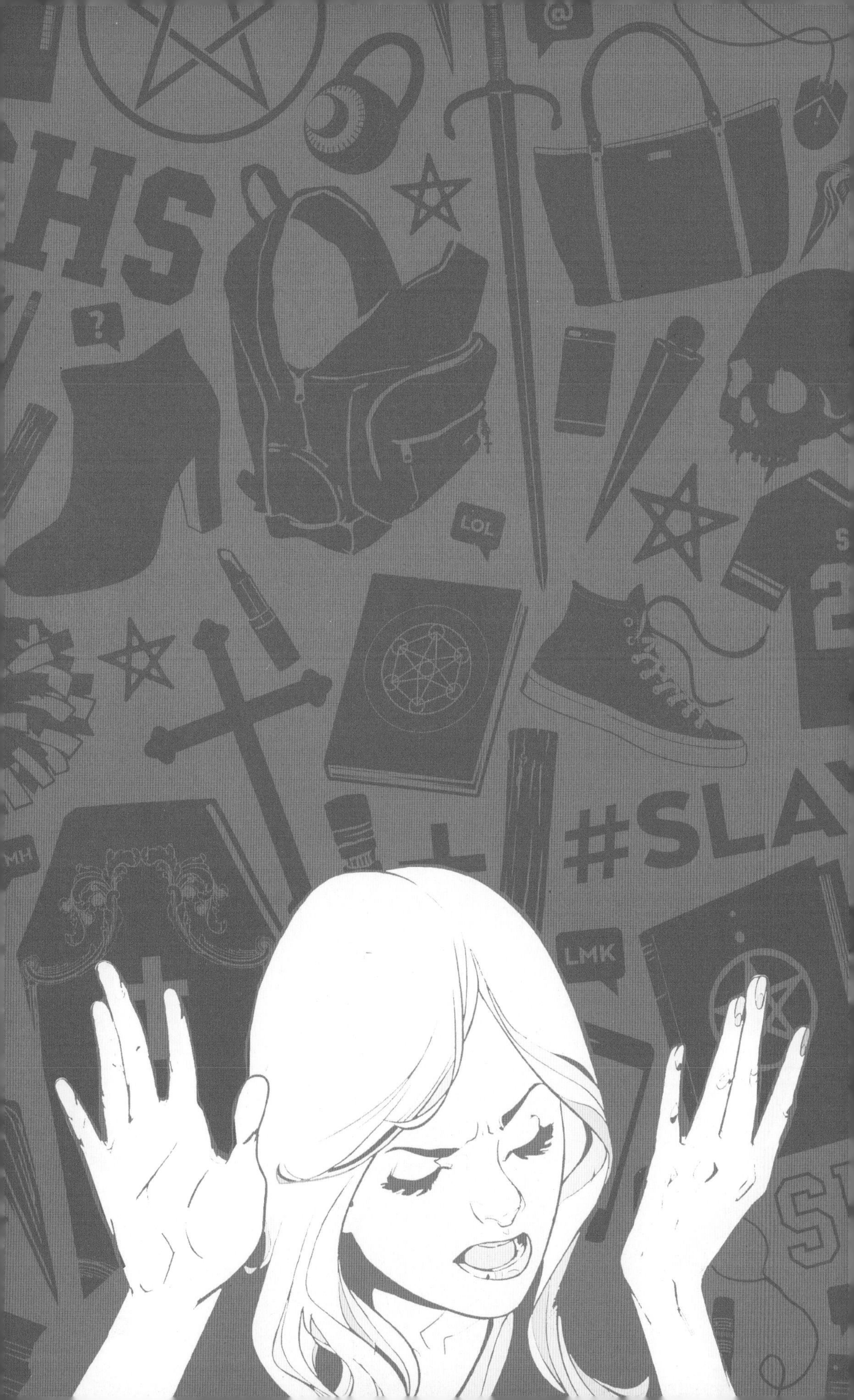
HS
LOL
#SLA
LMK

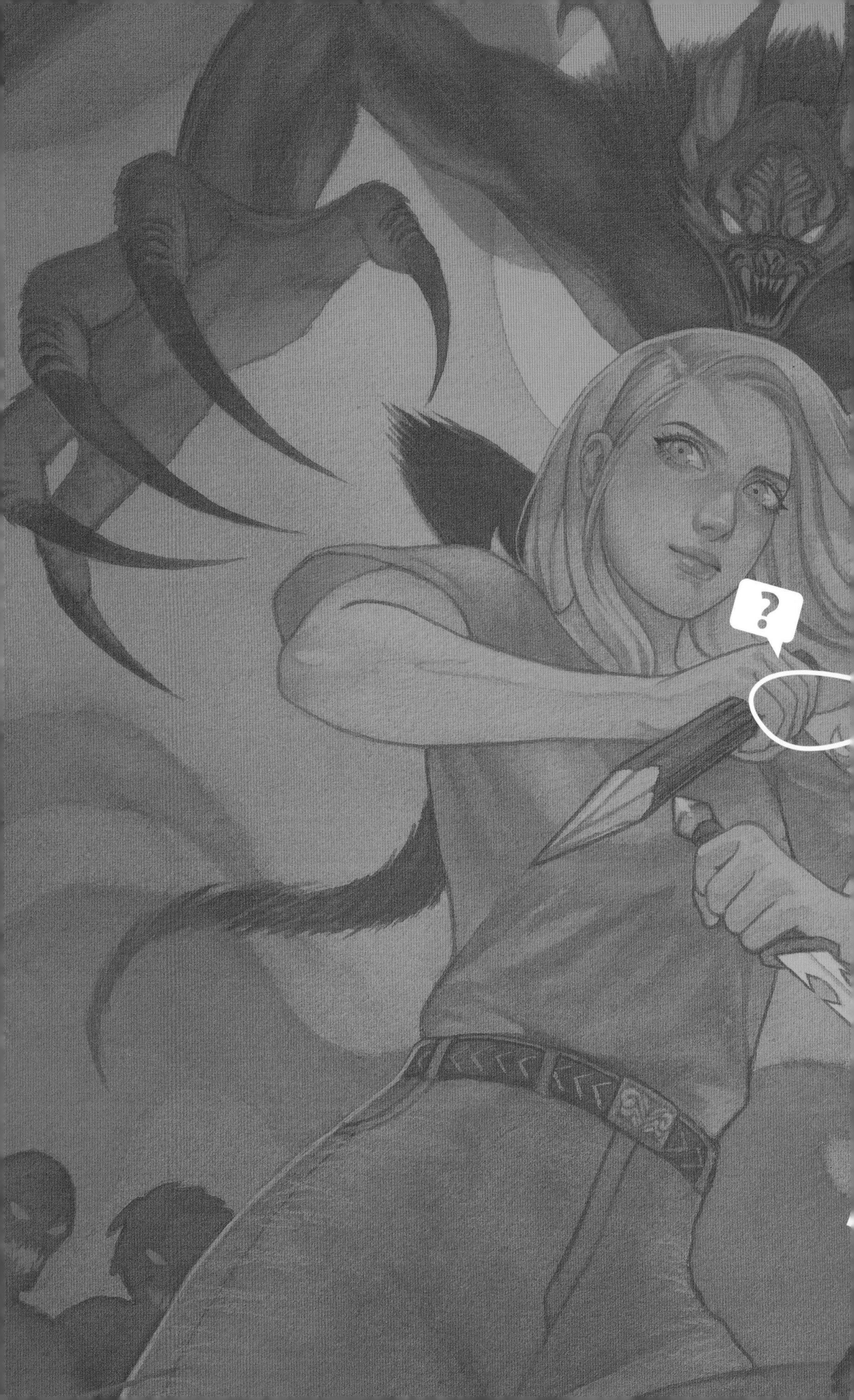

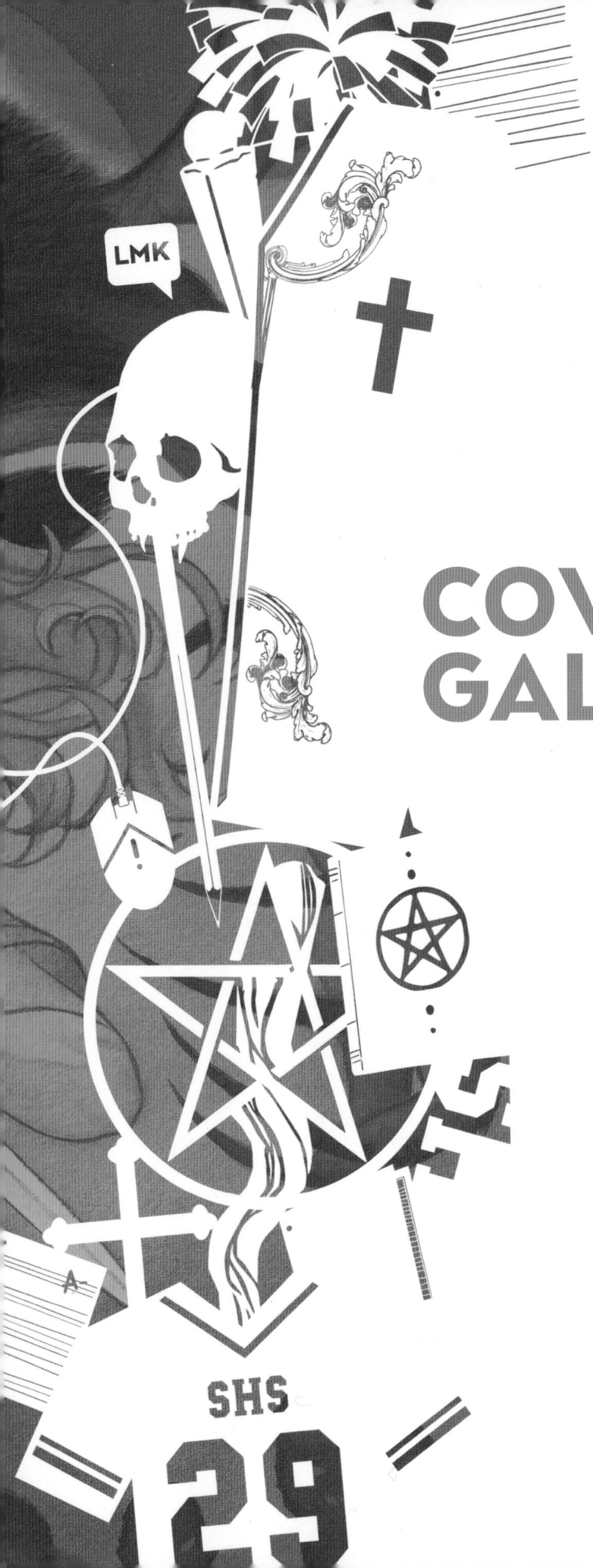
LMK
SHS
29

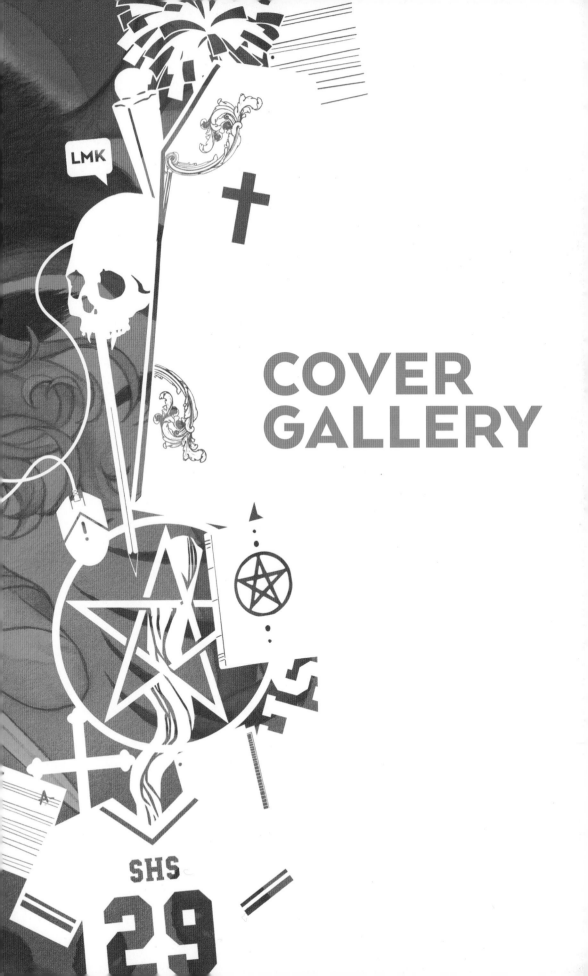

COVER GALLERY

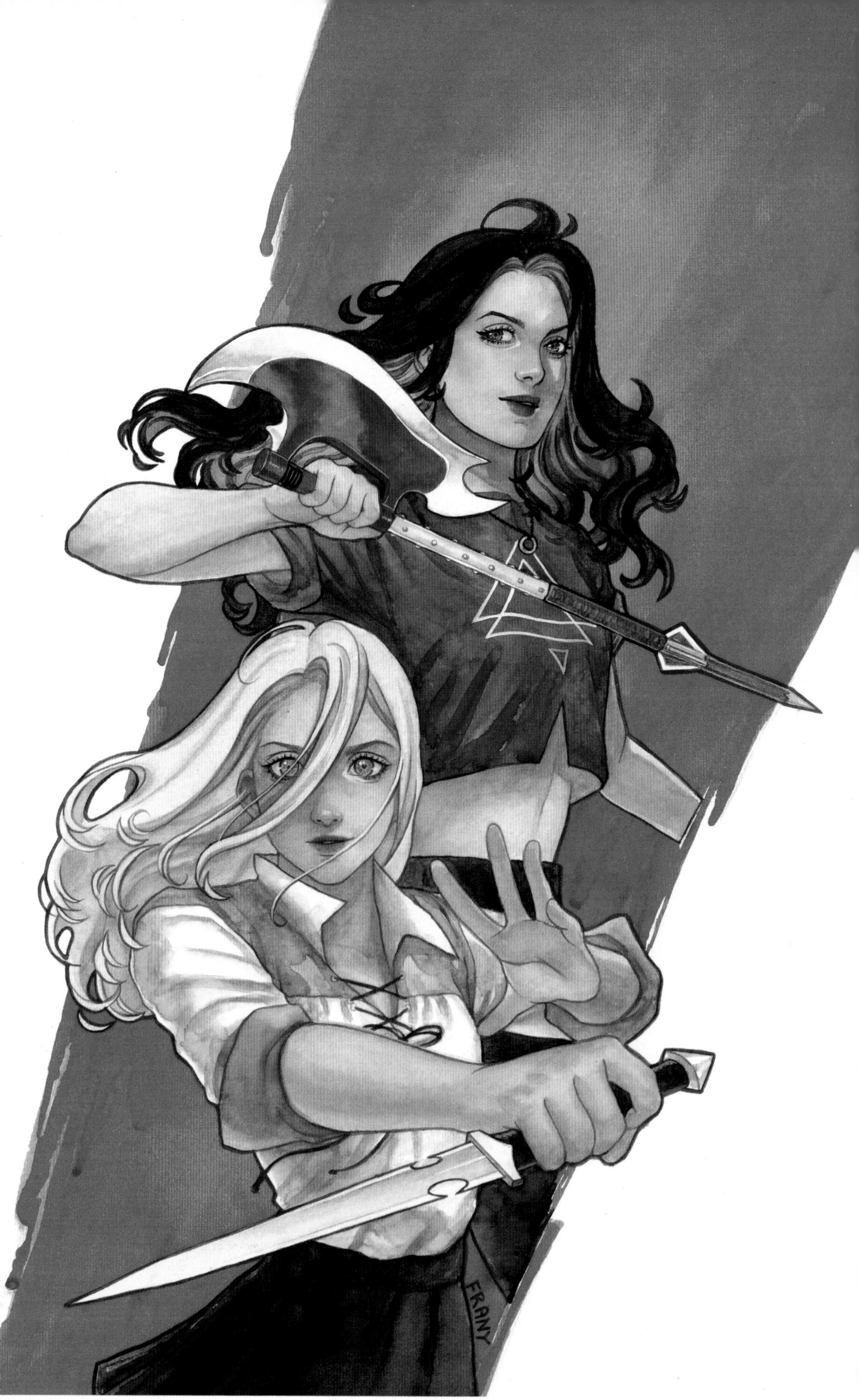
FRANY

Issue Thirty Three Main Cover by **Frany**

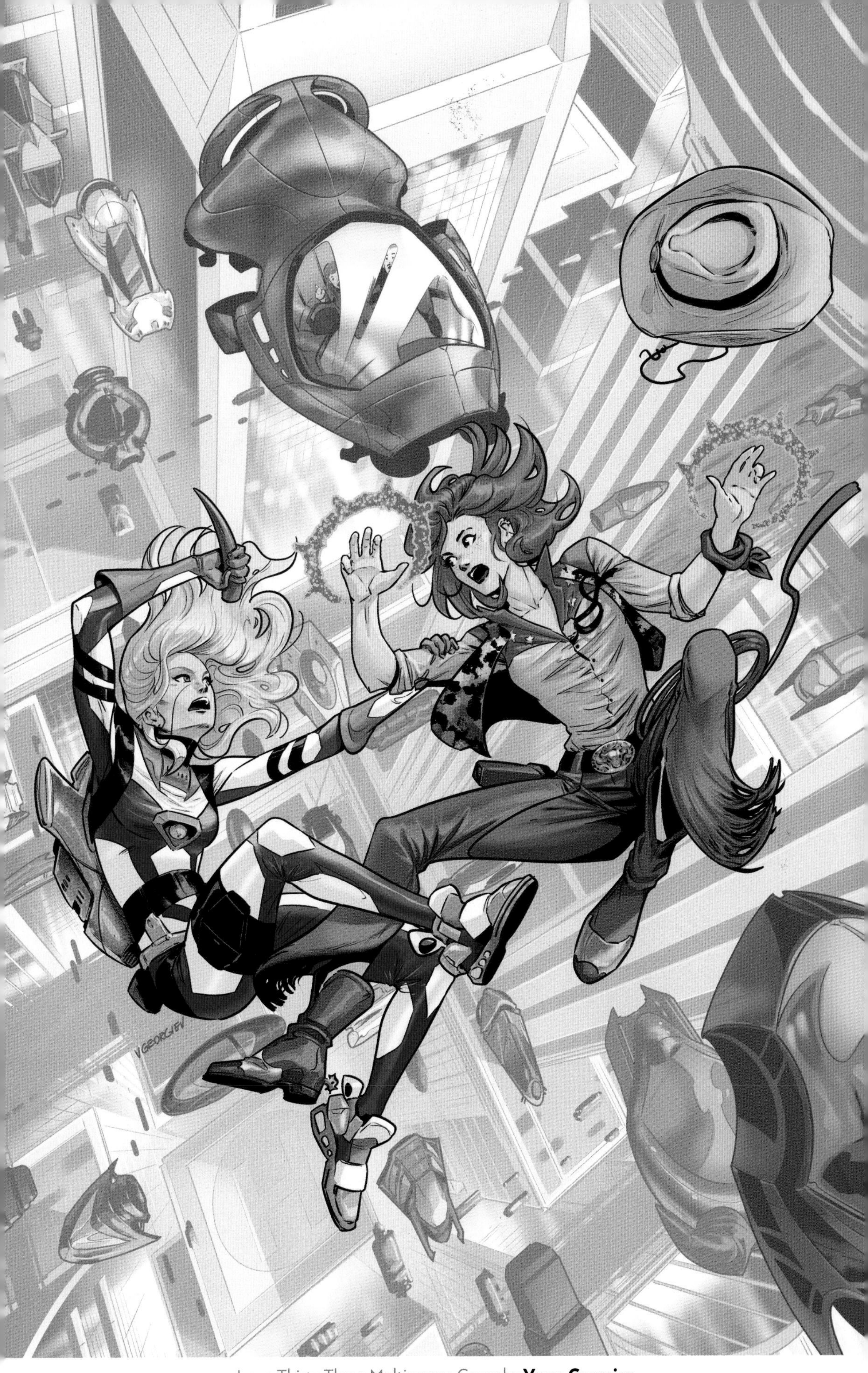
VGEORGIEV

Issue Thirty Three Multiversus Cover by **Vasco Georgiev**

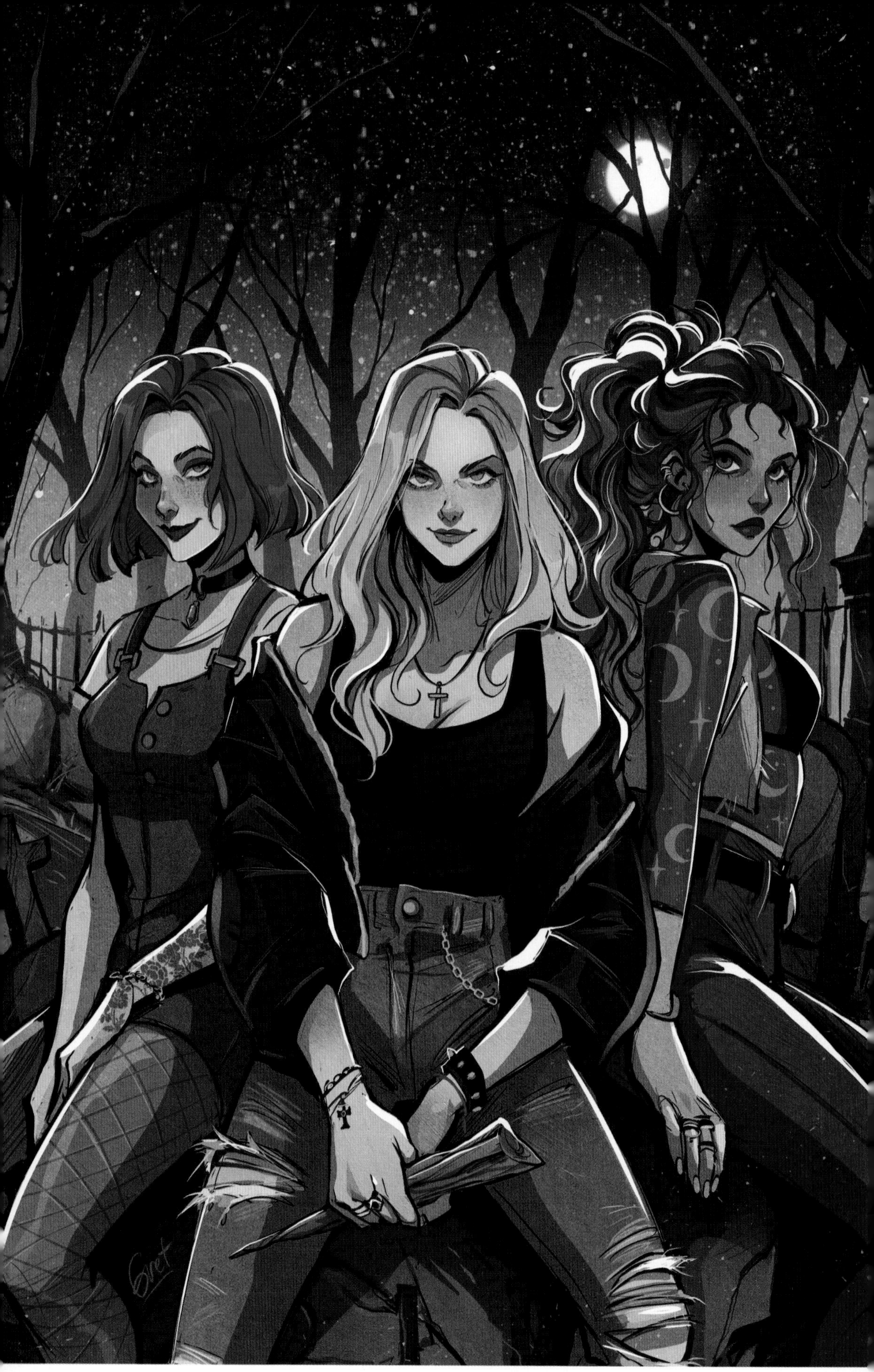
Gret

Issue Thirty Three Variant Cover by **Gretel Lusky**

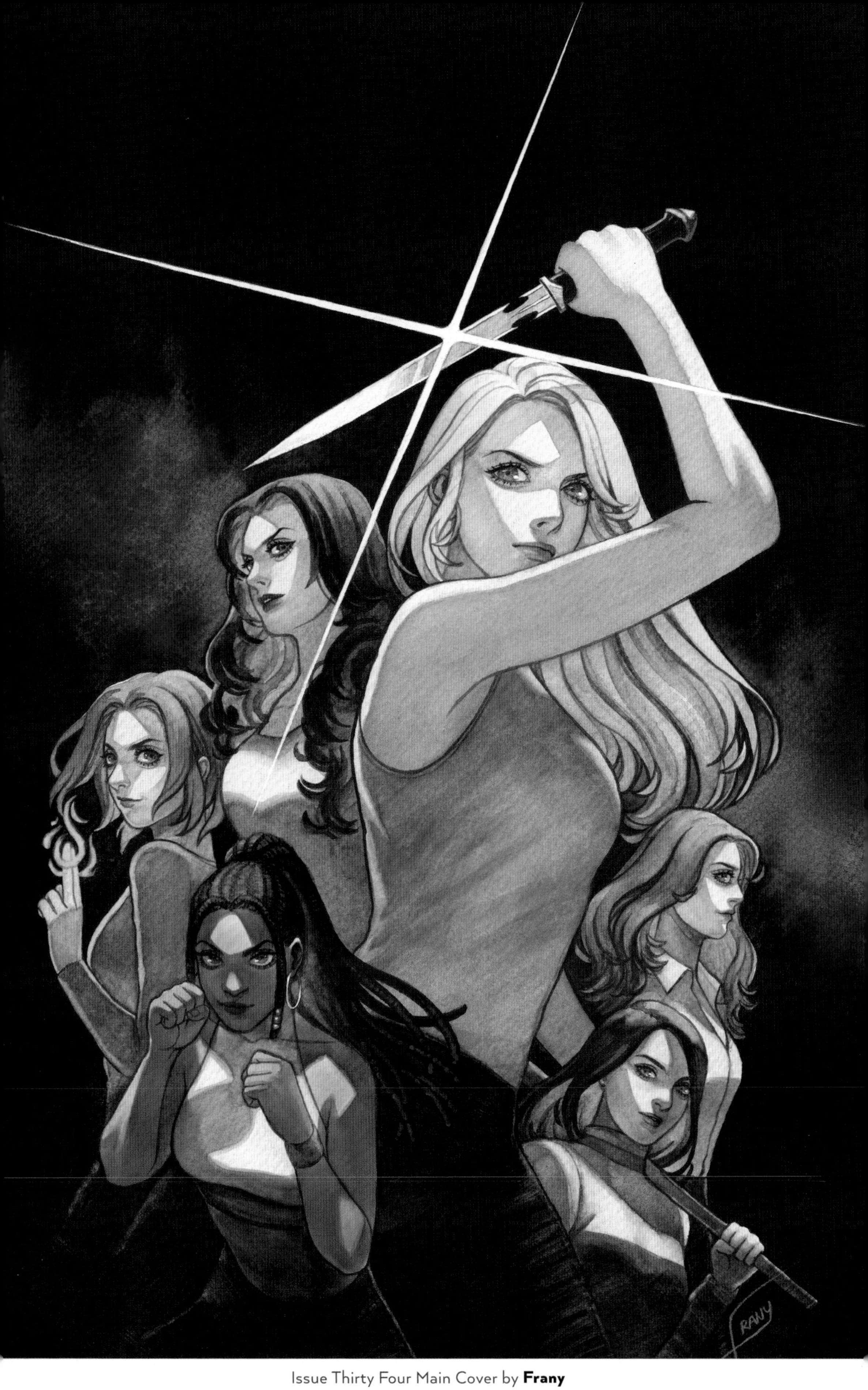

Issue Thirty Four Main Cover by **Frany**

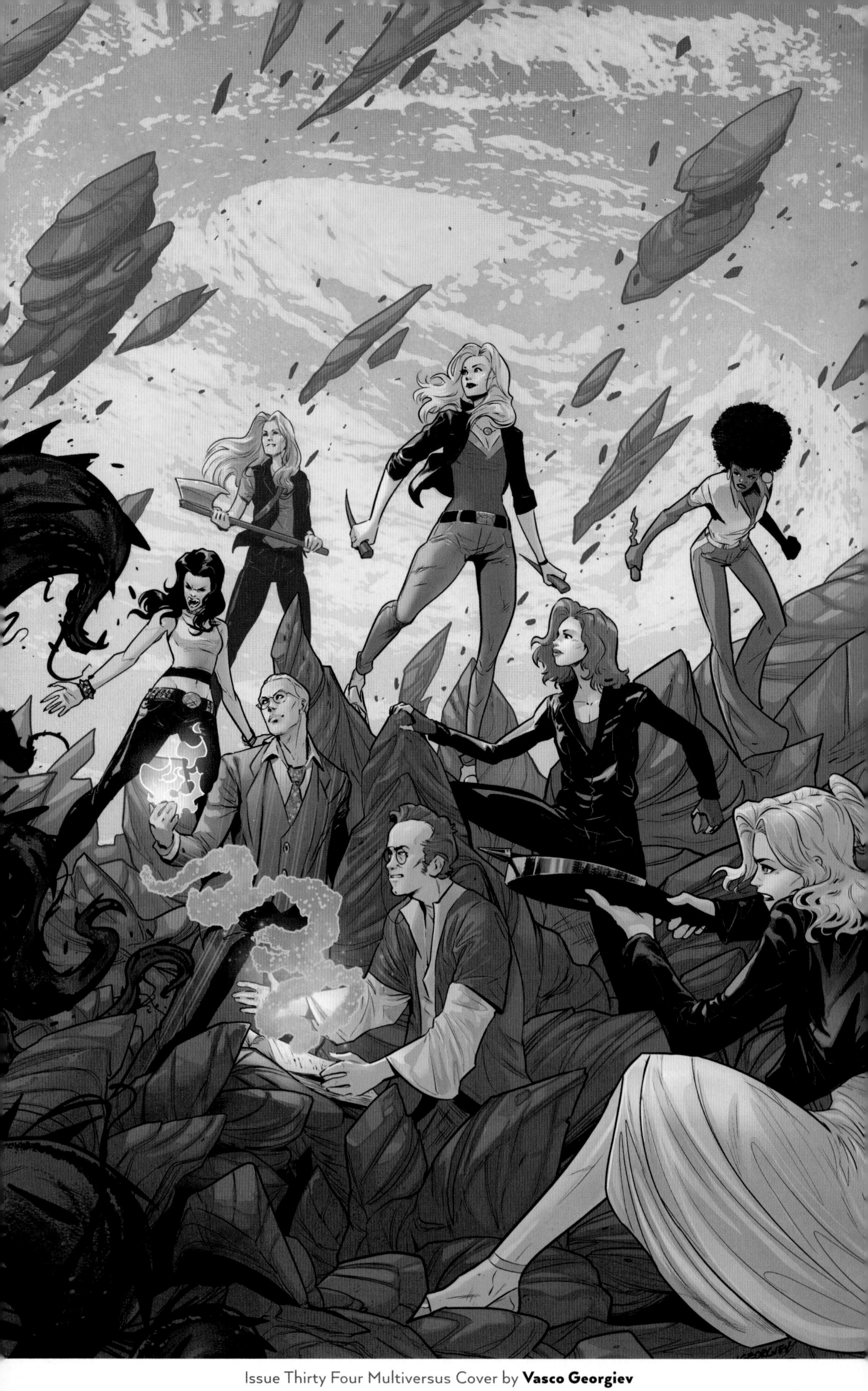

Issue Thirty Four Multiversus Cover by **Vasco Georgiev**

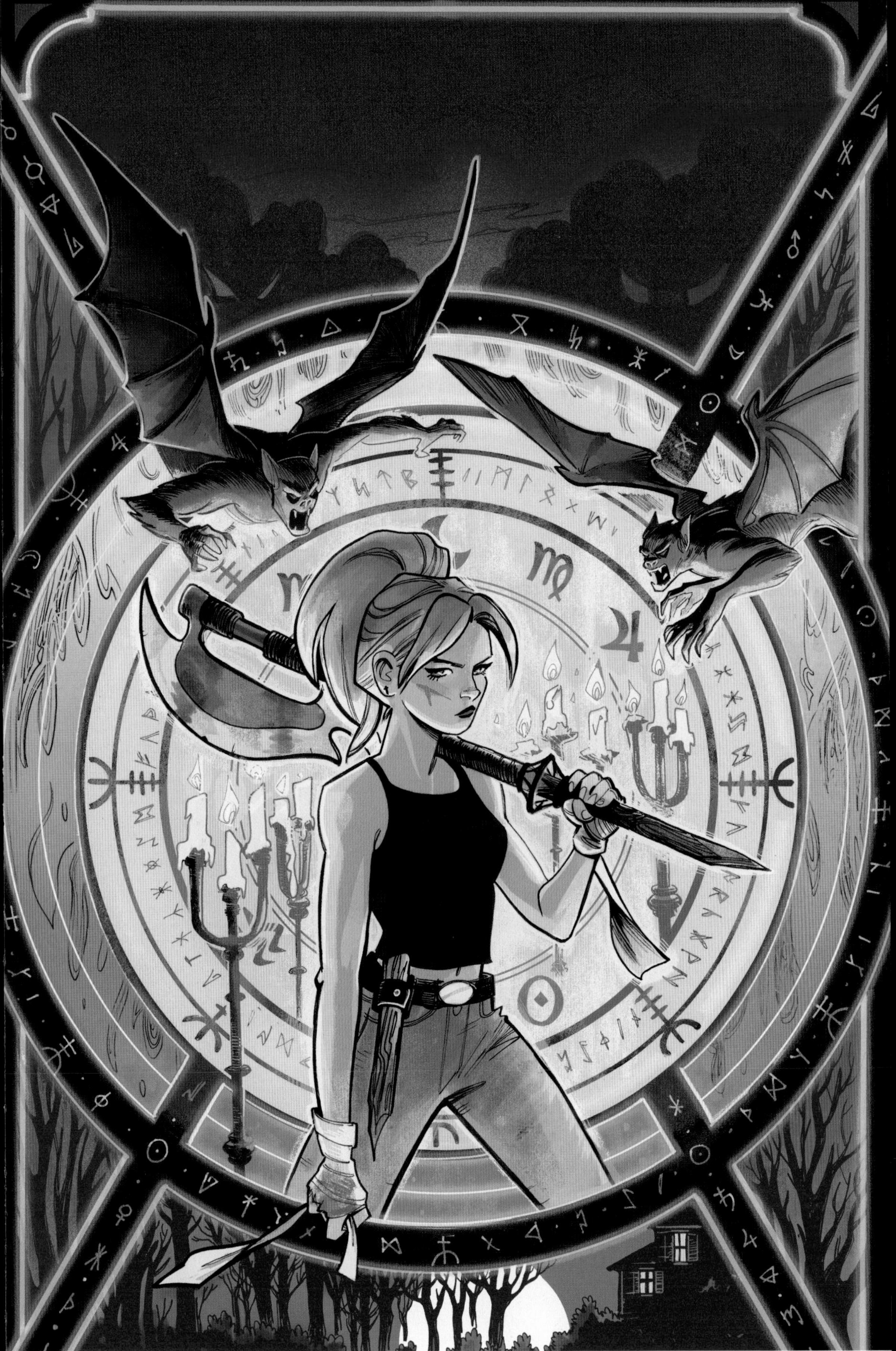

Issue Thirty Four Variant Cover by **Veronica Fish**

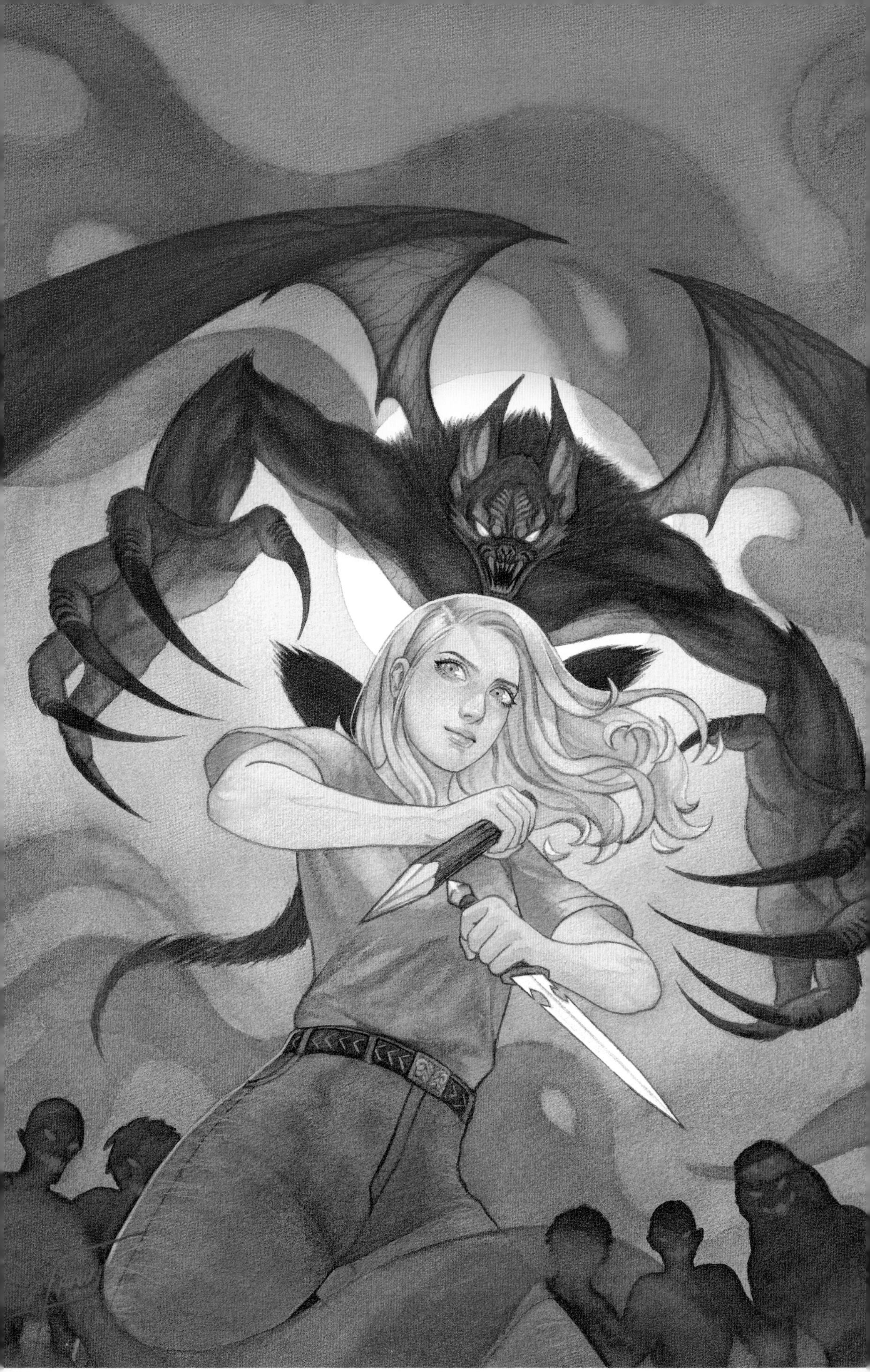

Buffy the Vampire Slayer 25th Anniversary Main Cover by **Frany**

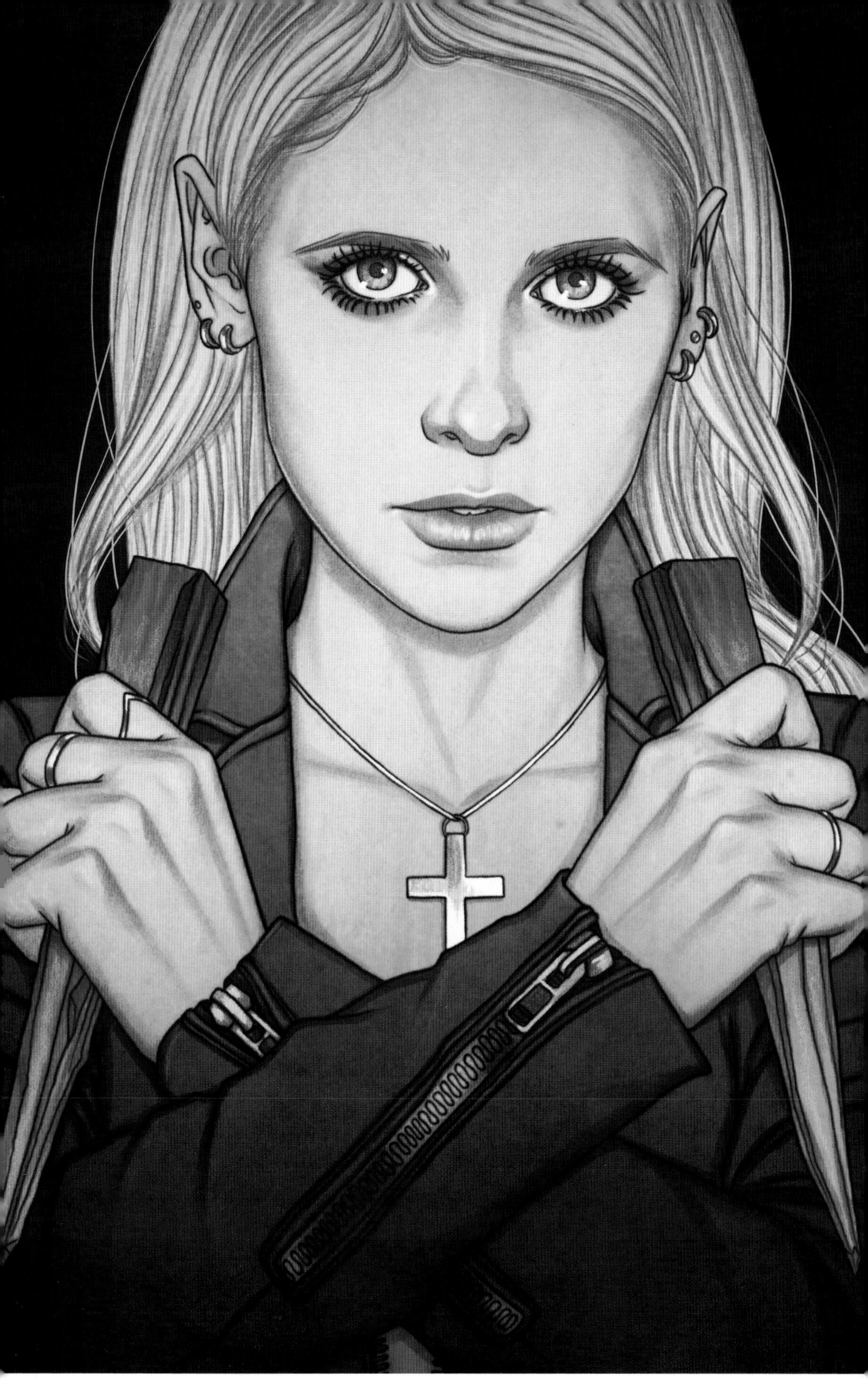

Buffy the Vampire Slayer 25th Anniversary Variant Cover by **Jenny Frison**

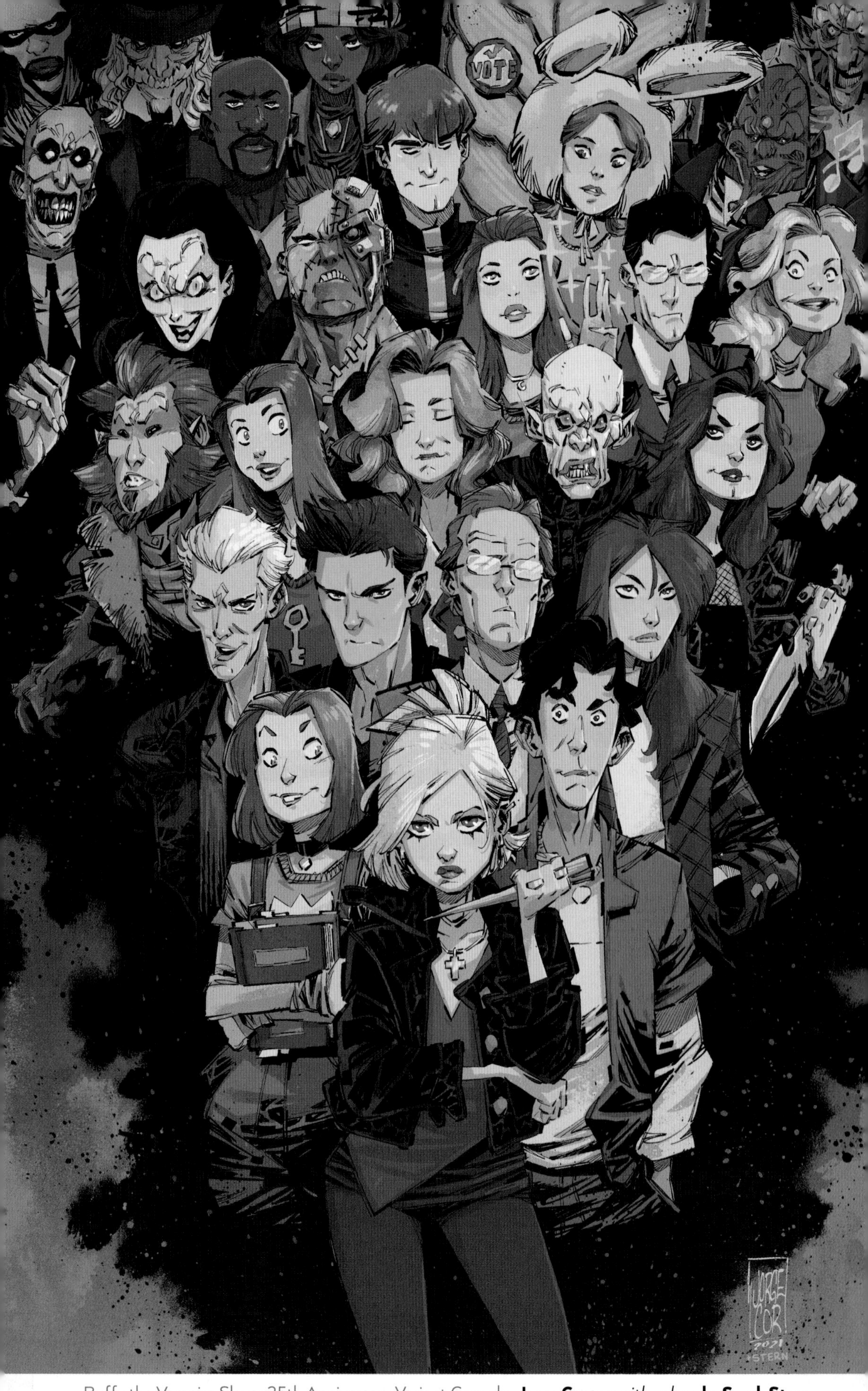
VOTE

Buffy the Vampire Slayer 25th Anniversary Variant Cover by **Jorge Corona** *with colors* **by Sarah Stern**

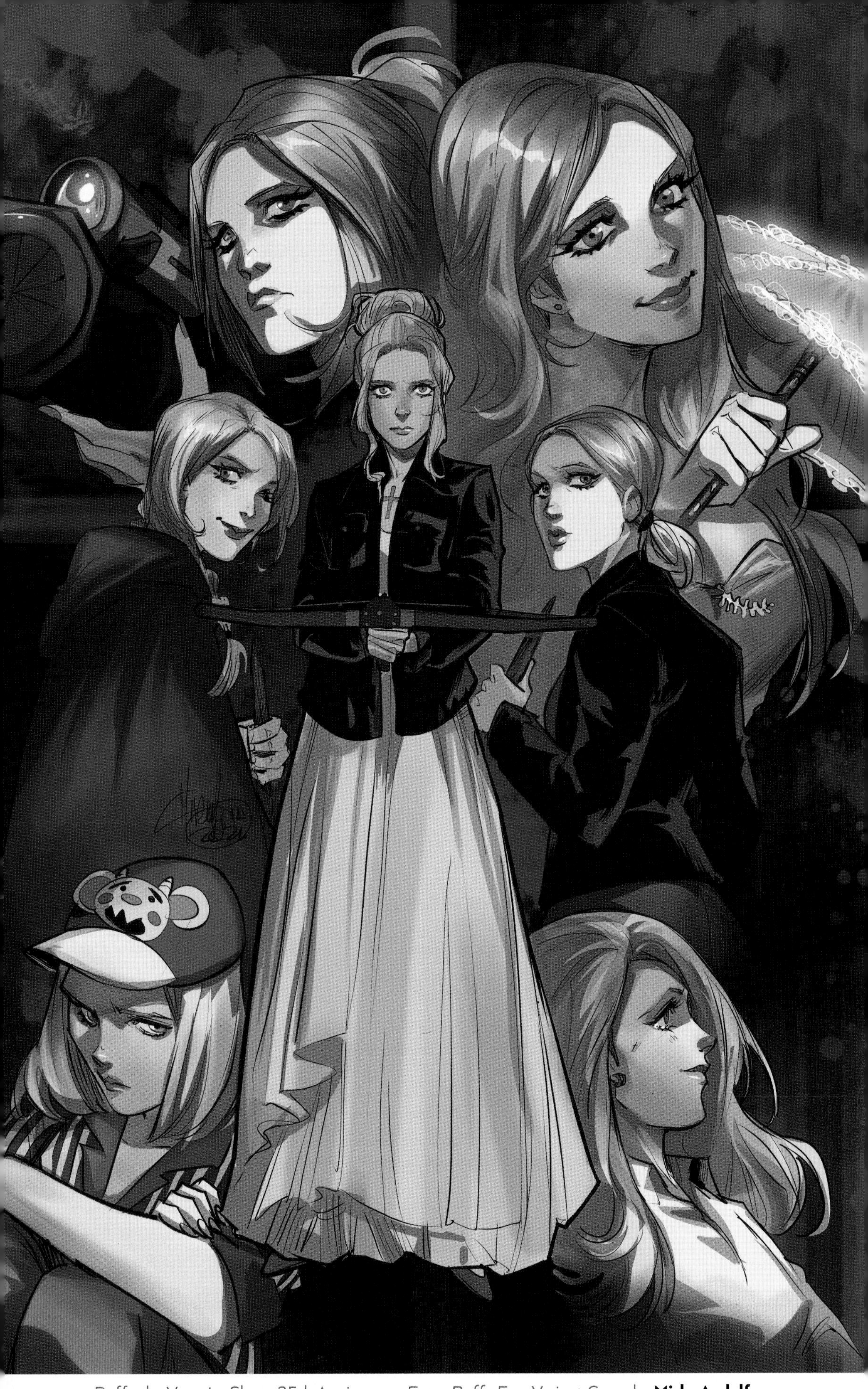

Buffy the Vampire Slayer 25th Anniversary *Every Buffy Ever* Variant Cover by **Mirka Andolfo**

SCRIPT TO PAGE: *25th Anniversary Special, page 5*

PANEL 1: Kendra's dropping off books in her locker, while Buffy and Willow wait next to her. Kendra's looking at Buffy. Willow's rolling her eyes.
KENDRA: The one with that peaceful little lakehouse so she could do laps or whatever. Anya owns the house, now, I guess.
KENDRA: Anyway. I figured Prom would be a break from the BS, but we should've known better.
WILLOW: Yeah. The BS is eternal.

PANEL 2: Close on Buffy, leading the way down the hallway again, with Kendra and Willow behind her. Buffy's looking a little embarrassed in admitting she wanted to go too.
BUFFY: I don't know, I mean, I was thinking about it too--

PANEL 3: Similar frame to Panel 2. Willow's eyes are huge in surprise/anticipation. Buffy still looking embarrassed.
WILLOW: Wait, Buffy, did someone ask you?
BUFFY: Maybe...

25th Anniversary Special, page 5

PANEL 4: Close on Buffy, Willow, and Kendra now outside of the library doors in the hallway.
KENDRA: Ooohkaaay! Here we go! Process of elimination. So. Can't be Robin. Dude's AWOL, same as Wes.
KENDRA (SMALL): ...none of us technically even have a Watcher since Giles turned down the Council's offer to be reinstated after the Silas business--

PANEL 5: Inside the library, looking at the door. Buffy, Willow, and Kendra are entering the library doors. Willow's eyes are wide with anticipation.
BUFFY: Yeah, Robin's not magically coming back from England and even if he did there's absolutely no way that--
WILLOW: Okay, but who is it?! Who--
FAITH (OP): Oh come on! What the hell is that?

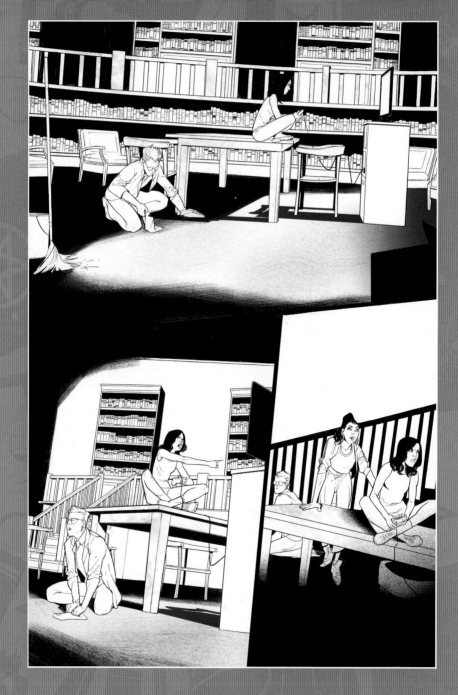

SCRIPT TO PAGE: *25th Anniversary Special, page 6*

PANEL 1: Biggest Panel on the Page.
Buffy's POV. Giles and Faith in the library. Faith is sitting on top of the table playing video games on a small flatscreen TV that was wheeled in, similar to this reference. Giles is scrubbing the bloodstain left from Silas' head. It's located beneath the table. He has large yellow kitchen gloves on, and he's sweating, having been at this for a while.
BUFFY: Whatcha doin' there, Giles?
KENDRA: ...wasn't Faith supposed to help?

PANEL 2: Everyone in the library. Giles is sitting back on his knees, exhausted, and staring at the ceiling. Faith is pointing at the screen with her hand that was maimed by Silas.
GILES: No, no - the one with superhuman strength is instead applying that skill to smashing controllers when the toy box doesn't do what she wants.
FAITH: Yeah well some A$$#*%& named *slickwilkee04* is trolling.
Suck it up, dude, and stop being a fu--

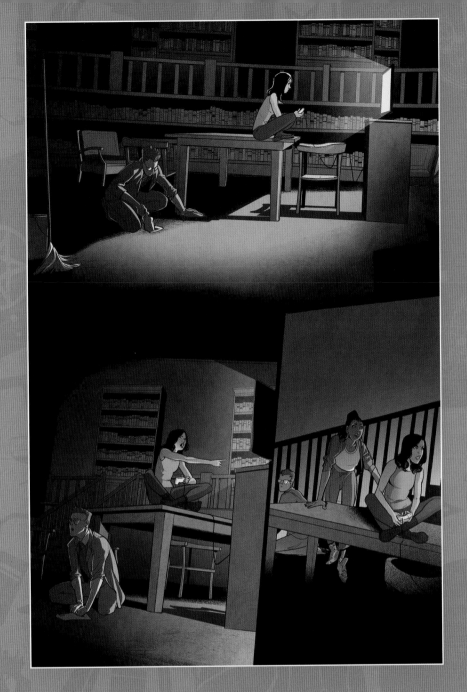

25th Anniversary Special, page 6

PANEL 3: In front of Faith now, the glow of the screen on her face. Now she's the one looking exasperated and towards the ceiling, the very definition of: ugh. Kendra's behind Faith, looking at the screen, interested. The top half of Giles' face is visible, just above the table, his eyes narrowed and angry and staring up at Kendra.
KENDRA: Whoa. This is cool...wait, can't you just kill him or something?
FAITH: Nah, we're on the same team. Dungeon delve co-op. Ugh. Whatever.
FAITH: ...none of you told me you had Eight Poets of Oald. This game rules... when you aren't playing with slick wilkee.
GILES (SMALL): ...Kendra you are standing directly in my scrubbing spot.

SCRIPT TO PAGE: *25th Anniversary Special, page 7*

PANEL 1: We're level with the table, everyone seated around it now. Buffy and Willow could just be taking their seats. Giles is at the head of the table, the library/books behind him. He is still wearing his gloves, his hands flat on the table like he's the serious company boss at an important meeting but the seriousness of the situation is upended by his gloves. Buffy and Faith will be sitting next to each other.
GILES: The good news is, Faith found the name of the funeral home where the Mayor's people are cremating Silas.
FAITH: Cordy's actually a useful little mole over there as the Mayor's assistant--
GILES: And apparently after this discovery, Faith considered her work day "done", but I digress.

PANEL 2: Buffy and Faith, seated next to each other. Buffy's speaking to the group, but Faith is looking at Buffy.
GILES: Not that it would have made a difference. Silas' bloodstain from the decapitation simply won't come off. Anyway.
BUFFY: Prom's canceled. FYI.
FAITH: Damn...
FAITH (SMALL): ...I mean, *whatever*.

PANEL 3: Close on a shrugging and smiling Buffy at the table, with an apologetic looking Giles in the background.
BUFFY: Well at least Joyce and Eric are out of the house for their anniversary dinner tonight, and there's the new season of--

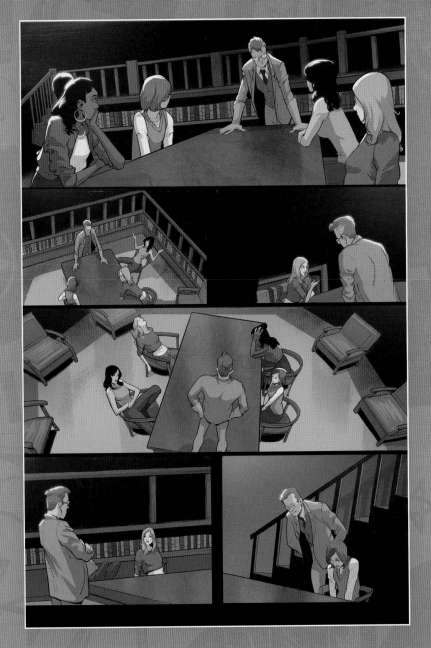

25th Anniversary Special, page 7

GILES: Actually, Buffy, I know I said tonight was an off night, but they're moving fast to get rid of Silas' corpse. It's set for a **traditional** burial tomorrow.

PANEL 4: Faith is grimacing. Gone is Buffy's optimism and now it's Buffy's turn for an UGH moment, her head thrown back to look at the ceiling. Kendra has her head in her hands. Willow looks guilty. Giles stands over the table, arms crossed with his yellow gloves still on.
GILES: That's not good enough. We need to go there and ensure Silas - his head especially - is destroyed to ensure the job is done. Tonight.
FAITH (SMALL): Great.
BUFFY (SMALL): Cool.
KENDRA (SMALL): Sounds good.

PANEL 5: On Buffy and Faith, with Giles in the background behind them, his arms crossed with his yellow gloves still on. Buffy is mocking Giles. Faith is rolling her eyes toward the ceiling.
GILES: Kendra, I was thinking you might be able to patrol, I don't need to remind you there's been an uptick in attacks, there. Buffy, Faith, we three--
BUFFY (MOCKING): --oh, we happy three--

PANEL 6: Giles is behind Willow now. Willow looks guilty. Giles is looking down at her in mild surprise.
GILES: ...will go to the funeral home. Willow--
WILLOW: I...uh...I'm sorry, Giles, I have to study for finals tonight!
GILES: Oh. Well...if...alright then. I understand.

SCRIPT TO PAGE: *25th Anniversary Special, page 8*

PANEL 1: Small panel. Close on Buffy in the library, sulking.
BUFFY: Guuhhh, but we already killed Silas. The guy's dead and he's still ruining my me time.

PANEL 2: Biggest Panel on the Page.
We're behind the heads of Buffy, Giles, and Faith, staring up at the Funeral Home. The funeral home itself is a bit spooky. An old, standalone building on a large lot. No other buildings in sight. An old, wooden sign in the ground reads: CAWTHORN FUNERAL HOME & MORTUARY. (This sign will be smashed/knocked down later). Buffy and Faith will have stakes on them that they'll use later, but don't necessarily need to be seen here.

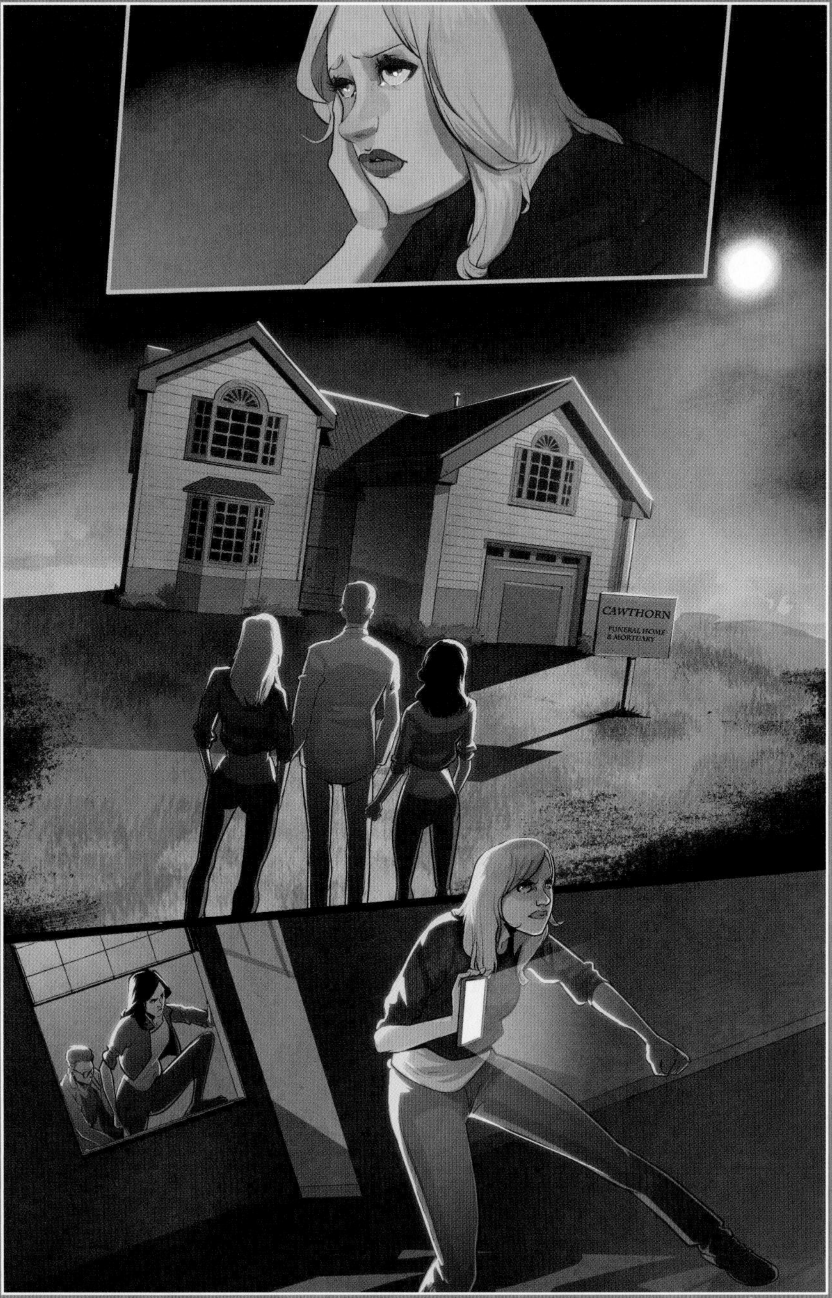
CAWTHORN
FUNERAL HOME
& MORTUARY

25th Anniversary Special, page 8

PANEL 3: Inside the funeral home, looking out an open, ground floor window. Buffy is already inside, using her phone flashlight to look around. Giles is still outside, helping Faith inside by giving her foot a boost.
GILES: I...oof...
FAITH (SMALL): Thanks, G--
BUFFY (SMALL): We got it from here, Giles. Keep watch. Anyone else comes in, text us.

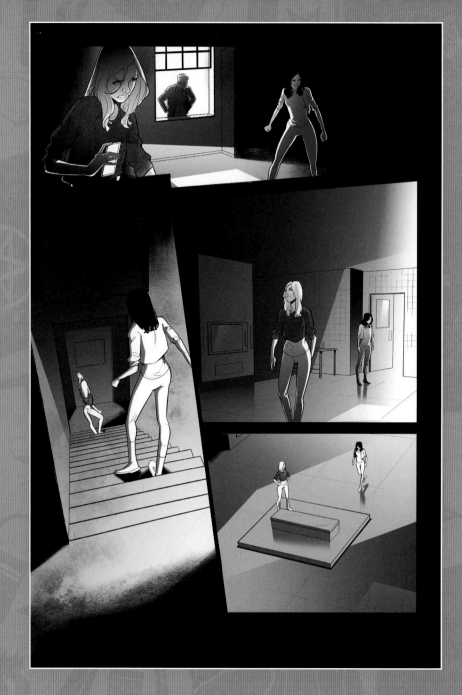

SCRIPT TO PAGE: *25th Anniversary Special, page 9*

PANEL 1: We're inside the funeral home, looking at an open window that Buffy, Faith, and Giles have opened. Buffy's already climbed in, and Faith is in the process of climbing in through an open window. We can see Giles outside the open window behind them. Buffy can be panel left. Giles in the middle, outside. Faith on the right, climbing in.
GILES (SMALL): ...fine but can we please rename that thread so it's not Ripper's Rebels?
BUFFY (SMALL): Ask Faith, she's the only one that can change it.
FAITH (SMALL): No way, man.

PANEL 2: We're at the bottom of the funeral homes' stairwell to the cellar, looking up at the cellar doorway, which is open. Buffy and Faith are in the doorway, looking down at the cellar. A sign on the wall reads CREMATORY & MORGUE with an arrow pointing down the stairs.
FAITH (SMALL): So...B...how're you gettin' on with, y'know, all the multiverse stuff?
BUFFY (SMALL): Well, I only had one panic attack today, so that's progress

PANEL 3: Buffy and Faith are in a sterile, clean basement with white tile walls. It looks like a morgue. In the center of one of the walls is a section made of metal, with a door in it. It's an incinerator (Reference).

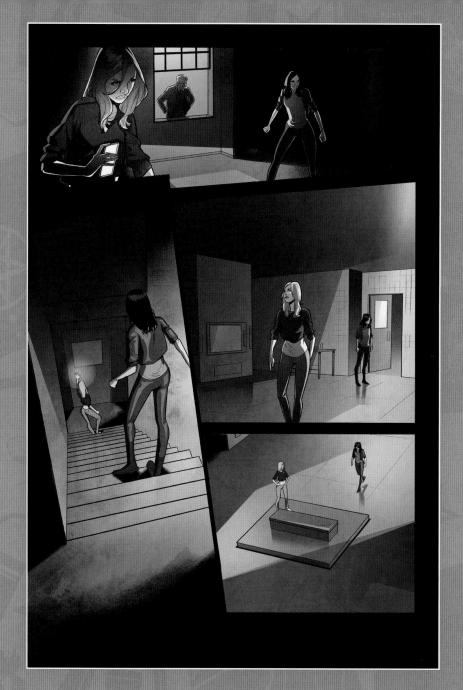

25th Anniversary Special, page 9

BUFFY: Honestly, the only thing I can do is try to focus on what I'm focusing on, you know? Drown the rest of the noise out. Don't got control over it…
FAITH: I meant like if you were gonna stick around here, around this Sunnydale, with so many other options out there, but yeah, that's cool.

PANEL 4: Buffy and Faith are standing over a metal tray in the center of the room. One top of it is a very cheap, plywood box the size of a human body. It's not a fancy casket, just a receptacle for remains. SILAS is stamped on it in blocky black letters, and below that, BURIALS & MAUSOLEUM.
BUFFY: Well…I guess I thought I never really had a choice--
BUFFY: Oh. Found him.
FAITH: Let's fire this bad boy up right now. Toss him in.
BUFFY: Better let Giles do it or else we'll probably burn the whole place down and then he'll be out there with his little *judge-y* face on.

CHARACTER DESIGN

PRELIMINARY SILAS SKETCHES
by Carmelo Zagaria

ALT /VERS

LONG HAIR

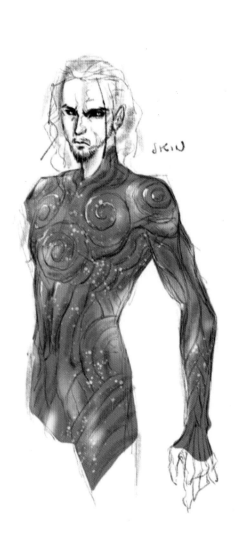

SKIN

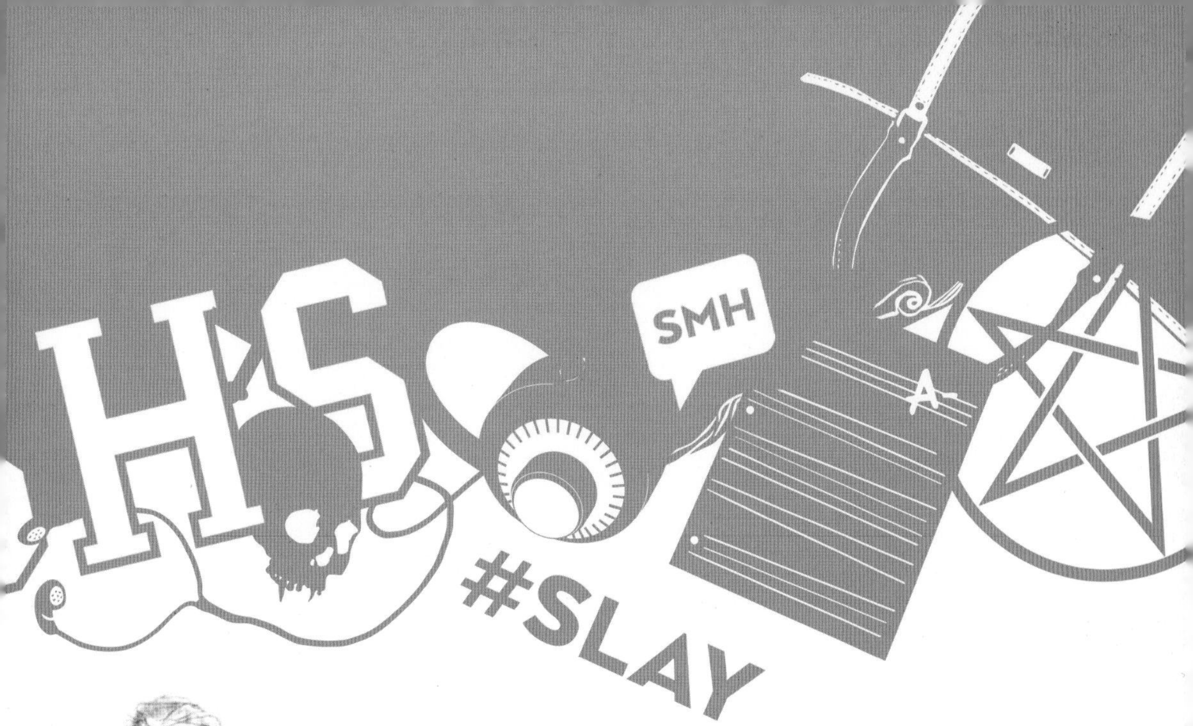
HS
SMH
A-
#SLAY

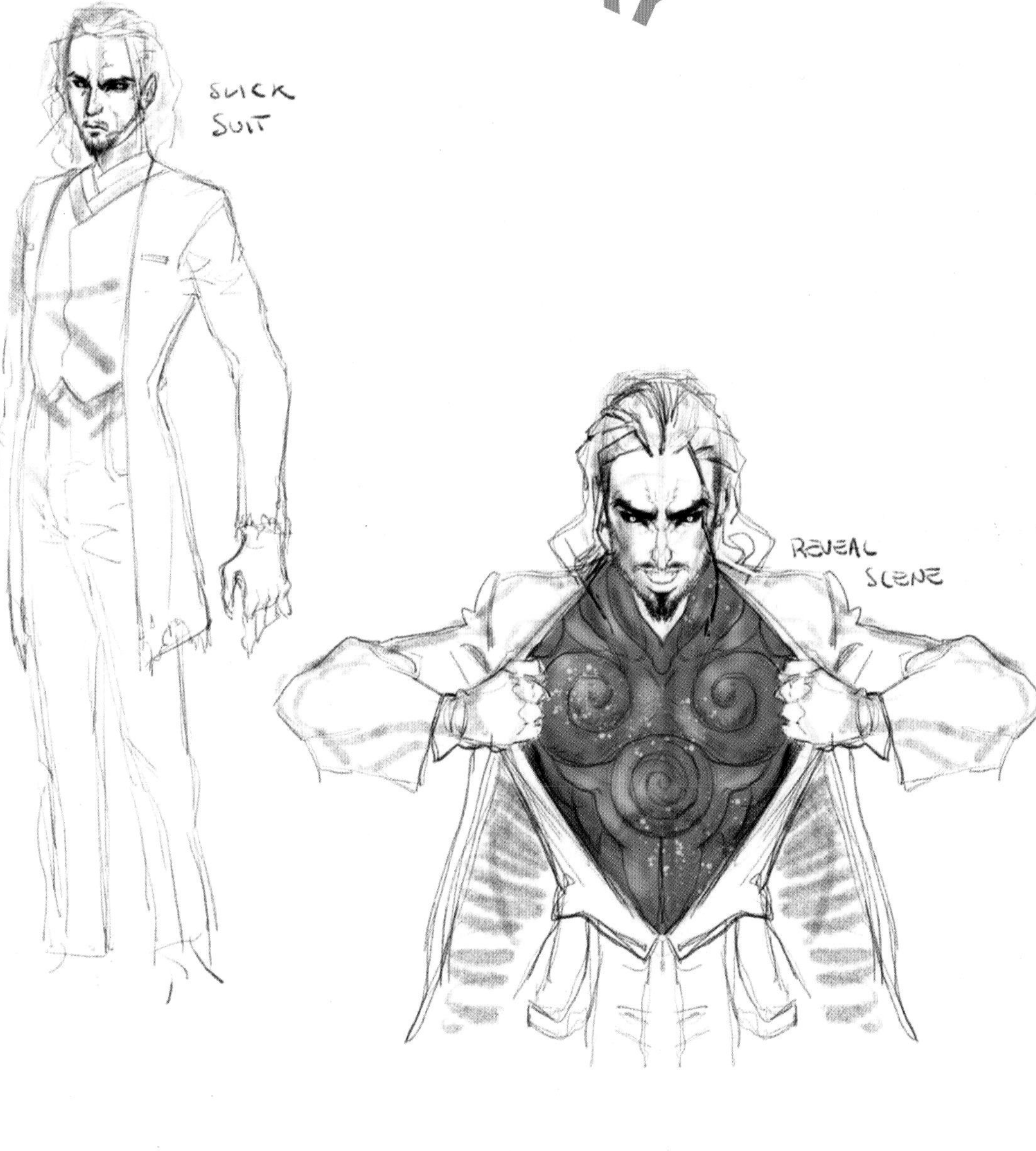
SLICK SUIT
REVEAL SCENE

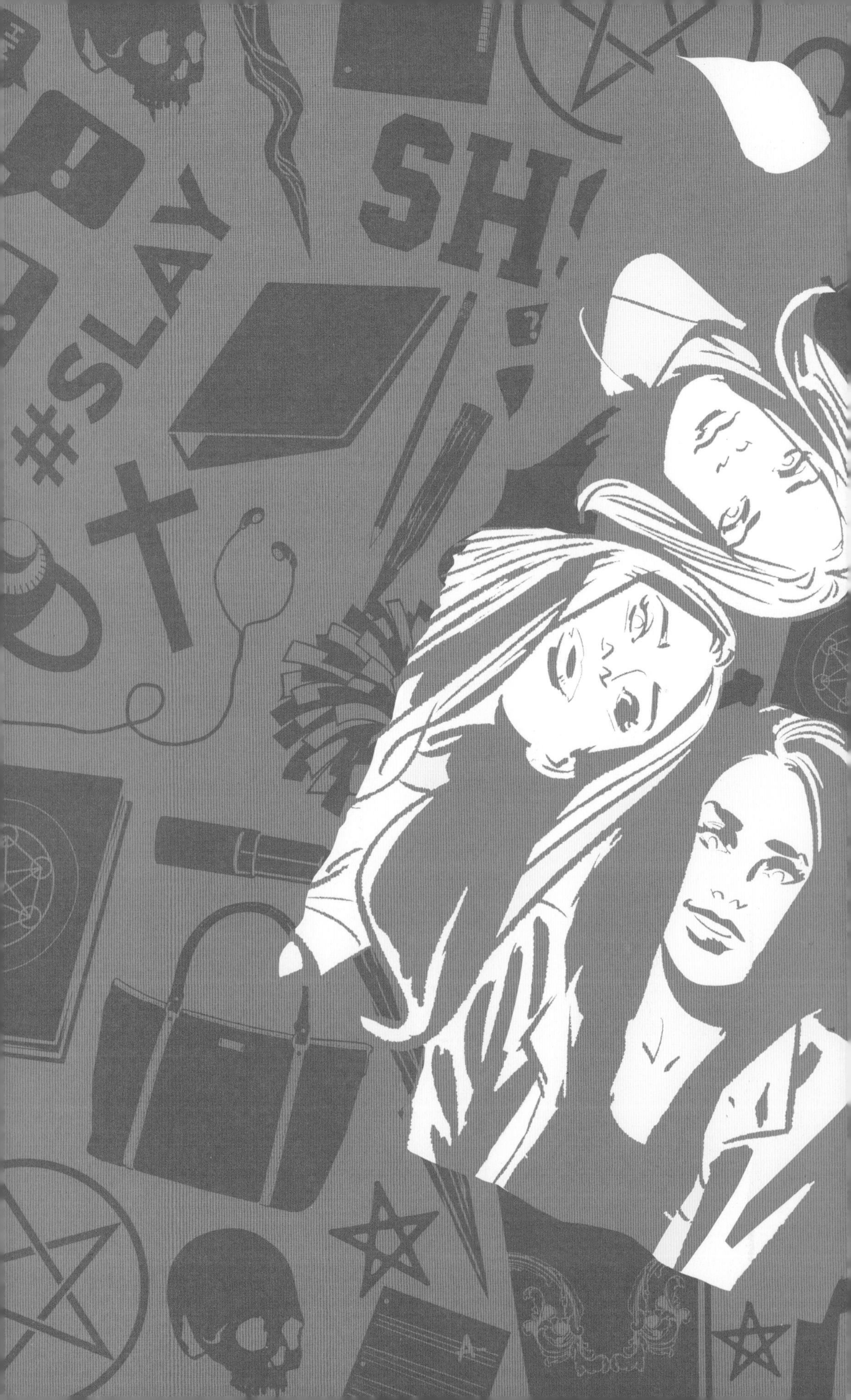
#SLAY
SH!

DISCOVER
VISIONARY CREATORS

KIERON GILLEN DAN MORA
TAMRA BONVILLAIN
ONCE & FUTURE
VOLUME ONE
THE KING IS UNDEAD

JAMES TYNION IV
WERTHER DELL'EDERA
MIQUEL MUERTO
SOMETHING is KILLING the CHILDREN
VOLUME ONE
SCOTT SNYDER

Brian Azzarello · Maria Llovet
FAITHLESS

GRANT MORRISON
DAN MORA
Klaus
How Santa Claus Began

SIMON SPURRIER × MATÍAS BERGARA
CODA
VOLUME ONE
"This one is really special!"
—JEFF LEMIRE
(New York Times bestselling writer of Black Hammer)

matt kindt
tyler jenkins
GRASS KINGS

BOOM! STUDIOS

AVAILABLE AT YOUR LOCAL COMICS SHOP AND BOOKSTORE

To find a comics shop in your area, visit www.comicshoplocator.com

WWW.**BOOM-STUDIOS**.COM

Once & Future
Kieron Gillen, Dan Mora
Volume 1
ISBN: 978-1-68415-491-3 | $16.99 US

Something is Killing the Children
James Tynion IV, Werther Dell'Edera
Volume 1
ISBN: 978-1-68415-558-3 | $14.99 US

Faithless
Brian Azzarello, Maria Llovet
ISBN: 978-1-68415-432-6 | $17.99 US

Klaus
Grant Morrison, Dan Mora
Klaus: How Santa Claus Began SC
ISBN: 978-1-68415-393-0 | $15.99 US
Klaus: The New Adventures of Santa Claus HC
ISBN: 978-1-68415-666-5 | $17.99 US

Coda
Simon Spurrier, Matias Bergara
Volume 1
ISBN: 978-1-68415-321-3 | $14.99 US
Volume 2
ISBN: 978-1-68415-369-5 | $14.99 US
Volume 3
ISBN: 978-1-68415-429-6 | $14.99 US

Grass Kings
Matt Kindt, Tyler Jenkins
Volume 1
ISBN: 978-1-64144-362-3 | $17.99 US
Volume 2
ISBN: 978-1-64144-557-3 | $17.99 US
Volume 3
ISBN: 978-1-64144-650-1 | $17.99 US

Bone Parish
Cullen Bunn, Jonas Scharf
Volume 1
ISBN: 978-1-64144-337-1 | $14.99 US
Volume 2
ISBN: 978-1-64144-542-9 | $14.99 US
Volume 3
ISBN: 978-1-64144-543-6 | $14.99 US

Ronin Island
Greg Pak, Giannis Milonogiannis
Volume 1
ISBN: 978-1-64144-576-4 | $14.99 US
Volume 2
ISBN: 978-1-64144-723-2 | $14.99 US
Volume 3
ISBN: 978-1-64668-035-1 | $14.99 US

Victor LaValle's Destroyer
Victor LaValle, Dietrich Smith
ISBN: 978-1-61398-732-2 | $19.99 US

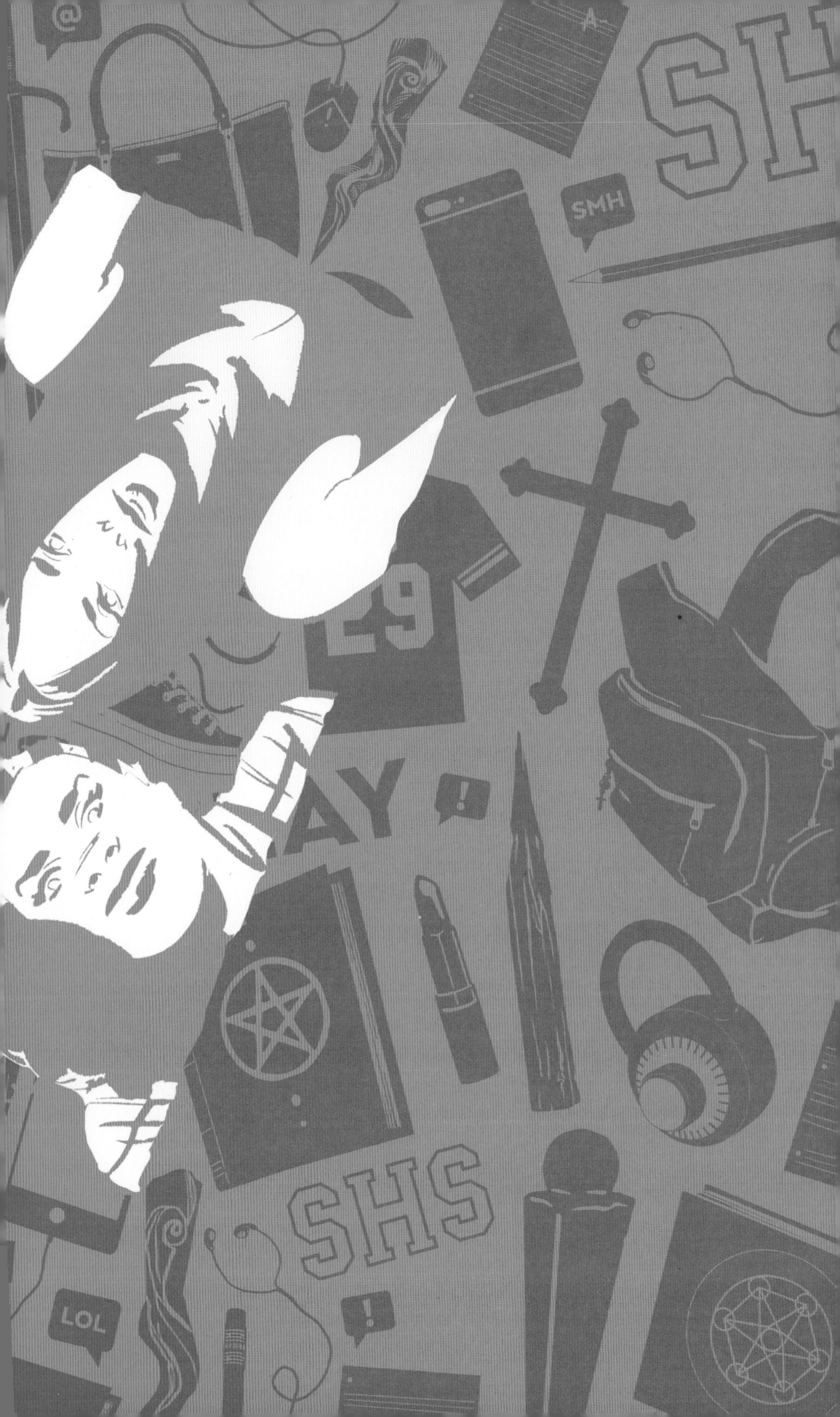
SMH
SHS
LOL